AMENDMENT SEVENTEEN:

A BLESSING? OR A CURSE?

Second Edition

MICHAEL JAMES GEANOULIS, SR.

Palmetto Publishing Group
Charleston, SC

Amendment Seventeen

Second Edition

Printed in the United States

ISBN-13: 978-1-64990-125-5

PROLOGUE

This is a tale of two governments in the United States, or to be more precise, a summary evaluation of two Senates that presided in the legislative branch since our Constitution was ratified in 1788. Each differed in the way they were elected. Each differed in the way they governed. The former Senate was elected by state legislatures; the latter, by the people at large as authorized by Amendment Seventeen (A17). For lovers of the pure democracy thought dangerous by our Founding Fathers who gave us instead a Democratic Republic, this tale may prove somewhat provocative—even inflammatory, but it must be told like it should have been told years ago.

In 1913, the Constitution was modified to provide for U. S. Senators to be elected by the people. Prior to 1913, for reasons thought best by our founders after penetrating debate on the matter, state legislators who had already been proven competent according to the vote of their neighbors were given the task of electing their respective Senators. The Founding Fathers believed, as I understand their scattered notes from the Constitutional Convention of 1787, that to realize the highest possible level of talented and gifted men (and now women) in the Senate, and to better check anticipated government incursions into rights and responsibilities reserved to the states and their people, this prescription would work best for long-term stability. The measure passed unanimously by a vote of 10 to 0.

I vaguely recollect an old college lecture about A17. The topic must have been less than stimulating, though, for I remember only a few boring items that lingered in one ear for a millisecond or so, then exited right out the other. Since A17 seemed like a needed corrective as it was portrayed, I never thought to ask, as I most certainly would if sitting in that class today: Why would anyone want to change the founders' attempt to give us a Senate populated with the highest and best humanity had to offer? What might be the outcome of this "needed corrective? And why are so many, including myself until recently, so casual about this profound change?

I was well into old age before I discovered the need to resurrect those mischievously buried records of that questionable effort to modify our representative republic, together with its neutering of the Federalism carefully crafted by the founders. And I was further motivated by numerous personal experiences that are chronicled in my memoir, *"The Big Gorge."* As a result, a series of "Eureka" moments left me wondering about the role of A17 on our declining status, both within our borders and without.

In debating the issue in 1913, justifications to change the way Senators were elected were alleged in a manner that was compelling. Wealth distribution was unfair; robber barons were enriching themselves at the expense of their employees; Senators were buying their seats; corruption was rampant; poverty was widespread; and our Democratic Republic was beginning to resemble an aristocracy. How utterly selfish, un-American, indecent and forgettable.

I found it thought-provoking, however, to have discovered a few eloquent and courageous notables who brought dissenting evidence to the table (See chapters 14, 15 and 16). But it was disheartening to find that most American voters at the time preferred to ignore or reject that evidence. They only knew that, for dubious reasons, the founders' prescription had to be rejected, while ignoring the possible impact of the proposed system.

Now that our country has had more than one hundred years of experience with each method in turn at the helm, and now that enough evidence has accumulated to reveal noticeable differences between the former and the latter Senates, a closer examination of those evolving differences seems obligatory. The most palpable of these are deteriorating fiscal management skills and a slow epidemic of business migrations to foreign lands.

A few corollary concerns remain virtually unchanged. Wealth distribution is still unfair; modern-day robber barons who resisted the pressure to migrate to friendlier business climates (and those who didn't) still enrich themselves at the expense of their employees; new forms of aristocracy endure along with the old; new varieties of corruption persist; and poverty rates, were it not for ballooning invasions into the future assets of our children and our grandchildren by way of the national debt, would be the same.

The details that gave us A17 were steeped in chicanery, un-tested theories, un-American activity, passions for the collective and a learning experience that should not be left in the forgotten dust bin of history.

The American majority voted to enact A17 for reasons that, at the time, seemed just, reasonable and proper though repeated resolutions to conduct impact studies were always rejected without comment. We are, after all, a democracy--a government of, by and for the people so said the popular wisdom of the time--what could be more reasonable, then, but to provide for a Senate influenced directly by and for the people?

We can never know exactly how America would have evolved in the absence of A17. But we should be curious and honest about the cause of emerging neo-problems like unmanageable debt, unstable families, fatherlessness and a growing inability to compete in a world economy.

The questions I proffered above beg for yet more in the form of the philosophical "if/then" variety. Now we must ask ourselves, (1) If we cannot tolerate the representative republic prescribed by our founders, then what would work better? A form closer to the socialist construct? Or the kind of democracy deemed as dangerous, *"ever a source of turbulence and contention; ever a threat to property rights and liberty,"* as alleged in Federalist #10?

Another source of higher wisdom should be an objective and honest attempt to estimate possible answers to, (2) If A17 had never been enacted to give Senate elections directly to the people, then what might our country's condition be like today? I have experienced an unsettling variety of extremes in response ranging from blank stares which seemed somewhat threatening, to reasonable expressions about progressive needs left in the private domain by prosperous founders who could never have been expected to comprehend such needs. But those needs, albeit complicated by financial stress both public and private, were slowly being remedied in a financially responsible manner even before A17 was enacted, as this report shall reveal.

Those satisfied with the latter publicly controlled Senate will reject the question out of hand, simply saying there would be little or no difference between the former Senate construct prescribed by the founders and the latter by the people at large, or that in any case we're better off with direct Senate elections.

Little or no difference? Then why the 70-plus year effort to get A17 enacted? Is that supposed to validate the determined effort to replace the founders' design? Such a claim reflects muddled thinking--especially as it relates to debt, deficits, and inflation. Fiscal management under the former Senate, best evidenced by inflation rates that hovered close to zero for more than 100 years, was far superior. But under the leadership of a post-1913 Senate, prices have doubled every 20 years or so while debt rockets to the moon.

Better off? Only if it can be established that the Pied Piper of Debt will never come looking for his dues. The jury is still out and the pressure builds. Living standards are beginning to decline as perpetually rising debt service costs, not counting the cost of inflation, will soon exceed one trillion dollars and more each and every year. This cannot end well.

A third query should provoke thought about whether or not we might have been better off if direct Senate elections were prescribed right from the start. I won't hazard an estimate for that one. I'm already on thin ice with what I've written already. I'll just let readers ponder those possibilities on their own. All that's needed is an exercise of the mind that transplants our most recent 100 plus years of experience with social and fiscal policies from 1913 to 1787 instead.

Scholars have long agreed that democracies are inherently fragile and unstable. Of all those efforts by early European explorers to plant self-government in this hemisphere, the American experience seems to be the only one that has survived in a manner that warrants respect--at least until 1913 (Canada should be included in this success story though it was spawned from monarchy early on).

Alexis de Tocqueville, for example, who expressed praise for the way our former Senate was constructed, further alleges in his highly regarded book, *"Democracy in America,"* that Mexico fell to anarchy and military despotism not long after it cloned our constitution almost word for word in 1824. It has since been amended more than 200 times, and today resembles a disorganized mess. It was not possible for me to determine the date, but at some point, they too, changed from indirect to direct election of their Senators. To be fair though, the method of electing Senators is the least of Mexico's problems. But we should still wonder, if only for academic reasons, what might have happened if Mexicans had preserved its indirect method of electing their Senators.

This may well boil down to a need to be more circumspect about the way we digest or ignore history and to reevaluate America's passion for the collective. For I believe that powerful emotions, better described as envious afflictions of the mind I would categorize as "utopianitis" or "collectivitis," are at the root of A17.

To this day four American states proudly refer to themselves as Commonwealths even though no examples have survived here, or most anywhere else, with possible exceptions like the Inuits of Greenland, where mutual sharing is a forced necessity. People everywhere, including the London investors for the Mayflower expedition, are, and have been, forever enamored with mandated sharing even though such experiments ordinarily fail miserably. There were many such failures reported by Tocqueville, who studied democracies throughout the western hemisphere. The history of Plymouth Plantation is a special case in point needing detailed elaboration in order to help me validate the founder's prescription for a Senate that should legislate at "arm's length" from the people.

Most Americans, who are fervently and irreparably attached to the false promises of the commonwealth, forgot, if indeed they ever knew or cared, that according to one of the Pilgrim settlers who documented the experience in detail, London investors demanded that "...*the houses, and improved lands, especially gardens and home lots, should remain undivided wholly to the planters at the end of seven years.*" (William Bradford, *Of Plymouth Plantation*," Ch. VI, 1620)

Bradford goes on to describe how some were inclined to play games while others worked thereby putting an end to this early form of communism after only one year. In Ch XIII, 1621, he says: *"On Christmas Day the governor called them all out to work, as was usual; but most of this new company excused themselves, and said it was against their consciences to work on that day. So he led the rest away and left them; but when they came home at noon from their work he found the new-comers in the streets at play, openly – some pitching the bar, and some at stool ball, and similar sports. So he went to them and took away their implements, and told them that it was against his conscience that they play and others work."* I got a chuckle for myself while revisiting this scene in my imagination. Too bad those marvelous little Androids weren't available to record the governor's annoyance and to give us some comic relief on the internet.

Bradford's journal continues: *"So they began to think how they might obtain a better crop than they had done, that they might not still languish in misery. And so they assigned to every family a tract of land according to the proportion of their number... This had very good success, for it made all hands very industrious and much more corn was planted than otherwise would have been by any means the Governor or anyone else could use. The women now went willingly into the field to set corn, and took their little ones with them, a thing which they would formerly have declared themselves unable to do.... the effect of their planting was well seen; for all had very near enough to last the year.... so that no general want or famine has been among them since."*

So ended this early American experiment with the commune and the "wholly undivided." The Pilgrims violated the London investors' mandate, but they survived when they otherwise would likely have perished. I am stymied that Massachusetts, in spite of this early flirtation with extinction, still refers to itself proudly as a Commonwealth that, in truth, was aborted after only one year of near-death experience with those "undivided" mandates. Do the voters of the Commonwealth of Massachusetts then, who unwittingly pride themselves as citizens of a commune, reflect the kind of "utopianitis" that gave us A17 and a Senate more closely controlled by some unknown percentage of the population who might be inclined to play while others work?

I will venture briefly into the problem of poverty or pauperism for I am utterly convinced that A17 actually gave permanence to those ailments. The 70-plus year effort to change the method of electing the Senate had roots in the desire for a closer relationship with the Senate which, ostensibly, would better facilitate the general welfare. But as none other than Andrew Carnegie, who I believe qualifies to comment because he gave away the bulk of his fortune for the benefit of the public, cautions: *"These who would administer wisely must, indeed, be wise, for one of the serious obstacles to the improvement of our race is indiscriminate charity."* He further posits, *"...In bestowing charity, the main consideration should be to help those who will help themselves."* (See Carnegie's *Gospel of Wealth*, Chapter 19)

In another little-known work authored by Tocqueville, *"Memoir on Pauperism,"* it was alleged that the wealthiest countries of Europe had the highest poverty rates because public relief for the poor stretched local budgets beyond the reasonable. Tocqueville therefore alleged:

"But I am deeply convinced that any permanent, regular administrative system whose aim will be to provide for the needs of the poor will breed more miseries than it can cure, will deprave the population that it wants to help and comfort, will in time reduce the rich to being no more than tenant farmers of the poor, will dry up the sources of savings, will stop the accumulation of capital, will retard the development of trade, will benumb human industry and activity, and will culminate by bringing about a violent revolution in the state, when the number of those who receive alms will have become as large as those who give it, and the indigent, no longer being able to take from the impoverished rich the means of providing for his needs, will find it easier to plunder them of all their property at one stroke than to ask for help."

To be sure, drudgery and poverty in 19th century America festered everywhere. And there were, beginning shortly after the Civil War and the Act of 1866, intolerable levels of bribery and corruption in America. Disgust, envy, and scorn, as a consequence, were directed at corrupt robber barons and colluding Senators alleged to be enriching themselves at the expense of economically abused workers. But there are traces of disingenuousness in those much-regurgitated themes.

Many will be surprised to learn that Senate bribery and corruption problems were virtually nonexistent until the passage of a poorly designed Election Act of 1866. This Act was very restrictive--nearly paralyzing the process of electing Senators in state legislatures. Those dreaded back-room deals suddenly became necessary in order to avoid gridlocks that occasionally left Senate seats empty. A redress of the Act of 1866 should have been seen as a better fix for real or imagined problems in bribery and corruption, not an amendment that merely transferred the possibility for such sins from state legislators to the people at large. (See Chapter 6).

While it's true there was everywhere corruption and economic stress of every kind, it's also true that overall living standards were rising and that America was serving as a beacon of freedom, hope and prosperity for the world. Immigrants persisted in migrating to our shores by the millions because they were fleeing economic stress that was even worse. They saw America as an opportunity to become successful job creators, innovators and wealth producers themselves.

An amendment that was supposed to cure bribery and corruption in high places merely transferred the possible source of these crimes from one place to another, and in the process cast doubt about America's long-term stability. Before 1913, state legislators were alleged to be colluding with Senators; since 1913, it's the people at large who collude with Senators. Such sins, from whatever the source, are still being committed across the entire political spectrum at rates, according to the data, that are higher than they ever were. Senators, Representatives, judges and administrators of every political stripe commit these crimes in spite of A17. Those rates for much-maligned Senators, surprisingly, have always been lower than the rest--as we shall see. I am deeply suspicious that relief from Senate bribery and corruption was not the primary goal of determined opponents of the founder's prescription for Senate elections.

Hundreds, if not thousands of strikes plagued 19th century America. Many were violent and were inspired by the inferior, unproven communist philosophy of Karl Marx. In one such strike in 1894, steelworkers illegally occupied a Carnegie steel plant in Homestead, Pennsylvania. But Carnegie vowed to turn his plant back to grass rather than be dictated to about how to run his business—a business that, incidentally, had suffered a steep decline in steel prices in 1893.

In 1894, an economic downdraft spawned a march on Washington by thousands of financially stressed unemployed workers, later referred to as Coxey's Army, who demanded relief in the form of government aid. This occurred, oxymoronically, during a decade which experienced a steep increase in overall wages and living standards with no inflation. Coxey's pleadings were rejected by an already financially-stressed government for reasons that could well be considered valid. But a government populated with Senators influenced directly by people who incessantly give tacit approval for debt financing, would have armed itself with green ink and coerced itself into the affairs of the several states through debt stimulus having untoward implications for divisive selective benevolence, inflation, retirement account devaluations, and higher levels of stress on the assets of unborn citizens through increased national debt.

Marx, himself a failure in the workplace, wrote hundreds of articles for American consumption in a truly splendid effort to replace the proven with the unproven, to provoke disgust for capitalist bosses and sweatshops, and to, indirectly at least, endorse the tireless effort to change the nature of our Senate.

While it's easy for me to allege that Marx influenced 19th century proceedings in support of A17, I could find little evidence except indirectly from socialist newspapers of the era and the vivid Madison-Marx philosophical comparison in my Epilogue. It was not possible to raise more than two of the entire set of Marx's essays in a google search at the Library of Congress website. This fact alone demonstrates the need for detailed research into the subversive nature and extent of communist influence in 19th century America and the passage of A17.

The former legislatively-appointed Senators knew better than those elected by the people, that the forces of economics are basic and eternal. No amendment, not a thousand amendments, nor a thousand gallons of green ink can change those forces, except temporarily. The occasional claim that A17 was necessary because "Things are different now" resonates dishonestly with me as a sophisticated form of corruption.

While dire warnings about flawed arguments were repeatedly rejected, evidence alleging the need for A17 came from a thousand places and was well received in the end. One possible consequence was a growing bias favoring labor which slowly evolved into scattered migrations of much-maligned American industrialists to cheaper labor in foreign lands, where business interests garnered more respect for their ability to create jobs and, by deduction, considerable relief from the debilitation of poverty.

Going forward, Americans should carefully evaluate the differences between the pre-1913 Senates, and those elected after that, along with their modes of governance. In spite of A17, or maybe even because of it, forms of aristocracies persist, moneyed influence and corruption are as bad, or worse than it ever was, a severe imbalance in wealth distribution is still intractable, and poverty rates, were it not for constant wealth transfers from the future, would be the same. Strict, painful discipline was required, but under the former system of appointing wise Senators, government had much better control over debt, inflation, and deficit spending. In 1890, when average wages were but a few pennies per hour, a dinner at an ordinary restaurant in New York cost 13 cents, 15 cents if you included a beer with your order…but I digress to a topic for another book to stimulate thought about the way we chase our economic tail, and to rub it in.

My words here should not be seen as pleading for a repeal. That is not possible, given the prevailing emotional state of mind in this country. But I do pray, with a sense of urgency, that my fellow citizens will, using this book as a primer, encourage a low-level repair that will at once allow public input for, while preserving state legislative control of, their respective Senate candidates. The founders' carefully considered prescription for states to check possible federal overreach, aka Federalism, should never have been violated… excepting, of course, any inclination of a state or group of states to disregard well-established principles of liberty, equality, and justice for each and every citizen, as the tragedy of our bloody Civil War excruciatingly demonstrated.

TABLE OF CONTENTS

INTRODUCTION

"What bitter anguish would not the people of Athens have often escaped, if their government had contained so provident a safeguard (Senate) against the tyranny of their own passions?"
(James Madison, Federalist #63)

At a recent Christmas party here in the historic town of New Castle, New Hampshire, this practicing recluse discovered, almost by accident, that he could break the ice with those he rarely interacts with and who know him only by the memory of his face at the post office, simply by approaching them with, "Hi, Merry Christmas. Hope Santa will be good to you," along with a quick, "My name is Mike. I'm 83 years old and I'm writing a book."

It was a neat thing to discover that their eyes and demeanor, while returning in kind, would light up a little as if chatting with Hemingway himself: "Wow, no kidding, a book? What will it be about?"

"It will call attention to the 17th Amendment," adding the entire word set to incite thought on the matter, "the title will be, *Amendment Seventeen: A Blessing? Or a Curse?*"

Almost without exception these revelers would then seem a little stunned and return with something like, "Amendment Seventeen? What (the hell) is Amendment Seventeen?"

The "what" question was dispiriting for me. It was echoed everywhere. It bothered me that virtually no one knew about this truly profound impact on our condition or how it may, or may not, have affected our long-term stability. But I stuttered a little, saying simply that "it changed the responsibility for electing U. S. Senators from State legislatures to the people."

The "why" of it all then emerged. Now we're in the weeds. This forgotten episode can't be explained by simply echoing those who sold A17 as necessary to prevent alleged Senate election corruption problems or - closer to the truth - inject a higher level of democracy. It's really a complex mystery couched in subterranean obfuscation, the need for wealth redistribution, ulterior motives and a universal utopian desire for a better life. It's concealed by a truckload of records safely tucked away in dusty cubicles of the Library of Congress, and it has a raucous 19th century history driven by 2 or 3 of the 7 deadly sins – from both the pro and the con sides of this overlooked disturbance.

The "why," at least in part; or in some measure impossible to determine, could be easily described, after looking deep into the congressional records, as a clever scheme to deposit part of our founder's venerable constitution into the circular and to replace it with a version more compatible with well-intentioned benevolent needs, which, by itself might be considered a good thing but for the threat to our long-term stability and the chicanery involved.

As I made the rounds, one of three things would happen: the good, the bad and the ugly.

The "good" came in the form of genuine interest from many along with some stimulating dialogue about the wisdom of founders Hamilton, Madison and others who were very well versed on the ancient record of European politics, the dangers of a pure democracy, and the critical need for those checks and balances in the Constitutional Republic given to us in 1787.

Stimulating, I say, because one apparently disinterested sort invited me, with a memorable determination in his manner, to change the subject. Ignorance or denial was, and continues to be, everywhere - even in high places as we shall see. The "ugly" was the frustration I felt over the discovery that most never even heard of this profound, potentially deadly Amendment (Effective date: May 31, 1913); or if they did, they didn't care - preferring instead to take on the demeanor of an embarrassed ostrich.

After a few such exchanges I began to cuss a little to myself right in front of images of the baby Jesus. Why do so many seem to have such difficulty understanding that tampering with the basic structure of our constitutional republic can be very dangerous? Why are so many unaware of this possibility – even uncaring?

I was, to be fair, in that same state of ignorance myself well into old age. But I went home frustrated nevertheless while my sympathetic wife, Norma, placated my threats to run around in the streets with my hair on fire by predicting sweetly, "Don't worry too much hon, once your book is published; once the word gets out, everyone will know all about the 17th Amendment. And they will appreciate your revelations, I'm sure of it." Norma is very good for my morale.

In order to be better understood, we will turn the clock back a few years; to the day when I began wondering, with a deep sense of alarm, why politicians from either side of the aisle, together with their constituents, seem totally and completely unable or unwilling to grapple with our growing vortex of debt. Why do they seem so indifferent about this hole being drilled to Hades, where no relief, repair, comfort, utopia, happiness, or benevolence is possible? You can get a better idea by attending the campaign rally of any presidential candidate and asking in the simplest possible terms: "What about the annual service costs on the national debt?" It won't matter who – Republican, Democrat, Independent – they will each be reduced to the nonsensical, then immediately proceed with new promises for yet more of the unaffordable.

After retiring from technical chores on the submarines that long ago brought me to the New Hampshire seacoast, I rediscovered books - non-fiction books mostly. I discovered that this was hardly the America I knew growing up; nor was it the America of yore proudly described for me by the likes of Mark Twain or Alexis de Tocqueville. I found reasons to suspect A17 as being partly responsible for the social and economic instability we see everywhere today; and I haunted the Library of Congress and other places for evidence to prove it. The troubleshooter in me demanded to know more about the "why" of A17, but I could find little more than the nonsensical and the irrational though well-intentioned, as we shall see.

Authors like Greaves[1] and Dilorenzo[2] began ringing my bell with their anxious calls to better understand downers like Roosevelt's 1930s depression and the relatively healthier financial conditions of the 19th century even with its periodic bank panic (assuming, of course, reliance on constant injections of debt and fiat paper are not seen as a permanent source of wealth and economic well-being, both public and private). And I discovered an uncomfortable need to know more about how it came to pass that, in a cosmic instant, $2 newspapers, rusting factories, family decay and opioid related suicides replaced 2 cent newspapers, vibrant industries, intact families, and the optimism of former times.

1 Greaves, P., "Understanding the Dollar Crisis," (1973)
2 Dilorenzo, T., "The Problem with Socialism," (2016)

Perplexing indicators like the great recession of 2006, forever wars, national debt service costs (rapidly approaching one trillion dollars annually), and fatherless rates began shaking my faith in the America I formerly would have described as our great American Constitutional Representative Republic and the envy of the world; not the pure democracy described as dangerous by the founders, nor the pure democracy esteemed by compassionate supporters of the 17th Amendment—our American Constitutional Representative Republic based on responsible democratic/republican principles.

Then came 19th century politicians like Senators George Hoar and Elihu Root and researchers Zywicki, Bybee, Holcombe and Hoebeke who waxed eloquently about the causes, consequences and dangers of the 17th Amendment.

Most importantly, I discovered researcher Ralph A. Rossum, Ph.D., who shocked me with comprehensive charts revealing a stark difference in the scarcity of Senate election corruption/deadlock rates before 1866, and the far more virulent variety that occurred *after* 1866, the year congress modified the way state legislatures chose their Senators (ACT of 1866).[3]

Rossum's data was a profound jolt for me; like the kind I experienced when my doctor told me, with little empathy, that I had cancer in my bladder (later healed); or the stunning discovery that my home had been burglarized while I was away sunning myself in the tropics.

It seemed that Rossum's disturbing findings might go a long way in helping to fully understand the process that brought us an amendment that threatened the mission of our most favorite political system in all the universe; and impugn the reputation of the Senate and those highly talented founders, to boot. Rossum upended my faith in American

---

3 Rossum, Ralph A., *"Federalism, the Supreme Court, and the Seventeenth Amendment,"* 2001

voters, too, because they put intense pressure on Congress to bring us all closer to the Senate contrary to our founders' prescription. He helped me discover the unsettling certainty *that the 17ᵗʰ Amendment was "necessary" to fix Senate election problems that never really existed as a practical matter until the defective ACT of 1866 came along* (see Chapter 7).

Why was our cherished Constitution blamed for Senate election problems that were caused, not by the Civil War Era as claimed by diversionists, but by a flawed election ACT of 1866? Why did Washington lawmakers deny resolutions to address the ACT's weaknesses? Should we suspect ulterior motives, though well-intentioned, lurking beneath the radar?

For the entire 77 years of our republic prior to that ACT, Rossum reported one (1) Senate deadlock problem and one (1) bribery case – _one_ _each_. But subsequent to 1866 and the ACT, deadlock rates blew out to 71. The totals for alleged and confirmed bribery and corruption cases (15) increased, as well; but not unreasonably given the difficulty State legislatures had in complying with an ACT that should have been repaired at the first indication of trouble.

But for that poorly designed election law, Senate corruption/deadlock problems would have been no more noticeable than any of the other unlawful acts committed by a variety of government officials over that same time span. After 1866, moreover, mushrooming Senate election problems presented opportunities for a variety of populists - who thought they knew better about how to appoint Senators than the founders did - to conscript improperly portrayed Senate election malfunctions as leverage to bring the Senate closer to the People using constant resolution drumbeats for the People to replace State legislatures in Senate elections.

"Hey, not to worry," said populists whose real goal was closer access to the treasury. "No need to repair the ACT of 1866. We can kill 2 birds with one stone: enacting Amendment 17 (1) removes (real or imagined) corrupt Senate candidates and State legislatures from the Senate election process, and (2) brings us a higher form of democracy by letting the people elect their Senators instead."

Conversations with honorable relatives and valued neighbors emerged which always remained cordial despite revelations that must have shocked and offended. For these, I apologize, but only for diplomatic reasons. Hard realities need to be told, especially those that contribute to what I honestly consider dangerous, both to our republic, and to our families and progeny if left untreated.

Some of these conversations probed the 19th century differences between Progressivism (with its previous cousins: socialism, egalitarianism, populism, Marxism, communism and etcetera); and capitalism, (with its so-called "robber barons," slave wages , boom/bust cycles, periodic unemployment, bank panics and extreme poverty) altogether challenging during a 19th century industrialist America replete with extremes in both poverty and wealth.

Washington politicians could learn much from our dialogues. We were always able to come up with resolutions for our differences—theoretically at least—even though the salient topic under discussion had the potential to blow up like a road-side bomb in Iraq. And I learned a few things. We all did (I think), especially the lesson to politely agree to disagree as necessary.

The subjects of poverty, income inequality, wealth redistribution and national debt interest costs were the worst. For my part, I now wish our founders contributed a few clauses to address the problem of eternal poverty in their final product, and tried a little harder to resolve the slavery issue which negatively impacted the concept of federalism (state/federal power sharing).

Even with readily available economic data accumulated over the life span of our republic (1790—2020), estimates of our present condition in the absence of Amendment 17, like estimates of modern Mexico in the absence of the Spanish invasion into the Aztec Empire, will be vexingly difficult to prove. But try we must, if only to better understand how we evolved; to challenge those who teach that Amendment 17 improved our condition; and to improve our critical thinking skills relative to its effects on our collective longevity, health, welfare, stability and happiness.

It will become apparent that A17 might never have seen the light of day but for that poorly conceived ACT of 1866; and regrettably, somewhat less apparent that our federal balance sheets might be, accordingly, in much better shape today.

The serious student of Amendment Seventeen should drop this book immediately and go directly to the superior scholarship of Rossum, Zywicki, Bybee and the rest, leaving me to fill information gaps; to make plausible estimates about the whole truth; to speculate about the causes and consequences of this colossal insult to our most honorable founders; and to practice those old troubleshooting skills I learned at DeVry Technical Institute – the first of which is to properly parse the difference between the symptom of a problem and the problem itself.

The primary mission of this book is to improve the understanding about the "why" or the "need" for Amendment Seventeen. A secondary motive was inspired by Benjamin Franklin's response to a gentle old lady who asked him, as he was leaving that venerable Constitutional Convention in Independence Hall on Chestnut Street, Philadelphia for the last time (1787), "Well, Mr. Franklin, what kind of government have you given us?"

His answer was not comforting to me when I first learned of this conversation many years ago in high school, if memory serves. But the implied warning in his answer proves even more disturbing when combined with the painful revelations of the unjustifiable hyperbole that brought us the 17th Amendment.

"We gave you a republic, madam; if you can keep it," he answered.

With that ominous clause, "if you can keep it," Mr. Franklin expected that we might have trouble keeping our republic. Would the trouble he envisioned present in the form of A17 today? Did that injection of higher democracy into Senate elections bring our republic down a notch or two? Would he be ignored if he were to come back from the grave long enough to advise us, after reviewing our deteriorating performance over the most recent 100 years, to restore the Senate in accordance with the original design as soon as possible?

Should we not, at the very least, shine as much light as possible on this controversy in order to inoculate ourselves from similar mischief, however remote the possibility for mischief going forward – assuming of course, we can all agree first on the need to fully investigate this one? If together, we are not able to agree, then......let this manuscript sit quietly on the shelf until the need becomes more urgent; or until future historians perform a post mortem on our debt-ridden carcass.

I hope, likewise, to enhance the public's interest in our history with a special emphasis on A17; to probe the weaknesses and strengths of both supporters and opponents; to elevate the distinct possibility that a federal election law (ACT of 1866) served, not to clear up Senate election problems as alleged, but to severely aggravate and foster them; to revive the theory and value of a sophisticated and wise Senate as a State ambassador to, and a necessary check on, the central government; to rediscover the value of checks and balances between the Senate and the House of Representatives; to investigate more meaningful and responsible alternatives for Progressive needs; to learn how we caught a potentially deadly arrow in our heel, and to remove it with as little collateral damage as possible.

My recent experience in discussing these matters with friends and relatives has me suspecting you will wonder: "Just who the hell does this guy think he is anyway? Does this blockhead not know this is an ancient argument having been shredded and diced a million times during the 19th century and beyond? Does this windmill jouster not realize that the people have spoken; that come hell, or high water, or debt costs beyond the moon, or runaway federal agencies, they will not give their hard-won Senate vote back to their State legislature; that they are quite content with this potentially deadly siren, thank you just the same?"

Consider me, instead, as something akin to a frustrated patriotic servant of my fellow traveler who, like Odysseus at the mast unable to resist that mythical siren and the death it represents, might appreciate in the end, these attempts to tie him down by the chains of our constitution as it was originally intended for us.

> *In questions of powers, then, let no more be heard of*
> *confidence in man, but bind him down from mischief by the*
> *chains of the Constitution.*
> *— Thomas Jefferson*

Chapter 1

THE BASICS

With that foreword, you might conclude, as do many of my friends here at the New Castle Men's Coffee Group who listen politely to my weekly curmudgeon-like rants, that I hope for a repeal of Amendment Seventeen. So, let's get that impossibility off of the table right now. Only a low-level repair is even remotely likely. This is mainly about understanding where we are and how we got here.

After inspecting the essence of those 19th century records, and listening to the casual regard for those ancient echoes right here in conservative New Castle, New Hampshire, we can conclude that repeal is not possible. We can only encourage a more detailed inspection of the record, the primary mission of this book, and promote a better understanding of the whole truth behind the evolution of A17.

Ralph (not his real name) captures the essence of it all between sips of coffee by saying, with deep concern, "Look at it this way, Mike. The people wanted A17 badly. They fought long and hard for it so we ought to just respect their wishes. It reflects our political philosophy of government by the people. I for one rather enjoy the right to vote directly for my Senator and would not, under any circumstances, give up that right."

Another unnamed, also highly respected member of the group, who is obviously concerned about a possible economic downdraft accompanying any effort to redress our unrelenting addiction to debt, cautions, "You should be careful about what you wish for, Mike. You could lose your coffee and donuts in the morning."

I responded weakly by suggesting a low-level repair thoughtfully recommended by one Wendell Garrison who prescribed that the people could bring a slate of senatorial candidates for State legislators to choose from. This would ameliorate real or imagined monied influence in State legislatures, return us to the federalism envisioned by our founders, pave the way for gradual debt relief, and restore responsible governance.[1]

But we're getting way ahead of ourselves. Before exploring further, let's make sure everyone has a reasonable grasp on (A): the original structure of our Constitution and the government given to us by the delegates from 12 States assembled in the Constitutional Convention in Philadelphia during that hot summer of 1787 (Rhode Island never sent delegates); and (B): the modified structure of our Constitution which, by way of A17, replaced State legislatures with the People in the election of United States Senators.

In 1787, we were given three branches of government by the Constitutional Convention:

The Administrative Branch (1), consisting of the President and his minions who would administer the laws passed by the legislature.

The Legislative Branch (2) to enact laws. It consisted of two houses: a lower or **House of Representatives** whose members were elected directly by the people, and an upper house or **Senate** whose members were controlled by State legislatures.

---

1 Garrison, Wendell P., *"The Reform of the Senate,"* 1891

The Supreme Court (3) charged with supporting and defending the U. S. Constitution by adjudicating relevant petitions. Its members are chosen by the President.

In 1913 the people, by way of A17, changed the Legislative Branch. Though it still consists of two houses, both are now elected by the people contrary to the founders' wish that the House of Representatives and the Senate have different constituents that could better provide a check and balance for each on the other. A17 weakened that wish (the sharing of power between the States and the Federal Government).

The concept of **Federalism,** or power sharing, was designed to delegate certain specific powers to the central government of the United States, while reserving powers not delegated to the United States, to the States and to its people respectively (U. S. Constitution, Amendment X).

> *"So, there are particular moments in public affairs, when the people, stimulated by some irregular passion, or some illicit advantage, or misled by artful misrepresentation of interested men, may call for measures which they themselves will afterwards be the most ready to lament and condemn."*
> (James Madison, Federalist #63)

Chapter 2

OVERVIEW

"The powers delegated by the proposed Constitution to the federal Government are few and defined. Those which are to remain in the State governments are numerous and indefinite."
James Madison, **Federalist #45**

Sad it is, that if you were to ask a random sampling of your friends or neighbors to define the mostly forgotten 17th Amendment for you, or to explain the reasons for it, most would respond as if challenged by a problem in differential equations. If you try a follow-up request for an estimate of the amendment's impact on our overall long-term happiness, economic health and wellness, you'd likely get a yawn or a comment about the weather.

People don't seem to care about history, or even its effect on our destiny. Our institutions of higher learning have a casual attitude about it, as well. According to researcher Mona Charon, 80% of our colleges no longer require a course in history in order to qualify for a degree. Such attitudes should change.[2]

---

2 Charon, Mona, *Sex Matters*, 2018

*"It is important that we know where **we** come from, because if you do not know where you come from, then you don't know where you are, and if you don't know where you are, you don't know where you're going. And if you don't know where you're going, you're probably going wrong."*
Terry Pratchett, Humorist

EXACTLY WHAT WAS THE 17ᵀᴴ AMENDMENT?

As of May 31, 1913, the effective date of the 17ᵗʰ Amendment to the Constitution of the United States, all U. S. Senators would henceforth be elected by direct popular vote, superseding the founder's carefully considered intention, and a Constitutional Convention vote of 10 to 0, that all U. S. Senators should be chosen by their respective State Legislatures.

The original, or pre 1913 Constitution, under Article I, Section 3 stated: "The Senate of the United States shall be composed of two Senators from each State, chosen by the legislature thereof, for six years; and each Senator shall have one vote." In the amended, or post 1913 version, the clause, "chosen by the legislature thereof," was replaced with "elected by the people thereof."

Simply put, State legislative influence on their respective appointments to the United States Senate, coupled with the founder's desire to check federal overreach into responsibilities that were reserved to the State and to its People (U. S. Constitution, Amendment X), was largely neutered as State legislatures were replaced by the People for the election of Senators.

WAS AMENDMENT SEVENTEEN NECESSARY?

In an essay supporting A17, author Sally Kohn asks, "Who do you trust more? Do you trust the American people to directly elect our government? Or do you want to give more power to state legislators for them to potentially abuse? Do you want to believe that the American people can wisely change and carry out the governance of our nation, including amending the Constitution? Or do you think that a few wealthy elites from centuries ago still know absolutely best how our country should be run today?"[3] Then she answers her own questions by saying she would put more faith in the American people than State legislators abusing their Senate appointment power in order to enrich themselves, while sidestepping the possibility that the people can be abusers, as well— maybe slightly more so given that no requirement is made for them to swear an oath that they will defend and protect the property rights and constitutional freedoms of others.

Prior to Amendment 17, a healthier state of checks and balances existed between the State and the federal; and between the House of Representatives controlled by the People and the Senate controlled by State legislatures which in turn, were also controlled by the People. *This structure further ensured that the House and Senate were each responsible to separate constituencies.* But Ms. Kohn would abandon that, arguing instead to support an amendment that favors the People in both the House of Representatives AND the Senate.

Actually, A17 was not needed – not for the reasons given anyway, i.e.: to correct alleged bribery, power brokering, back room deals, deadlocks and corruption during the seating of U. S. Senators – problems that were relatively insignificant until the flawed election ACT of 1866 appeared on the scene, as we shall detail in chapter 6.

After 1866, and accumulating Senate election problems manifesting mostly in gridlocks, Progressives argued convincingly that Senate elections by the People instead of by State legislatures was the answer, even though simpler solutions were available. The amendment was considered "necessary" to "strengthen" our democracy.

---

3 (Kohn, Sally, *"The 17th Amendment is Good for America,"* Huffington Post, 2011)

"The closer the people are to their Senators the better off we are," echoed repeatedly throughout the land. "We are, to be sure, a democracy are we not? As in government of the people, by the people and for the people?" Actually, for reasons to be explored, the answer is, no. *We were not given a democracy. We were intentionally and purposefully given a constitutional representative republic complete with checks and balances to neutralize special interests of every kind.*

> *"It has been observed by an honorable gentleman, that a pure democracy, if it (were) practicable, would be the most perfect government. Experience has proved, that no position in politics is more false than this. The ancient democracies, in which the people themselves deliberated, never possessed one feature of good government. Their very character was tyranny; their figure deformity."*
> (Alexander Hamilton, *Speech to Congress, June 21, 1788*)

The exaggerated record suggested that ulterior motives were at work under the radar. Of the 1,180 Senators elected from 1789 to 1909, only fifteen (.0127 percent) were contested due to allegations of corruption, and only seven were actually denied their seats. A federal election law enacted in 1866, according to Rossum and others, was more likely the root cause of election problems – not the criminal activity of shady characters.

It was popularly alleged that, in any event, so-called "Robber Barons" were fleecing people who were constantly struggling with bank panics, unemployment and poverty; that an amendment would better protect people from unfair activities in both the marketplace and the Senate, considered to be a loathsome bastion for millionaires; and that elites were colluding to enrich each other at the expense of the people.

Another likely motivator for A17 had its roots in the horrible overcrowded conditions of urban areas, the worst example of which, thanks to the emotionally-charged journalism of one Jacob Riis, was New York. The release of "How the Other Half Lives," in which Riis graphically described the appalling state of survival for half of the city, marked a major decline in public attitudes against rich, improperly regulated landlords who were increasingly seen as caring only about the health of their bank accounts. The disgust extended to so-called "Robber Baron" industrialists as the first source of misery for the poor, who, because of inadequate pay, couldn't afford to move away from the slums. Economic stress was apparent everywhere even as per capita Gross Domestic Product and wages steadily increased, oxymoronically, throughout the Progressive Era and beyond (see Figure 1).

Figure 1

U.S. Real GDP Per Capita, 1800-2004 (In 2004 Dollars)

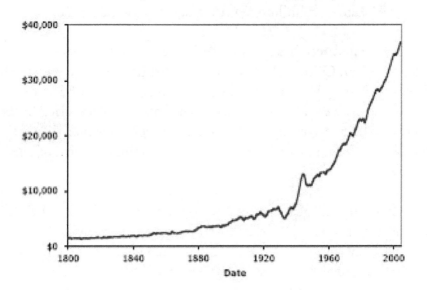

SOURCE: US BUREAU OF THE CENSUS, HISTORICAL
STATISTICS OF THE UNITED STATES

What was the attraction that convinced the People, States, and Congress to trade a reasonably well working Constitution for an unproven, potentially dangerous unknown? If amendment proponents were truly concerned about election deadlocks and empty seats, they would have sooner repaired the ACT of 1866. We must remember that the founders, having significant fear of pure democracies, rejected a well-considered motion for direct Senate elections 9 to 1, later approving Senate elections by respective State legislatures, 10 to 0.

Scholars Hoebeke, Rossum, Zywicki and Bybee estimated that alleged Senate election problems of the 19th century may have been inflated to enhance the possibility of success for an amendment that the founders would have rejected if the history of their debates on the matter is any indication. Should we not wonder, then, since the founders had reasonable doubts about the success of direct democracy, why either or both of two alternatives were not properly considered instead: (1) modify the ACT of 1866 to address the confusion introduced by multiple parties and candidates, or (2) leave the matter for the States themselves to resolve as they were doing for the virtual trouble free 76 years prior to the ACT?

The data previously introduced, which revealed stark differences in deadlock/corruption totals before and after the ACT of 1866, suggests that it would have been much simpler and more expedient to modify the ACT rather than hazard an amendment that could prove dangerous to our long-term stability.

Senate checks on the lower House and on government overreach were important. If the Senate should be a "place of sober second thought," we should consider the possibility that A17 was unnecessary - even dangerous - as we shall attempt to prove; especially as the question relates to forever wars and our national debt with its burgeoning annual service costs and inflation subsequent to 1913, the effective date of the Amendment. (See Fig. 2)

Figure 2
ANNUAL DEBT SERVICE COST SINCE FOUNDING OF U.S.

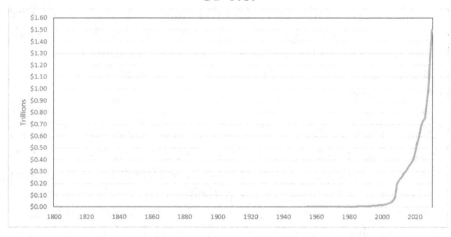

[Not to be confused with the National Debt. Fig 2 represents only its annual costs that, unlike the National Debt itself – a mind-boggling illusion having too many zeroes that can be kicked down the road until the next asteroid hits - must be redeemed annually or the Piper comes calling. Note the most recently tallied $0.4 trillion debit ($400 billion) for 2018 alone.]

New Hampshire and Kentucky recently came up with parallel ideas that might work to avoid confusion and retain a measure of State control of the Senate as originally intended: Let each State legislature create a short, bipartisan list of candidates. Then let the people choose from that list.

> *"The State legislatures also ought to have some means of defending themselves against encroachments of the National Government."*
> (George Mason, In Convention, 1787)

WERE MITIGATING FACTORS AT WORK UNDER THE RADAR?

The record reveals considerable competition and economic stress during the so-called Gilded Age at all levels (including many wannabe tycoon bankruptcies) even as wages and per capita Gross Domestic Product - oddly and counterintuitively - inched constantly upward. Nagging demands for relief of unemployment and poverty were nevertheless unrelenting. So called "bourgeoisie" Robber Barons were reviled and implicated as the primary cause of financial stress for "proletariat" workers whose wealth producing skills were being "used" to subsidize posh Newport lifestyles. Of these increasingly odious dichotomies in class warfare - let's call them a bourgeoisie/proletariat clash for convenience and convention - the latter would, of course, predominate in numbers alone with successful efforts to replace a frugal, State-controlled Senate, condescendingly referred to as a millionaires' club, with a more generous version directly controlled by the people.

Troublesome slavery issues also presented problems for the founder's desire to have a balance of power between state and federal governments. A terrible civil war was caused, in large part, by intense irreconcilable differences between state and federal factions that may not have occurred if certain States had not insisted in preserving the vile institution of slavery.

Since slavery has long been relegated to the ash heap of history; and since the record for per capita GNP showed steady increases over the Progressive period (1870-1910), it seems reasonable, given the alleged harm we are about to explore, that we should reconsider the legacy of our founders and the questionable amendment.

WOULD THE FOUNDER'S HAVE APPROVED OF THE AMENDMENT?

Since election corruption problems could have been treated by ordinary means, and because the effort to cure a problem in our constitutional republic with more democracy would have been seen as dangerous, the founders would have rejected A17. A motion for popular Senate elections by Pennsylvania delegate, James Wilson, in the Constitutional Convention of 1787 failed by a vote of 9 to 1. A later motion, by John Dickenson of Delaware, for Senators to be elected by State legislatures passed 10 to 0.

Federalism, or a sharing of power between state and federal governments, was thought best by the founders. Now that the institution of slavery is a reviled relic of the past, the state/federal balance, as delineated in the 10th Amendment, should be revisited.

The thinking was that State control of the Senate would better serve to discourage the central government's inclination to reach into responsibilities reserved to the State and its People (U.S. Constitution, 10th Amendment). To achieve this, they provided for State legislatures to choose and supervise, even recall, their respective U. S. Senators. The provision was lost with A17.

HOW DID WE BENEFIT FROM AMENDMENT SEVENTEEN?

Proponents of A17 say that corruption and bribery rates in Senate elections were reduced, even eliminated, by transferring control of the Senate from State legislatures to the People.

Opponents claim Senate election problems were caused primarily by poorly conceived election laws of 1866 – not the way Senators were elected under the original Art I, Sec 3. They further allege that the influence of so-called dark money since 1913 actually increased because it had easier influence on, and access to, candidates heretofore influenced more by their respective State legislatures. Despite the blatant use of money to win indirect Senate elections, 100 years after Amendment Seventeen was enacted found modern Senate elections swamped with campaign money in ways that far outpace elections under the indirect elections system.

Proponents further assert that democracy was enhanced by bringing people closer to the Senate. But the founders were altogether convinced that the closer you get to a pure democracy (closer control of the government by the people) the higher the risk for problems. This is essentially why we were given a constitutional representative republic complete with checks and balances—not a pure democracy. Here is what James Madison, who studied 2 crates of books on the political histories of European democracies sent to him by Jefferson (then in Europe), had to say about democracies:

> *"Hence it is that such democracies have ever been spectacles*
> *of turbulence and contention; have ever been found*
> *incompatible with personal security or the rights of property;*
> *and have in general been as short in their lives as they have*
> *been violent in their deaths."*
> (James Madison, Federalist #10)

At about the time our original 13 States adopted their new constitution, Alexander Tyler, a Scottish history professor at The University of Edenborough, had this to say about "The Fall of The Athenian Republic":

> *"A democracy is always temporary in nature; it simply*
> *cannot exist as a permanent form of government. A*
> *democracy will continue to exist up until the time that voters*
> *discover that they can vote themselves generous gifts from the*
> *public treasury. From that moment on, the majority always*
> *votes for the candidates who promise the most benefits from*
> *the public treasury, with the result that every democracy*
> *will finally collapse due to loose fiscal policy, which is always*

followed by a dictatorship."
Tyler (1787) further States:

*The average age of the world's greatest civilizations from
the beginning of history has been about 200 years. During
those 200 years, nations always progressed through the
following sequence: From bondage to spiritual faith; from
spiritual faith to great courage; from courage to liberty; from
liberty to abundance; from abundance to complacency; from
complacency to apathy; from apathy to dependence; from
dependence back into bondage.*

If the Amendment were to accomplish anything, it might well manifest
more in the form of a discovery that we should be more careful about
what we do to ourselves.

WAS THE AMENDMENT GOOD OR BAD FOR US?

Although it took a while to develop, a sharp difference in attitudes toward the debt can be seen in the debt cost growth rate of change (Figure
2) and the growth of the debt itself, before and after 1913, the year A17
became effective. Likewise, for inflation rates. The national debt was
barely perceptible by today's standards for the 100 years prior to 1913
while debt service costs over that same time span were minimal, as well.
After replacing a frugal, prudent Senate with a more progressive variety
in 1913, however, national debt levels began accelerating unchecked to
astronomical heights with associated debt service costs now predicted to
soon reach $800 billion and beyond - annually. For the years between
2020 and 2030 net interest costs on the national debt will total nearly
$7 trillion.

For the 100 years prior to the enactment of A17, inflation, aka the
Consumer Price Index (CPI, Fig 3) hardly moved above zero under the
wiser, thriftier Senate of old, even as Gross Domestic Product (GDP)
numbers per capita (Fig 1), wages, and living standards gained steadily.

Since 1913, however, price averages for goods and services have slowly doubled every twenty years or so—slow enough to desensitize the unwary into believing that their retirement accounts will retain their value over time, or that our ability to compete in world markets will remain unchanged.

There seems to be an emerging dichotomy of a kind: (1) supporters of A17 allege that such economic differences were nothing more than ordinary happenstance that would have occurred no matter how Senators were elected; that in any event, social and political forces were changing in efforts to improve the general welfare whereas nothing was being done when miserly Senators were supervising budgets and the balances thereof; (2) opponents, on the other hand, would use the foregoing economic data as proof that State legislatures, as our founders anticipated, were vetting and selecting – even recalling - Senate candidates with a higher level of sophistication and care for the long haul.

Figure 3
Cost Price Index Over Two Centuries

Bureau of Labor Statistics
[Note the virtual absence of inflation prior to Amendment 17 (1913)]

SOURCE: RANDALL G. HOLCOMBE. REPRODUCED WITH PERMISSION[4]

So then, why the 86-year hassle to pass an amendment that could possibly do more damage than good? Wasn't it a bit disingenuous to portray corruption problems as needing a constitutional amendment to fix when repairable by ordinary means? Isn't it time to suspect subterranean motives by those willing to risk long term damage for the sake of short-term gain? Were we so collectively naive that we would embrace an amendment billed as an "improvement" without an impact assessment of some sort? No objective impact study was ever conducted before, during or subsequent to, the debate and final passage of the 17th Amendment.

> *"But whenever the American people has made up its mind, when its judgment is formed, when its will is determined, that will is sure to be carried into effect. Whether through Senates or over Senates, through courts or over courts, through presidents or over presidents, through constitutions or over constitutions the irresistible current will make its way."*
> (Senator George Frisbie Hoar, 1893)

---

4 Holcombe, Randall G., *The Growth of the Federal Government in the 1920s*

Chapter 3

ESTIMATES OF THE AMENDMENT'S IMPACT

A requirement to assess the impact of any resolution to change the way Senators were elected was never established. Expressions of possible danger to the Constitution were rare during that 19th century effort. There was little in this regard except for eloquent statements of theory and support for the existing method of Senate elections by Senator George F. Hoar of Massachusetts (Chapter 12); a deeply prescient estimate from Senator Elihu Root of New York (Chapter 13); and a post-mortem revealing evidence of a political shift to the left detailed by Bybee.[5]

Rossum reported a partisan alinement as well. Democrats were typically in support of most 19th century amendment resolutions while Republicans generally rejected them with little comment.

Our founders spent more time on the construction of the Senate than on any other topic. But our 19th century Congress, oxymoronically, spent much of their time in repeated attempts to reconstruct what the founders unanimously supported: Senate elections by State legislatures.

---

5 Bybee, Jay S., *"Ulysses at the Mast: Democracy, Federalism, and the Siren's Song of the Seventeenth Amendment,* 1997

Tasking State legislatures with the vetting and seating of Senators would bring a higher level of quality, sophistication and wisdom into the U. S. Senate according to the founders. Those devoted to commonly held democratic principles (often confused with republican principles) would insist that the amendment was, at long last, a needed improvement. What could be more reasonable, they ask? But reasonable could represent subjective and selective mischief of the kind Madison and company labored to avoid by way of checks and balances that, in part, no longer exist thanks to the passage of A17.

Prior to the enactment of A17, Senators were intrinsically linked to their home state's interests. Since Senators were elected by State legislatures, they were directly responsible to those same State legislatures. If a Senator voted against the interest of the State he or she represented, he or she could be immediately recalled. *This system prevented undue influence of special interests at the Congressional level and cannot be emphasized strongly enough.* States, not special interests or dark money, held the greatest sway and control over the votes of their respective Senators. A17 changed all that.

The underlying premise was simple. States were better equipped to understand and respond to the needs of their citizens than the national government as State governments were *closer* to the people. Because of Amendment 17, the premise is different now.

The people elected their State legislature – who appointed members of the Senate – and the people elected members of the House of Representatives – who acted as checks on the Senate. The people would watch the State legislatures and the State legislatures would watch their respective Senator. This falls into line with the principal of separate representation at respective levels of government – People through the House of Representatives, States through the Senate. These principles were negatively impacted by A17.

The Constitution sought to diffuse power wherever it was able and was structured to push power down governmental levels – towards the people – not away from them. Citizens were directly represented by the House. States were directly represented by the Senate. Both were naturally aligned to guard against federal overreach. *Congress was originally intended to be an arena of balanced competition between citizen, state and federal interests.* The State portion of that balance was reduced with the passage of A17.

The Congressional structure was specifically and thoughtfully put in place to protect States and individuals against power consolidation and undue influence by the federal government. Protection from such influence and consolidation was compromised with the passage of A17.

Some researchers have alleged a cause/correlation between the advent of A17 and federal government intrusion into responsibilities reserved "to the States and to its people."

The Amendment did nothing to cure the problem of alleged corruption. Instead, it gave special interests and dark money easier access to Senate candidates who were formerly more isolated from such influences by their respective State legislatures.

Senators are no longer beholden to State legislatures, but to the same constituents held by the House of Representatives, i.e., the people at large. Senators became incentivized to promote unchecked growth of the federal system because Sena*tors were now beholden to the people directly—dependent on them for reelection – not to their State legislatures.* As a consequence of A17 we now have a higher form of democracy rejected by the founders for being possible "spectacles of turbulence and contention." (Madison, Federalist #10)

The record shows glaring differences in the intensity of business cycles and depressions, inflation rates, growth of the federal government and

national debt growth rates before and after 1913, the effective date for
A17.

The State's power, voice and inherent ability to resist the federal government is noticeably reduced. Consider the indicators listed here to
stimulate thought.

1. Government spending ratchets out of control not long after the
   effective date for A17 (Figure 4).

2. Inflation rates, as reported by the Consumer Price Index (CPI),
   averaged slightly above zero for 100 years prior to A17; but sub-
   sequently began a steep upward bias (Figure 2).

3. The mind numbing, growing vortex of annual debt service costs
   was virtually non-existent prior to A17 because of strict financial supervision by a wiser Senate.

4. Federalism---otherwise known as a mutual federal/state check
   on, and balance of, each on the other—considerably reduced by
   A17.

5. Bicameralism was considerably neutered with A17. The goals of
   both are essentially the same now.

6. A17 encouraged government program growth and divisive selective benevolence that, as some conservatives charge, encouraged a debilitating culture of dependency.

7. Supreme Court decisions, especially as they relate to the 10th
   Amendment of the United States Constitution which provides
   for a separation of State and federal powers, may have been influenced by populism and A17. Each of nine justices swears to
   support and defend the United States Constitution. Presumably,

that should include Amendment X which States: "The powers not delegated to the United States by the Constitution, nor prohibited by it to the States, are reserved to the States respectively, or to the people."

Figure 4
Real Per Capita Federal Expenditures 1800 - 1990
(constant 1990 dollars)
SOURCE: RANDALL G. HOLCOMBE. REPRODUCED WITH PERMISSION[6]

[Note the difference in growth of federal spending before and after Amendment 17 (1913)]

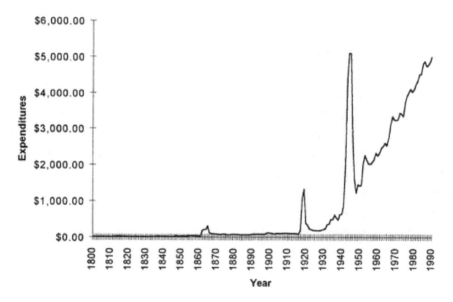

---

6 Holcombe, Randall G., *The Growth of the Federal Government in the 1920s*

Chapter 4

NOTES FROM THE CONSTITUTIONAL CONVENTION (1787)

Constitutional Convention Excerpts

[Note: The following notes from the Constitutional Convention were lifted from a variety of sources in the Library of Congress. They are presented here in excerpted form to emphasize, (1) the founders fear of direct democracy, (2) the detailed attention and time that the founders were willing to spend on the construction of the Senate in efforts to get it right. No topic received more attention from the delegates than that given to the United States Senate, (3) a desire for the highest possible level of checks and balances in order to minimize troublesome concentrations of special interests. The period between May 31 through June 9, 1787 was the most telling. Those interested in a more detailed study of the proceedings of the Constitutional Convention of 1787 should refer to:

https://www.usconstitution.net/constconnotes.html or
https://www.nhccs.org/Mnotes.html

A narrative from the notes of James Madison is also available in book form.[7] What would we give for a modern recording of the dialogue that took place at the Philadelphia, Pennsylvania State House on Chestnut Street (now Independence Hall) in the summer of 1787?]

May 31, 1787

Mr. Gerry: The evils we experience flow from the excess of democracy. The people do not want virtue, but are the dupes of pretended patriots. In Massachusetts it had been fully confirmed by experience that they are daily misled into the most baneful measures and opinions by the false reports circulated by designing men, and which no one on the spot can refute. One principal evil arises from the want of due provision for those employed in the administration of government. It would seem to be a maxim of democracy to starve the public servants. He mentioned the popular clamor in Massachusetts for the reduction of salaries, and the attack made on that of the governor, though secured by the spirit of the constitution itself. He had, he said, been too republican heretofore; he was still, however, republican, but had been taught by experience the danger of the levelling spirit.

Mr. Mason argued strongly for an election of the larger branch by the people. It was to be the grand depository of the democratic principle of the Government. It was, so to speak, to be our House of Commons. It ought to know and sympathize with every part of the community, and ought therefore to be taken not only from different parts of the whole Republic, but also from different districts of the larger members of it, which had in several instances, particularly in Virginia, different interests and views arising from difference of produce, of habits, etc. *He admitted that we had been too democratic, but was afraid we should incautiously run into the opposite extreme. We ought to attend to the rights of every class of the people.* (emphasis added). He had often wondered at the indifference

---

7 1Larson, E. and Winship, M., Editors, *"The Constitution Convention,"* 2005

of the superior classes of society to this dictate of humanity and policy; considering that, however affluent their circumstances or elevated their situations might be, the course of a few years not only might, but certainly would, distribute their posterity throughout the lowest classes of society. Every selfish motive, therefore, every family attachment, ought to recommend such a system of policy as would provide no less carefully for the rights and happiness of the lowest than of the highest order of citizens.

Mr. Madison considered the popular election of one branch of the national legislature as essential to every plan of free government. He observed that in some of the States one branch of the legislature was composed of men already removed from the people by an intervening body of electors; that if the first branch of the general legislature should be elected by the State legislatures, the second branch elected by the first, the executive by the second together with the first, and other appointments again made for subordinate purposes by the executive, the people would be lost sight of altogether and the necessary sympathy between them and their rulers and officers too little felt." He was an advocate for the policy of refining the popular appointments by successive filtrations, but thought it might be pushed too far. He wished the expedient to be resorted to only in the appointment of the second branch of the legislature and in the executive and judiciary branches of the government. He thought, too, that the great fabric to be raised would be more stable and durable if it should rest on the solid foundation of the people themselves than if it should stand merely on the pillars of the legislatures.

Mr. Gerry did not like the election by the people. The maxims taken from the British constitution were often fallacious when applied to our situation, which was extremely different. Experience, he said, had shown that the State legislatures, drawn immediately from the people, did not always possess their confidence. He had no objection, however, to an election by the people if it were so qualified that men of honor and character might not be unwilling to be joined in the appointments. He seemed to think the people might nominate a certain number, out of which the State legislatures should be bound to choose.

Mr. Butler thought an election by the people an impracticable mode.

The remaining clauses of the fourth resolution, relating to the qualifications of members of the national legislature, being postponed, as entering too much into detail for general propositions, The committee proceeded to the fifth resolution, that the second (or Senatorial) branch of the national legislature ought to be chosen, by the first branch, out of the persons nominated by the State legislatures.

Mr. Spaight contended that the second branch ought to be chosen, by the State legislatures, and moved an amendment to that effect.

Mr. Butler apprehended that the taking of so many powers out of the hands of the States as was proposed tended to destroy all that balance and security of interests among the States which it was necessary to preserve, and called on **Mr. Randolph**, the mover of the propositions, to explain the extent of his ideas, and particularly the number of members he meant to assign to this second branch.

Mr. Randolph observed that he had, at the time of offering his propositions, stated his ideas, as far as the nature of general propositions required; that details made no part of the plan and could not perhaps with propriety have been introduced. If he was to give an opinion as to the number of the second branch, he should say that it ought to be much smaller than that of the first; so small as to be exempt from the passionate proceedings to which numerous assemblies are liable. He observed that the general object was to provide a cure for the evils under which the United States labored; *that in tracing these evils to their origin every man had found it in the turbulence and follies of democracy; that some check, therefore, was to be sought for against this tendency of our governments,* *and that a good Senate seemed most likely to answer the purpose* (emphasis added).

Mr. Wilson opposed both a nomination by the State legislatures- and an election by the first branch of the national legislature because the second branch of the latter ought to be independent of both. He thought both branches of the national legislature ought to be chosen by the people, but was not prepared with a specific proposition. He suggested the mode of choosing the Senate of New York, to wit, of uniting several election districts for one branch in choosing members for the other branch, as a good model.

Mr. Madison observed that such a move would destroy the influence of the smaller States associated with larger ones in the same district, as the latter would choose from within themselves, although better men might be found in the former. The election of Senators in Virginia, where large and small counties were often formed into one district for the purpose, had illustrated this consequence. Local partiality would often prefer a resident within the county or State to a candidate of superior merit residing out of it. Less merit also in a resident would be more known throughout his own State.

Mr. Sherman favored an election of one member by each of the State legislatures.

Mr. Pinckney moved to strike out the "nomination by the State legislatures."

On this question," Massachusetts, Connecticut, New York, New Jersey, Pennsylvania, Virginia, North Carolina, South Carolina, Georgia—no, 9. Delaware, divided. On the whole question for electing by the first branch out of nominations by the State legislatures, Massachusetts, Virginia, South Carolina—aye, 3. Connecticut, New York, New Jersey,

Pennsylvania, Delaware, North Carolina, Georgia—no, 7. So the clause was disagreed to, and a chasm left in this part of the plan.

June 6, 1787

Mr. Mason contended that some powers under the proposed new form of government must be left with the States. The States, he concluded, should be made "a constituent part of, the National Establishment."

All civilized Societies would be divided into different Sects, Factions, & interests, as they happened to consist of rich & poor, debtors & creditors, the landed, the manufacturing, the commercial interests, the inhabitants of this district or that district, the followers of this political leader or that political leader, the disciples of this religious Sect or that religious Sect. In all cases where a majority are united by a common interest or passion, the rights of the minority are in danger. What motives are to restrain them? A prudent regard to the maxim that honesty is the best policy is found by experience to be as little regarded by bodies of men as by individuals. Respect for character is always diminished in proportion to the number among whom the blame or praise is to be divided. Conscience, the only remaining tie, is known to be inadequate in individuals: In large numbers, little is to be expected from it. Besides, Religion itself may become a motive to persecution & oppression. These observations are verified by the Histories of every Country ancient & modern. In Greece & Rome the rich & poor, the creditors & debtors, as well as the patricians & plebeians alternately oppressed each other with equal unmercifulness. What a source of oppression was the relation between the parent cities of Rome, Athens & Carthage, & their respective provinces: the former possessing the power, & the latter being sufficiently distinguished to be separate objects of it? Why was America so justly apprehensive of Parliamentary injustice? Because Great Britain had a separate interest real or supposed, & if her authority had been admitted, could have pursued that interest at our expense. We have seen the mere distinction of color made in the most enlightened period of time; a ground of the most oppressive dominion ever exercised by man over man. What has been the source of those unjust laws complained of among ourselves? Has it not been the real or supposed interest of the major number? Debtors have defrauded their creditors. The landed interest has borne hard on the mercantile interest. The Holders of one species of property have thrown a disproportion of taxes on the holders of another species. The lesson we are to draw from the whole is that where a majority are united by a common sentiment, and have an opportunity, the rights of the minor party become insecure. In a Republican Government the Majority if united have always an opportunity. The only remedy is to enlarge the sphere, & thereby divide the community into so great a number of interests & parties, that in the 1st place a majority will not be likely at the same moment to have a common interest separate from that of the whole or of the minority; and in the 2nd place, that in case they should have such an interest, they may not be apt to unite in the pursuit of it. It was incumbent on us then to try this remedy, and with that view to frame a republican system on such a scale & in such a form as will control all the evils which have been experienced.

Mr. DICKENSON considered it as essential that one branch of the Legislature should be drawn immediately from the people; and as expedient that the other should be chosen by the Legislatures of the States. This combination of the State Governments with the national Government was as politic as it was unavoidable. In the formation of the Senate we ought to carry it through such a refining process as will assimilate it as near as may be to the House of Lords in England. He repeated his warm eulogiums on the British Constitution. He was for a strong National Government but for leaving the States a considerable agency in the System. The objection against making the former dependent on the latter might be obviated by giving to the Senate an authority permanent & irrevocable for three, five or seven years. Being thus independent they will speak & decide with becoming freedom.

Mr. READ: Too much attachment is betrayed to the State Governments. We must look beyond their continuance. A national Government must soon of necessity swallow all of them up. They will soon be reduced to the mere office of electing the National Senate. He was against patching up the old federal System: he hoped the idea would be dismissed. It would be like putting new cloth on an old garment. The confederation was founded on temporary principles. It cannot last; it cannot be amended. If we do not establish a good Government on new principles, we must either go to ruin, or have the work to do over again. The people at large are wrongly suspected of being averse to a General Government. The aversion lies among interested men who possess their confidence.

Mr. PIERCE was for an election by the people as to the 1st branch & by the States as to the 2nd branch; by which means the Citizens of the States would be represented both individually & collectively.

General PINKNEY wished to have a good National Government & at the same time to leave a considerable share of power in the States. An election of either branch by the people scattered as they are in many States, particularly in S. Carolina was totally impracticable. He differed from gentlemen who thought that a choice by the people would be a better guard against bad measures, than by the Legislatures. A majority of the people in S. Carolina were notoriously for paper money as a legal tender; the Legislature had refused to make it a legal tender. The reason was that the latter had some sense of character and were restrained by that consideration. The State Legislatures also he said would be more jealous, & more ready to thwart the National Government if excluded from a participation in it. The Idea of abolishing these Legislatures would never go down.

Mr. WILSON would not have spoken again, but for what had fallen from Mr. Read; namely, that the idea of preserving the State Governments ought to be abandoned. He saw no incompatibility between the National & State Governments provided the latter were restrained to certain local purposes; nor any probability of their being devoured by the former. In all confederated Systems ancient & modern the reverse had happened; the Generality being destroyed gradually by the usurpations of the parts composing it.

June 7, 1787

Mr. PINKNEY according to notice moved to reconsider the clause respecting the negative on State laws, which was agreed to and tomorrow for fixed the purpose. The Clause providing for yearly appointment of the 2d. branch of the national Legislature, having lain blank since the last vote on the mode of electing it, to wit, by the 1st. branch, **Mr. DICKENSON** now moved "that the members of the 2d. branch ought to be chosen by the individual Legislatures."

Mr. SHERMAN seconded the motion; observing that the particular States would thus become interested in supporting the national Government and that a due harmony between the two governments would be maintained. He admitted that the two ought to have separate and distinct jurisdictions, but that they ought to have a mutual interest in supporting each other.

Mr. DICKENSON had two reasons for his motion. 1. Because the sense of the States would be better collected through their Governments; than immediately from the people at large; 2. Because he wished the Senate to consist of the most distinguished characters, distinguished for their rank in life and their weight of property, and bearing as strong a likeness to the British House of Lords as possible; and he thought such characters more likely to be selected by the State Legislatures, than in any other mode. The greatness of the number was no objection with him. He hoped there would be 80 and twice 80 of them. If their number should be small, the popular branch could not be balanced by them. The legislature of a numerous people ought to be a numerous body.

Mr. WILLIAMSON preferred a small number of Senators, but wished that each State should have at least one. He suggested 25 as a convenient number. The different modes of representation in the different branches, will serve as a mutual check.

Mr. BUTLER was anxious to know the ratio of representation before he gave any opinion.

Mr. WILSON: If we are to establish a national Government, that Government ought to flow from the people at large. If one branch of it should be chosen by the Legislatures, and the other by the people, the two branches will rest on different foundations, and dissensions will naturally arise between them. He wished the Senate to be elected by the people as well as the other branch, and the people might be divided into proper districts for the purpose & moved to postpone the motion of **Mr. Dickenson**, in order to take up one of that import.

Mr. MORRIS 2nded. him.

Mr. READ proposed "that the Senate should be appointed by the Executive Magistrate out of a proper number of persons to be nominated by the individual legislatures." He said he thought it his duty, to speak his mind frankly. Gentlemen he hoped would not be alarmed at the idea. Nothing short of this approach towards a proper model of Government would answer the purpose, and he thought it best to come directly to the point at once. His proposition was not seconded nor supported.

Mr. MADISON: if the motion [of **Mr. Dickenson**] should be agreed to, we must either depart from the doctrine of proportional representation; or admit into the Senate a very large number of members. The first is inadmissible, being evidently unjust. The second is inexpedient. The use of the Senate is to consist in its proceeding with more coolness, with more system, & with more wisdom, than the popular branch. Enlarge

MICHAEL JAMES GEANOULIS, SR.

their number and you communicate to them the vices which they are meant to correct. He differed from **Mr. Dickenson** who thought that the additional number would give additional weight to the body. On the contrary it appeared to him that their weight would be in an inverse ratio to their number. The example of the Roman Tribunes was applicable. They lost their influence and power, in proportion as their number was augmented. The reason seemed to be obvious: They were appointed to take care of the popular interests & pretensions at Rome, because the people by reason of their numbers could not act in concert; were liable to fall into factions among themselves, and to become a prey to their aristocratic adversaries. The more the representatives of the people therefore were multiplied, the more they partook of the infirmities of their constituents, the more liable they became to be divided among themselves either from their own indiscretions or the artifices of the opposite faction, and of course the less capable of fulfilling their trust. When the weight of a set of men depends merely on their personal characters; the greater the number the greater the weight. When it depends on the degree of political authority lodged in them the smaller the number the greater the weight. These considerations might perhaps be combined in the intended Senate; but the latter was the material one.

Mr. GERRY: 4 modes of appointing the Senate have been mentioned. 1. by the 1st. branch of the National Legislature. This would create a dependence contrary to the end proposed. 2. by the National Executive. This is a stride towards monarchy that few will think of. 3. by the people. The people have two great interests, the landed interest, and the commercial including the stockholders. *To draw both branches from the people will leave no security to the latter interest (emphasis added)*; the people being chiefly composed of the landed interest, and erroneously supposing, that the other interests are adverse to it. 4. by the Individual Legislatures. The elections being carried through this refinement, will be most likely to provide some check in favor of the commercial interest against the landed; without which oppression will take place, and no free Government can last long where that is the case. He was therefore in favor of this last.

Mr. DICKENSON: The preservation of the States in a certain degree of agency is indispensable. It will produce that collision between the different authorities which should be wished for in order to check each other. To attempt to abolish the States altogether, would degrade the Councils of our Country, would be impracticable, would be ruinous. He compared the proposed National System to the Solar System, in which the States were the planets, and ought to be left to move freely in their proper orbits. The gentleman from Pa. [**Mr. Wilson**] wished he said to extinguish these planets. If the State Governments were excluded from all agency in the national one, and all power drawn from the people at large, the consequence would be that the national Government would move in the same direction as the State Governments now do, and would run into all the same mischiefs. The reform would only unite the 13 small streams into one great current pursuing the same course without any opposition whatever. He adhered to the opinion that the Senate ought to be composed of a large number, and that their influence from family weight & other causes would be increased thereby. He did not admit that the Tribunes lost their weight in proportion as their number was augmented and gave a historical sketch of this institution. If the reasoning of [**Mr. Madison**] was good it would prove that the number of the Senate ought to be reduced below ten, the highest no. of the Tribunitial corps.

Mr. WILSON: The subject it must be owned is surrounded with doubts and difficulties. But we must surmount them. The British Government cannot be our model. We have no materials for a similar one. Our manners, our laws, the abolition of entails and of primogeniture, the whole genius of the people, are opposed to it. He did not see the danger of the States being devoured by the National Government. On the contrary, he wished to keep them from devouring the national Government. He was not however for extinguishing these planets as was supposed by

Mr. Dickenson - neither did he on the other hand, believe that they would warm or enlighten the Sun. Within their proper orbits they must still be suffered to act for subordinate purposes for which their existence is made essential by the great extent of our Country. He could not comprehend in what manner the landed interest would be rendered less predominant in the Senate, by an election through the medium of the Legislatures then by the people themselves. If the Legislatures, as was now complained, sacrificed the commercial to the landed interest, what reason was there to expect such a choice from them as would defeat their own views. He was for an election by the people in large districts which would be most likely to obtain men of intelligence & uprightness; subdividing the districts only for the accommodation of voters.

Mr. MADISON could as little comprehend in what manner family weight, as desired by **Mr. Dickenson** would be more certainly conveyed into the Senate through elections by the State Legislatures, than in some other modes. The true question was in what mode the best choice would be made? If an election by the people, or through any other channel than the State Legislatures promised as uncorrupt & impartial a preference of merit, there could surely be no necessity for an appointment by those Legislatures. Nor was it apparent that a more useful check would be derived through that channel than from the people through some other. The great evils complained of were that the State Legislatures run into schemes of paper money &c. whenever solicited by the people, & sometimes without even the sanction of the people. Their influence then, instead of checking a like propensity in the National Legislature, may be expected to promote it. Nothing can be more contradictory than to say that the National legislature without a proper check, will follow the example of the State Legislatures, & in the same breath, that the State Legislatures are the only proper check.

Mr. SHERMAN opposed elections by the people in districts, as not likely to produce such fit men as elections by the State Legislatures.

Mr. GERRY insisted that the commercial & monied interest would be more secure in the hands of the State Legislatures, than of the people at large. The former have more sense of character, and will be restrained by that from injustice. The people are for paper money when the Legislatures are against it. In Massachusetts the County Conventions had declared a wish for a depreciating paper that would sink itself. Besides, in some States there are two Branches in the Legislature, one of which is somewhat aristocratic. There would therefore be so far a better chance of refinement in the choice. There seemed, he thought to be three powerful objections against elections by districts. 1. it is impracticable; the people cannot be brought to one place for the purpose; and whether brought to the same place or not, numberless frauds would be unavoidable. 2. small States forming part of the same district with a large one, or large part of a large one, would have no chance of gaining an appointment for its citizens of merit. 3. a new source of discord would be opened between different parts of the same district.

Mr. PINKNEY thought the 2nd branch ought to be permanent & independent, & that the members of it would be rendered more so by receiving their appointment from the State Legislatures. This mode would avoid the rivalships & discontents incident to the election by districts. He was for dividing the States into three classes according to their respective sizes, & for allowing to the 1st. class three members-to the 2d. two, & to the 3d. one. On the question for postponing **Mr. Dickinson's** motion referring the appointment of the Senate to the State Legislatures, in order to consider **Mr. Wilson's** for referring it to the people:

Mass. no. Ct no. N. Y. no. N. J. no. Pa. ay Del. no. Md. no. Va. no. N. C. no. S. C. no. Geo. no.

Col. MASON: Whatever power may be necessary for the National Government a certain portion must necessarily be left in the States. It is impossible for one power to pervade the extreme parts of the U.S. so as to carry equal justice to them. The State Legislatures also ought to have some means of defending themselves against encroachments of the National Government. In every other department we have studiously endeavored to provide for its self-defense. Shall we leave the States alone unprovided with the means for this purpose? And what better means can we provide than the giving them some share in, or rather to make them a constituent part of, the National Establishment. There is danger on both sides no doubt; but we have only seen the evils arising on the side of the State Governments. Those on the other side remain to be displayed. The example of (the Continental) Congress does not apply. (That) Congress had no power to carry their acts into execution as the (new) National Government will have.

On **Mr. DICKINSON's** motion for an appointment of the Senate by the State Legislatures:

Mass. ay. Ct. ay. N. Y. ay. Pa. ay Del. ay. Md. ay. Va. ay N. C. ay. S. C. ay. Geo. ay.

The first draft of the Constitution submitted to the Constitutional Convention of 1787 by Edmund Randolph provided as follows:

"*Resolved*, that members of the second branch of the National Legislature (Senate) ought to be elected by those of the first (House) out of a proper number of persons nominated by the individual legislators, etc."

The draft of the Constitution submitted by **Mr. Pinckney** was practically the same, to wit:

"The Senate shall be elected and chosen by the House of Delegates." (Changed to State Legislatures)

The draft submitted by **Mr. Hamilton** provided as follows:

"The Senate to consist of persons elected to serve during good behavior; their elections to be made by electors chosen for that purpose by the people. In order to do this the States to be divided into election districts." (failed)

Gouverneur Morris of Pennsylvania proposed that the Senators be appointed by the President to serve for life and without compensation. (Failed)

Mr. Wilson of Pennsylvania urged that the election of Senators be made by the people.

The vote was taken on the election by the lower branch of the legislature and was **lost, 9-1.**

Mr. Dickinson afterwards moved that they be elected or chosen by the individual legislators. A substitute was offered for this referring the election to the people. The substitute was defeated, and the method of choosing through the State legislatures was thereupon **adopted, 10-0.**

One cannot in reading the proceedings and debates of the convention fail to notice the amount of discussion on the subject of the Senate and the mode or manner of electing Senators.

Gouverneur Morris thought it desirable that the Senate be made up of men of great and established wealth, that thus they might keep down the "turbulency of democracy."

Roger Sherman: "The people immediately should have as little to do as may be about the Government. They lack information and are constantly liable to be misled."

Mr. Gerry: *"The evils we experience flow from the excess of democracy. The people do not want virtue but are the dupes of pretended patriots."* (Emphasis added)

Mr. Dickinson: The Senate should bear as strong a resemblance to the House of Lords of England as possible.

Chapter 5

A CONSTITUTIONAL IDENTITY CRISIS

"Woodrow Wilson, Theodore Roosevelt, Herbert Croly, and John Dewey argued explicitly and energetically that the Constitution was outdated." Quoted in **"Leaving the Constitution,"** by Ronald J. Pestritto; a review of *Politics and Administration: A Study in Government* by Frank J. Goodnow.

Posted June 8, 2006 to:
http://www.claremont.org/publications/crb/id.1009/
article_detail.asp

In at least one scene from "The American Heritage" TV Series, director and narrator David Barton proudly boasts, while waving an ancient copy of the United States Constitution in front of the camera, that "the United States - the world's longest living republic - has been operating on this same piece of paper for more than 200 years!"

Is this well-informed historian unaware of the A17 change to the Constitution? Is he in denial?

"Well, Dave," I hate to say it, even think it. "Forgive me – I mean no harm – but the whole truth needs to be told so as to alert everyone about the possibility that Ben Franklin was right to worry about that little old lady's ability to keep the Republic he gave her; and to set about making things right for Ben, wherever he is."

Nay, it needs to be shouted from the rooftops, Dave. *"The Constitution we are operating on today is not the same as the wrinkled, venerated copy you resurrected from 1787 and waved before the camera!"*

There, with that emotional outburst, I may have blown it. I was astutely warned by my literary coach to project only the middle ground. "Stay balanced in this controversy," he rightfully advised, "lest you cause angst and rejection from the multitude out there who might be at peace with this progressively modified constitution." – ("Yup"), I grouch angrily to myself, ("together with the potential trillions in debt costs it represents"). Sorry, folks, can't help it. I fume while knowing I will eventually be forgiven for the high respect I hold for our founders and the Republic they gave us. I admit to being a little pissed. But I'd like a chance to redeem myself and try to get back on that middle track. I promise to take anger management classes, soonest.

PROGRESSIVES AND THEIR PREDECCESSORS

Let us probe further for plausible answers to a question raised earlier: Why did we need to transform the original constitution to the Progressive version? Or rather, why did we need an amendment to fix Senate election problems caused, not by a defective Constitution in need of repair as alleged, but by the deficient election ACT of 1866 compounded by improperly stated bribery, corruption allegations and the possibility of ulterior motives?

Here are a few of Zywicki's viewpoints on the "why" of it all: "...the Seventeenth Amendment...one small element in the larger Progressive Movement..."; "...an outgrowth of the Progressive Movement..."; and "...a largely successful attempt to wrest control of the government from the wealthy and powerful, and to transfer it to 'the people' who could

then use the government as an instrument for positive social change...
through increased democracy."

Zywicki further States, "The full story of Amendment Seventeen cannot
be understood without examining the role of special interests seeking a
more aggressive role by the federal government in passing legislation
designed to redistribute wealth to those special interests."[8]

The shift from the thinking of the founding fathers presented in several ways, from different sources. First came the rejection of Jefferson's
natural rights theory, the idea that all men are created equal with certain
unalienable rights to freedom and property. Second, that social and economic conditions had changed so greatly that the regime of the founders
was inadequate to address modern circumstances. Third, due to changing conditions, *government was no longer the threat it was perceived to be
by the Founders but could instead be entrusted with increased (Progressive)
power to meet the needs of a new era.*

> *"It would seem, then, to be no bad specimen of argument,
> to say, inasmuch as great wealth is an instrument which
> is uniformly used to extort from others, their property in
> their personal qualities and efforts -- that it ought to be
> taken away from its possessor, on the same principle, that
> a sword or a pistol may be wrested from a robber, who
> shall undertake to accomplish the same effect, in a different
> manner."*
> Skidmore, T, 1829[9]

Progressives thought direct election would eradicate the evils which resulted from election of Senators by State legislatures, and to act as a

---

8 Zywicki, Todd J., *Beyond the Shell and Husk of History: The History of the Seventeenth
Amendment and its Implications for Current Reform Proposals*, 45 Clev. St. L. Rev. 165
9 Skidmore, Thomas, *The Rights of Man to Property*, 1829

democratic vaccine to immunize the Senate from corrupt and ineffective legislation.

According to Higgs, the fundamental characteristics of the Progressive Movement was not a desire to aid those suffering economic privation, but a tendency for interest groups of all kinds to demand that the government transfer wealth to them.[10]

The original Constitution of the United States was partly abandoned and replaced with a Progressive version both in theory and in practice; in high places, up to and including the Supreme Court – and the low.

Some charge the Progressive era (1880-1910) for this influence. But this story may well involve a much wider variety of value systems and philosophies over a much greater time span.

Progressivism, a term more politically correct and therefore more acceptable than its previous cousins, likely evolved from the lesser appealing varieties like socialism, populism, Marxism, communism, egalitarianism, communalism, new ageism, collectivism, Leninism, libertarianism or liberalism. While it may be arguable about what distinguishes any one from any of the rest, they all have compatible roots or branches with each other. Consider the following variations:

The philosophy of Jean-Jacques Rousseau (1712-1778) teaches that private property is the original basis of all inequality in a civil society. Philosopher Thomas Hobbes (1588-1679) viewed human beings as essentially selfish and thought that democracy could easily degenerate into chaos, poor government and eventually civil war. The kind of governments that would have been approved by Hobbes would include benevolent dictators and enlightened despots, neither of which was permanently trustworthy.

---

10 Higgs, Robert, *Crisis and Leviathan*, 1987

Pierre-Joseph Proudhon (1809-1865), philosopher, politician, anarchist and collaborator with Philosopher and Sociologist Karl Marx (1818-1883), advocated a social contract which didn't involve an individual surrendering of sovereignty to any government or individual. According to his view, the social contract was not between individuals and the state, but rather between individuals themselves refraining from coercing or governing each other, each maintaining complete sovereignty upon oneself.

Philosopher David Hume (1711-1776) stressed that the contract theory of government was not supportable because a normal contract requires the agreement of all parties—not just the majority which often operates to the detriment of the minority.

Thomas Skidmore (1790-1832), radical American Philosopher and Politician, thought Thomas Jefferson's declarations about natural rights and self-evident truths to be "nonsense on stilts."

Skidmore elaborates:

"Such was particularly the case, with regard to what was called the Agrarian Law. This law forbid any man to own more than five hundred acres of land; any excess over that quantity, was taken away and reserved to the public, or given to the poor. This law also gave to the soldiers, and to the common people, who had none, lands conquered from their enemies. Anterior to the introduction of this law, the Patricians, or in other words, the Aristocracy, turned all these lands to their own benefit. They were, therefore, extremely unwilling to give them up; and such was the structure of their political fabric, at the time, that they alone had the power of originating all laws, the Agrarian, as well as every other. They were therefore disposed, as often as they dared, to render it nugatory, or of little effect. For four hundred years, it was the source of much civil commotion and bloodshed in Rome, and often came near being the cause of subjecting them to conquest by their enemies. At last, the [21]

Aristocracy obtained the entire ascendency over the people, and from that day began the decline of the Roman Empire."[11]

The modern equivalent of the Siren Song of Odysseus – Marxism, communism, socialism, progressivism, etc., was everywhere attractive to large swaths of struggling masses mired in grinding poverty; to entire countries like North Korea, Cuba, Russia, Venezuela – even to the people of the United States with its detested Robber Barons and unequal wealth distribution.

Henry George, self-taught Social Economist, gained lasting success and influence for his penetrating book into technological progress, boom/bust business cycles, unemployment and poverty. He sold millions of copies around the world. Only the Bible had a better sales record in the Progressive Era. George's complex theories are beyond the scope of this book.[12] Those curious about the oxymoronic relationships between progress and poverty together with all of its complex derivatives in the Progressive Era might find Henry George worthy of detailed study. I could find little more than motivators for struggling businesses to flee to friendlier business climates in foreign lands. We will revisit Henry George in later chapters.

Frank J. Goodnow (1859-1939), American Educator and Political Scientist, taught that the public will should be articulated through administration; and that greater emphasis should be laid upon social duties and less on the individual rights promoted by the founders.

> "The rights which [an individual] possesses are...conferred
> upon him, not by his Creator, but rather by the society to
> which he belongs."
> (Frank J. Goodnow, Politics and Administration: A Study

---

11 Skidmore, Thomas, *The Rights of Man to Property*, 1829

12 George, Henry, *Progress and Poverty: An Inquiry into the Cause of Industrial Depressions and of Increase of Want with Increase of Wealth: The Remedy*, 1879.

in Government, quoted in "Leaving the Constitution," by Ronald J. Pestritto; Claremont.org, 2006)

Woodrow Wilson (1856-1924), Progressive Statesman and 28th U. S. President thought the U.S. Constitution to be deficient on many levels and should be updated.[13]

Wilson rejected the natural rights of Jefferson to favor, instead, rights as a positive grant from government. He further states:

> *"Men as communities are supreme over men as individuals."*
> (Woodrow Wilson, "Socialism and Democracy," 1887, Hillsdale College Reader, p 645)

In a 1912 campaign speech, Theodore "Teddy" Roosevelt directly opposed the founder's conclusions about direct democracy by saying, in an obvious reference to the pending vote on A17 and the direct election of Senators: *"I believe in the right of the people to rule...that they will make fewer mistakes in governing themselves than any smaller class or body of men."* A noteworthy Congressman Campbell from New Hampshire responded by saying, with obvious sarcasm, that this was *"equivalent to allowing an appeal from the umpire to the bleachers."*

(*The Right of the People to Rule,* Theodore Roosevelt speech at Carnegie Hall, NY, 20 March 1912; American Rhetoric.com; see also Hillsdale College Reader, pp. 683-692)

Herbert Croly (1869–1930), leading Progressive theorist and founder of The New Republic magazine, criticizes the Founders' fear of tyranny of the majority and rejects the idea that government exists to protect individual rights. According to Croly, "Pure Democracy has again become not merely possible, but natural and appropriate."

---

13 Wilson Campaign speech, 1912, from the Hillsdale College Reader, pp 635-643

Partly because of such stimuli, there developed A17 and a multitude of costly, unproductive, inflationary and irreversible initiatives that were enacted during the Roosevelt and Johnson administrations. Such developments might not have occurred under a Senate supervised by the States. I counted more than 100, often redundant, U.S. Government Agencies and Departments just for the first four letters of the alphabet. Many of the functions covered by those agencies and departments were supposed to be "reserved to the States and to its People" (10th Amendment). (see: https://www.usa.gov/federal-agencies/)

The purpose and scope of the United States government has drifted all the way from the 1787 philosophy of liberty and freedom to the need for federal government micromanagement of everything from aspirin doses to education curricula to musical medical bills to welfare benefits. Some things government does well, though I can't think of any examples right now; and some, nay many things, it does not. But such benevolence could have been more wisely and judiciously applied without risking counterproductive deficits and permanent structural damage to the Constitution. The pendulum occasionally swings too far.

Progressives lacked a solid theory to support the election amendment. As Zywicki postulates: "The accuracy of this traditional story of Progressivism....has fallen into question in recent years." He then echoes Gabriel Kolko: "...historians have examined and substantially debunked the conventional explanation for the motives of Progressives and Progressivism."[14]

Zywicki further quotes Higgs and Hoebeke: "The fundamental characteristics of the Progressive Movement was not a desire to aid those suffering economic privation, but a tendency for interest groups of all kinds to demand that the government transfer wealth to them."

---

14 Kolko, G., *"The Triumph of Conservatism,"* 1963

Partly because of the invisible influence of Progressivism and A17, the current administrative state violates the Constitution in a variety of ways. Congress was, and is, vested with legislative authority. But somehow, agencies, assuming a role belonging to Senators, now legislate and regulate in ways that a pre-1913 Senate might not have tolerated. Moreover, agencies violate the separation of powers with impunity by giving themselves the ability to legislate, adjudicate, regulate and enforce their own rules.

Maybe, for academic reasons at least, we should wonder how we would have evolved if our founders had operated more under the philosophy of Hobbs, Immanuel Kant, Karl Marx and other forms of progressivism in 1787 to begin with. But then, since A17 brought us closer to those philosophies more than 100 years ago (1913), we might need only inspect the 200-year record of federal spending, inflation and debt service costs of Figures 2, 3, 4 and 5 – while noting the difference in the before and after A17 – to understand.

Progressives did some good things. We should applaud many of their accomplishments. But these snippets from the writers at Britannica. com, who made a thorough analysis of the Progressive movement, seem noxious to the founders' legacy; and threatening to our stability:

".... promoted a new governing philosophy that placed *less emphasis on rights*..."

".... stressed *collective* responsibilities and duties..."

"... battles that had to be fought in order to bring about a *democratic revival*..."

"... *excessive individualism and vulgar commercialism*..." (as opposed to the collective and less vulgar government-controlled markets?)

"... core progressive commitment to moderate the American *obsession with individual rights and private property...*"

"... sanctioning a dangerous commercial power inimical to personal freedom..."

"... progressive's championing of mass democracy..." (the founders thought pure democracy to be deadly and so gave us a republic)

[see: https://www.britannica.com/topic/progressivism]

Progressivism defined: "Near the end of the nineteenth century, Progressive political theorists began to view the principles of the American founding as archaic and obstructive. They argued that *the modern age brought new problems, which required new principles, as well as a move away from the republicanism of the founding to a state ruled by administrative experts* (emphasis added). Progressivism came to dominate American politics in the 20th century, and remains a powerful political force today."

"Archaic?" "Obstructive?" "New problems?" "New principles?"

What, exactly, are these "new problems?" Do these "new problems" have anything to do with the explosion of wealth that motivated Progressives to promote a revised, living constitution; or rather, an amendment to modify the Constitution and the Senate in order to facilitate "new principles" that move us "away from the democratic republic of the founding with its free markets to a state ruled by administrative experts?"

Do these "new problems" have anything to do with the wide spectrum of wealth and opportunity made available by the legacy of our "archaic" founding principles in liberty and freedom; or the skill, ingenuity and inventiveness that unleashed a torrent of wealth that stuck to some more than to others? Was it considered "obstructive" that lovers of our constitution tried desperately to save it in its original form; and struggle yet to this day to revive it?

Are "new principles" now necessary to compensate for human deficiencies, or the oft occurring natural calamity bestowed upon us by disinterested natural forces or the creator of lights? If so, should not such positions have been openly stated to begin with instead of the deception and the chicanery that upended a proud Constitution which made us the envy of the world?

Would it not have proven better to properly fund and administer those aforementioned inequities rather than chance the alarming hindsight of the most recent 100-year experience of A17? And, to echo the Honorable Senator George Frisbee Hoar from Massachusetts who labored long and hard to preserve the Senate in its original form: *"Shouldn't we just leave well-enough alone?"*

BAD POLITICIANS

It is true, as alleged, that you will occasionally find a Senator who deserves the accommodations reserved for sneak thieves and pirates. Such criminals deserve to be locked up. But all bad politicians should be held accountable on a par with those holding Senate seats. A quick scan of the hundreds of misconduct allegations brought against both Senators and Representatives listed at https://www.govtrack.us/misconduct illustrates the distinct probability that weaknesses in human nature knows no political stripe, no particular date, no constitutional clause, no constitutional amendment or ten such amendments, and no reasonable substitute for our criminal justice system in policing such problems – either before, or after, 1913 and A17.

Such weaknesses deserve legal redress, in any case, to be sure. But honestly, which kind of Senate makes more sense? The pre-1913 version that budgeted and spent within reason - virtually free of debt? Or the faster, looser, fiscally undisciplined variety who, since 1913, indebted us all to the tune of the recently projected one trillion dollars annually for debt service costs alone?

Which view would you rather have in your rear-view mirror? (1) The post-1913 view you could easily describe from memory and the record? Or (2) the view you could only describe by imagining the influence of a wiser, more thoughtful, clearer-thinking pre-1913 type of Senator? The kind of Senator who would have been better able to face intense problems with slow, deliberate, objective problem-solving, clearer-thinking abilities of the kind not possible if supervised directly by the People instead of their respective State legislatures?

Which of the two (pre/post 1913) Senate types would have been more likely to approve of the Viet Nam War, the War on Poverty, the War Powers Act, annual billion-dollar debt costs and trillion-dollar budget deficits?

Which of these Senators would you rather have today? Those vetted and selected by more knowledgeable State legislators? Or the personable variety who depend, for their election or reelection, on regular folks more easily seduced with promises of every kind from a treasury that's empty except for immorally contrived debits on the assets of those not yet born?

Would it not have been more desirable to have evolved over the past 100 years under the influence of a Senate populated with the highest and best that State legislatures had to offer?

ULTERIOR MOTIVES

Did Progressives really care about alleged election problems? Did Senate gridlocks or empty Senate seats really concern them? No, not for a second. Their real concern was to modify the Constitution and maximize popular control of the federal government; and, by deduction, wealth transfer programs for which a wiser, more deliberative Senate would have demanded a higher level of quality control and fiscal responsibility. With the help of compassionate supporters, Progressives partially neutered the Senate and a critically important section of the constitution to get it done.

Progressives told us that the limited government established by the founders was outdated; that social and economic ills of modern society required action; that history had progressed to such an extent that a powerful central government no longer posed the threat to life, liberty, and property that it did in 1787.

Progressives saw the limited federal government of the founders as a barrier to much-needed "progress"; and that the rise of big corporations and the Industrial Revolution required more government regulation. They desired a move away from the enumerated powers, separation of powers and federalism, to a more active central government.

Progressives argued that the Constitution was a product of its time, designed to defend against the issues of the day. This, in contrast to Abraham Lincoln's view that *natural truths are applicable to all men at all times.*" (Excerpt from a Lincoln letter to Henry Pierce, 1859)

Progressives wanted the national government to be a dynamic agent, directly responsive to changing social and economic conditions. To accomplish the foregoing, passage of A17 and the direct election of Senators was needed.

> *"I believe there are more instances of the abridgment of the freedom of the people by gradual and silent encroachments of those in power than by violent and sudden usurpations."*
> James Madison, Address at the Virginia Convention, June 16, 1788

DENIAL

There seems to be universal denial about the relationship between the Progressive movement and A17. The primary example for this, my favored Hillsdale College, will be discussed at length in chapters 8 and 9. The Senate itself presents shocking examples (chapter 7).

Author Richard Epstein stunningly makes no reference to the connection between A17 and the Progressive Movement that "rewrote Article I, Section 3 of the Constitution."[15] And Randall G. Holcombe, previously cited, describes a sharp difference in government growth rates between the 19th and 20th centuries, while noting only that "seeds were sown in the Progressive era."

Would it not have been reasonable to suggest that those seeds were fertilized by a Progressive 17th Amendment and a new kind of Senate more agreeable to wealth redistribution for a variety of special interests? And the seduction of voters with financial promises funded by the printing press and an empty treasury, or rather, a treasury filled with improperly authorized IOUs for creditors not yet born?

What with Rossum's startling revelation about the blowout of election problems subsequent to the passage of the election ACT of 1866, and his equally startling disclosure about the dearth of such problems prior to 1866, should we not wonder: why didn't lawmakers see the difference between the before and after the ACT and simply repeal or repair it as a much safer and easier alternative to a profoundly misdirected, unfortunate, unproven, complicated, inappropriate, weighty and dangerous Constitutional amendment? Couldn't they have also seen that the ACT's requirement for majority consensus actually paved the way for direct elections that resulted in the very pluralities that the ACT attempted to avoid?

---

15 Epstein, Richard A., *How Progressives Rewrote the Constitution*, 1943

"Contemporary liberals believe that we must live under a living constitution but, of course, to live under a living constitution, which lives and breathes and grows and changes with the winds of progressive elites, is to live under no constitution at all. The very nature of a living constitution is to not fix things, or put certain things beyond the bounds of ordinary political change."
Watson, Brad C. S., May 2020[16]

---

16 From: *How the Academics Made Progressivism All American*, A lawliberty.com podcast interview with Brad C. S. Watson, hosted by Richard M. Reinsch. [Mr. Watson is a professor of Politics at Saint Vincent College.]

Chapter 6

AN ACT TO REGULATE SENATE ELECTIONS (1866)

The United States Congress is authorized to supervise elections for its Senators and Representatives under Article I, Section 4 of the United States Constitution.

Since the devil is in the details, and because citing government bills "can be tricky" (*How to Cite Government Bills*; Cort, Danielle, 2017), alternative citation methods are brought for those who may want to explore this implausible ACT on their own.

First alternative (best): United States. Congress. Senate. *An ACT to Regulate the Times and Manner of Holding Elections for Senators in Congress.* 39th Cong. 1st Session. Chapter 245. July 26, 1866. pp. 243-244. Second alternative: 14 Stat. 245 (1866).

Note the emphasis on the ACT's requirement for a "majority" (viz a plurality) which presented a profound source of difficulty for those States having multiple candidates and/or multiple parties. Note also, the simple prescriptions suggested by Senator Root, Todd Zywicki and others for "pluralities" and "run-offs" in lieu of "majorities."

For convenience, the ACT is copy/pasted herewith.
From the Congressional Record of the THIRTY-NINTH CONGRESS Sess. I. Ch 245, 1866:

———

CHAP. CCXLV -- *AN ACT TO REGULATE THE TIMES AND MANNER OF HOLDING ELECTIONS FOR SENATORS IN CONGRESS.* July 25, 1866

Be it enacted by the Senate and House of Representatives of the United States of America in Congress assembled, That the legislature of each state which shall be chosen next preceding the expiration of the time for which any Senator was elected to represent said State in Congress, shall, on the second Tuesday after the meeting and organization thereof, proceed to elect a Senator in Congress, in the place of such Senator so going out of office, in the following manner: Each house shall openly, by a *viva voce* of each member present, name one person for Senator in Congress from said State, and the name of the person so voted for, who shall have a majority of the whole number of votes cast in each house shall be entered on the journal of each house by the clerk or secretary thereof; but if either house shall fail to give such majority to any person on said day, that fact shall be entered in the journal. At 12 o'clock, meridian, of the day following that on which proceedings are required to take place, as aforesaid, the members of the two houses shall convene in joint assembly and a journal of each house shall then be read, and if the same person shall have received a majority of all the votes in each house, such person shall be declared duly elected Senator to represent said State in the Congress of the United States: but if the same person shall not have received a majority of the votes in each house, or if either house shall have failed to take proceedings as required by this act, the joint assembly shall then proceed to choose, by a *viva voce* vote of each member present a person for the purpose of aforesaid, and the person having a majority of all the votes of the said joint assembly, a majority of all the members elected to both houses being present and voting, shall be declared duly elected: and in case no person shall receive such majority on the first day, the joint assembly shall meet at 12 o'clock meridian, of each succeeding day during the session of the legislature, and take at least one vote until a Senator shall be elected.

Sec. 2. *And be it further enacted*, That whenever, on the meeting of the legislature of any State, a vacancy shall exist in the representation of each state in the Senate of the United States, said legislature shall proceed, on the second Tuesday after the commencement and organization of its session, to elect a person to fill such vacancy, in the manner hereinbefore provided for the election of a Senator for a full term; and if a vacancy shall happen during the session of the legislature, then on the second Tuesday after the legislature shall have been organized and shall have notice of such vacancy.

Sec. 3. *And be it further enacted*, That it shall be the duty of the governor of the State from which any Senator shall have been chosen as aforesaid to certify his election, under the seal of the State, to the President of the Senate of the United States, which certificate shall be countersigned by the secretary of state of the State.

Approved, July 25, 1866.

———

In *"Federalism, The Supreme Court, and the Seventeenth Amendment,"* as stated earlier, Rossum reported one (1) deadlock and one (1) case of alleged bribery investigated by the Senate in the entire 77 years prior to 1866, the date of the ACT; whereas subsequent to 1866 and the emergence of the questionable ACT, with its difficult "majority" and "time" constraints, the numbers of deadlock and alleged corruption cases blew way out of proportion: to seventy-one (71) and fifteen (15) respectively. Rossum also found Senate election deadlock/corruption rates to be a mere .074 percent of 1,180 Senate elections throughout the 19th century.

To understand why there were so many more election problems after 1866, and the onset of rumored back room deals, some of which were likely influenced by money as charged, a closer look at the "majority" requirements of the ACT is necessary. States having multiple candidates and/or multiple parties simply were unable to comply with majority and time requirements. During subsequent debates over resolutions to change the way Senators were elected, proposals to modify the ACT of 1866 as the best way to repair election problems were ignored because influential resolution supporters discovered that bringing the people closer to the Senate was thought to be more desirable anyway - problems with the ACT or the collective wisdom of our founders notwithstanding.

Apparently, it was not noticed or maybe even ignored, that the ACT of 1866 with its weak formula for Senate elections should have been seen as the object in need of repair – not the constitution, the assault on which was improperly influenced according to respected scholars.

To better understand those election paradoxes before and after 1866, we need to review the circumstance that gave birth to that defective ACT.

Both Houses of Congress are required under Article 1, Section 4, to be the judge and qualifier of its own members. Aggravating questions about the legitimacy of Senate elections, however, were annoying for a Senate who had better things to do than sort through the quagmire of State rules governing said elections.

In 1857, members of the Indiana legislature asked Congress to reject the credentials of two Senators alleged to be improperly elected because of quorum issues. That same year, the Pennsylvania legislature unsuccessfully petitioned the Senate to set aside the election of Senator Cameron because of a concurrent majority problem. Then again, in 1866, in the middle of important reconstruction matters, the Senate was pressured to unseat Senator Stockton from New Jersey because he voted, contrary to the rules, for his own seat in a close contest. The upshot? A hastily drawn ACT thought to improve, standardize and simplify State legislative elections for Senators (for more detail, see Rossum, R., 1946, Chapter 6).

The hastily constructed election ACT of 1866, which required majorities viz pluralities had unforeseen consequences. Gridlocks began to soar. Between 1866 and 1913 there were seventy-one gridlocks. The ACT, according to analysts, could have avoided such problems if it had provided for pluralities or runoffs. Isn't it ironic that the pluralities Congress sought to avoid may have paved the way for the pluralities of popular elections under A17?

With the record for deadlock and corruption rates before and after 1866 such as it was, how could lawmakers not have seen that the ACT - unable to get proper attention partly because of pressing reconstruction issues and/or possible ulterior motives - was the primary cause of Senate election problems? Why couldn't they have seen how, for the 77 years prior to 1866 and the ACT (which could have been easily modified), States were more appropriately and efficiently supervising their own respective Senate elections?

It might still prove wise to amend the Constitution—considered by many to be the greatest political document ever devised--to satisfy the need for poverty relief and to remove monied influence. But to justify A17 as necessary to repair alleged election problems or human weaknesses that were in truth, influenced more by defective federal legislation and the creator of lights seems profoundly disingenuous - even fraudulent.

As for the sins of monied influence and corruption, consider the "Misconduct" problems described by govtrack.us, which reveals an inclination for politicians of every stripe to be influenced by the devil far more often in, say, the decade of 2010 than their counterparts in any of the decades prior to May 31, 1913 - the date when such problems were supposed to be neutralized by A17. The data reflects the same in the categories of bribery and corruption for both Senators and their counterparts in the House of Representatives. (see: https://www.govtrack.us/misconduct)

As charged earlier, the openly stated justification for repeated amendment efforts were to repair election problems in bribery, power brokering, back room deals and corruption during the seating of U. S. Senators; and to neutralize monied influences that tainted Senate elections. But there were secondary motives deemed more important: a closer connection between the people and the Senate. This argument seems to be boiling down to the difference between the efficacies of democracies and republics; between the social needs of Progressives and the long-term stability of our Republic.

Rossum, Zywicki and others claim that gridlocks and other dubious justifications for that questionable amendment could have been avoided simply by amending the 1866 ACT to allow Senate elections by plurality and/or run-offs. But who really cares about Senate corruption problems or seats left empty, when the real, much more important goal, is popular control of the United States Senate which the researchers allege actually created a new, more virulent form of monied influence?

Bybee and others contend that the people simply preferred a higher form of democracy and were willing to sacrifice federalism to achieve it. People were alleging that Senators were being seated by their respective legislatures contrary to their wishes; and that Senate elections were being bought and sold (an exaggerated disorder that was fertilized by the problematic mandates of the ACT of 1866). Even so, the Senate could find only three (3) verifiable cases of bribery subsequent to the ACT. Though few in number, those cases contributed to a general feeling of discontent.

There were two more complex, mitigating factors worthy of note: the corrupting influence of machine politics and corporations – conditions, proponents claimed, that only direct elections by the people could alleviate. Opponents countered that the people could be influenced more than State legislatures. They further asserted that it was foolish to claim that the people, who elected State representatives unwisely, could be trusted to be the wiser when voting directly for their Senators. Senator Elihu Root made the point by asking: "Why reform the system while the whole proposition rests upon the postulate of the incapacity of the people of the United States to elect honest and faithful legislatures?" Zywicki alleged, moreover, that A17 may have worsened corporate influence by turning attention away from the legislature to the candidates themselves. Direct election enabled lobbyists to focus on Senators rather than entire state legislatures.

While there were a few rejectionable self-righteous Senators prior to 1866 who were deemed pompous, haughty, vain, smug, conceited, arrogant, egotistical, and obnoxious, - especially when it came to slavery issues - maybe even stubborn poverty issues that, in truth, belong to the State and its People to resolve in any event, it's worth repeating that alleged deadlock and corruption problems reached a grand total of one (1) each over 77 years prior to the ACT of 1866; whereas after 1866, those totals blew way out to 71 and 15 respectively - Ratios of 1 to 71; and 1 to 15.

Consider this divergence in the literature cited here in an effort to defend the aforementioned "rejectionable." Tocqueville celebrated the American Senate thusly: "Scarcely an individual is to be seen in it who has not had an active and illustrious career: the Senate is composed of eloquent advocates, distinguished generals, wise magistrates, and Statesmen of note, whose arguments would do honor to the most remarkable parliamentary debates of Europe."[17]

---

17 Tocqueville, Alexis, *Democracy in America*, 1835

In contrast, the Beards describe the Senate in politically correct terms by saying: "Some of them were political leaders of genuine talents but a majority possessed no conspicuous merits except the ownership of strong boxes well filled with securities."[18]

Contemporary writers, apparently unaware of the damage unwittingly triggered by the ACT of 1866, allege that the Civil War was the turning point for the sharp upturn in Senate election problems. *No - emphatically. The turning point was the ACT of 1866 – not the Civil War.* There is no shortage of misleading statements in the literature on this topic. Schiller and Stewart gave eloquent treatment on the need for A17 to cure bribery and corruption. But by their own admission, focused only "on the years between 1875 and 1913," thereby leaving untouched the relatively cleaner 77 years prior to the unfortunate impact of the ACT of 1866.[19] The full extent of this story may never be fully and accurately understood, even by distinguished scholars.

As for allegations, however real or imagined, about Senators being chosen in back room deals: why heck, how else could elections have been achieved given those 1866 restrictions, multiple candidates, time constraints and third parties? In any event, everyone knows back room deals are often used to iron out kinks in legal proceedings of every kind. What kind of "back room deals" took place during the hasty construction of that questionable election ACT of 1866? Was not the formerly venerated United States Constitution itself fabricated in a room closed off from the public in 1787 Philadelphia?

Would it be allowable to speculate, as politely as possible, that dubious Senate elections might be but a symptom; that the real problem, whole truth be known, might be found in sociopolitical circles whose philosophy in liberty and freedom is not entirely compatible with that of our

18 Beard, Charles and Beard, Mary, *The Rise of American Civilization*, 2 vols. 1930)
19 Schiller, Wendy J. and Stewart, Charles III, *Electing the Senate: Indirect Democracy before the Seventeenth Amendment*

founder's ideas about liberty and freedom? It is difficult for this violated curmudgeon to imagine how passage of A17 could have been otherwise possible?

> *"In these critical moments, how salutary will be the*
> *interference of some temperate and respectable body of*
> *citizens, in order to check the misguided career, and to*
> *suspend the blow meditated by the people against themselves,*
> *until reason, justice, and truth can regain their authority*
> *over the public mind?"*
> (Hamilton or Madison, Federalist #63)

Our venerable constitution was partially neutered by opportunists who were determined to take control of the United States Senate away from State legislatures using improperly portrayed and exaggerated election problems as red herrings.

Chapter 7

DIRECT ELECTION OF SENATORS

[Note: The following appraisal of Amendment Seventeen was copied from the Art/History section of Senate.gov (link below). It illustrates widespread casual regard for accuracy in the way A17 is portrayed – even in high places like the Senate itself. I took the liberty of editing the piece [**in bold**] because it was incomplete, incorrect, misleading and improper; and because it appeared to be an unwarranted exercise in denial to validate A17. As some scholars have indicated, and as I try to demonstrate here, the amendment controversy may well have been avoided by simply modifying the defective ACT of 1866 to legitimize pluralities or even repealing the ACT of 1866 altogether. By spending some extra effort understanding the difference in tone between the original and the bold **edits**, the reader will arrive at a better understanding of the evolution of Amendment 17.]

Direct Election of Senators
Undated; Author (unknown or withheld)

——

"Voters have elected their Senators in the privacy of the voting booth since 1913. The framers of the Constitution, however, **by a vote of 10 to 0,** did not intend Senators to be elected in this way and included in

Article I, section 3, "The Senate of the United States shall be composed of two Senators from each state, chosen by the legislature thereof for six Years; and each Senator shall have one Vote."

The election of delegates to the Constitutional Convention [1787] established the precedent for state selection. The framers believed that in electing Senators, state legislatures would cement their tie with, **or act as a check on,** the national government, which would increase the chances for ratifying the Constitution. They also expected that Senators elected by state legislatures would be able to concentrate on the business at hand without pressure from the populace.

This process seemed to work well until the ~~mid-1850s~~ **mid-1860s.** At that time, growing hostilities **[caused mostly by a defective election ACT of 1866]** in various States resulted in vacant Senate seats. In Indiana, for example, the conflict between Democrats in the southern half of the state and the emerging Republican Party in the northern half prevented the election of any candidate, thereby leaving the Senate seat vacant for two years. ~~This~~ **[The enactment of the defective election ACT of 1866]** marked the beginning of many contentious battles in state legislatures, as the struggle to elect Senators reflected **[the defective ACT of 1866].** ~~the increasing tensions over slavery and States' rights that led to the Civil War.~~ **[Note: Slavery tensions had little effect on Senate election problems which didn't really blow out of control until the negative impact of the ACT of 1866].**

After ~~the Civil War~~ **the ACT of 1866,** problems in Senatorial elections by the state legislatures multiplied. In one case in **1866** ~~the late 1860s~~, the election of Senator John Stockton of New Jersey was contested on the grounds that he had been elected by a *plurality* rather than a *majority* in the state legislature. Stockton based his defense on the observation that not all States elected their Senators in the same way and presented a report that illustrated the inconsistency in state elections of Senators. In response, Congress passed a law in 1866 regulating how and when

Senators were elected in each state. This was the first change in the process of Senatorial elections created by the Founders, **and this 1866 change, which required majority votes while rejecting plurality votes, caused the problem; the Constitution was inexplicably charged with election problems that belonged, instead, with the 1866 change**. The law ~~helped but~~ did not ~~entirely~~ solve the problem, **but in fact greatly aggravated it**. And deadlocks in some legislatures continued to cause long vacancies in some Senate seats.

Intimidation and bribery marked **a few of** the States' selection of Senators. Nine bribery cases were brought before the Senate between 1866 and 1906 **[versus one (1) prior to 1866 (note the reference to 1866)]**. In addition, 45 deadlocks occurred in 20 States between 1891 and 1905 **[versus one (1) prior to 1866]**, resulting in numerous delays in seating Senators. In 1899 problems in electing a Senator in Delaware were so acute **[because of an inability to comply with the Act of 1866]** that the state legislature did not send a Senator to Washington for four years.

The impetus for reform began as early as 1826, when direct election of Senators was first proposed. In the 1870s, **[or after 1866]** voters sent a petition to the House of Representatives for a popular election. From 1893 to 1902, momentum increased considerably. Each year during that period, a constitutional amendment to elect Senators by popular vote was proposed in Congress, but the Senate fiercely resisted change, despite the frequent vacancies and disputed election results **caused by the deficient ACT of 1866**. In the mid-1890s, the Populist Party incorporated the direct election of Senators into its party platform, although neither the Democrats nor the Republicans paid much notice at the time. In the early 1900s, one state initiated changes on its own. Oregon pioneered direct election **[aka direct democracy]** and experimented with different measures over several years until it succeeded in 1907. Soon after, Nebraska followed suit and laid the foundation for other States to adopt measures reflecting the people's will. **[A James Wilson**

motion for popular Senate elections was rejected by the founders, 9 to 1 in 1787, partly because the "people's will" already had an outlet in the House of Representatives, and partly to facilitate State legislative checks on the federal government]. Senators who resisted reform had difficulty ignoring the growing support for direct election of Senators.

After the turn of the century, momentum for reform grew rapidly. **Yellow journalist,** William Randolph Hearst, expanded his publishing empire with *Cosmopolitan* and championed the cause of direct election with **overstated** muckraking articles and strong advocacy of reform. Hearst hired a veteran reporter, David Graham Phillips, who wrote scathing pieces on Senators, portraying them as pawns of industrialists and financiers. The pieces became a series titled "The Treason of the Senate," which appeared in several monthly issues of the magazine in 1906. These articles galvanized the public into maintaining pressure on the Senate for reform.

Increasingly, Senators were elected based on state referenda, similar to the means developed by Oregon. By 1912, as many as 29 States elected Senators either as nominees of their party's primary or in a general election. As representatives of a direct election process, the new Senators supported measures that argued for federal legislation, but in order to achieve reform, a constitutional amendment was **[NOT]** required. In 1911 Senator Joseph Bristow of Kansas offered a resolution proposing a constitutional amendment. The idea also enjoyed strong support from Senator William Borah of Idaho, himself a product of direct election. Eight southern Senators and all Republican Senators from New England, New York, and Pennsylvania opposed Senator Bristow's resolution. The Senate approved the resolution largely because of the Senators who had been elected by state-initiated reforms, many of whom were serving their first term and therefore may have been more willing to support direct election. After the Senate passed the amendment, which represented the culmination of decades of debate about the issue, the measure moved to the House of Representatives.

The House initially fared no better than the Senate in its early discussions of the proposed amendment. Much wrangling characterized the debates, but in the summer of 1912 the House finally passed the amendment and sent it to the States for ratification. The campaign for public support was aided by Senators such as Borah and political scientist George H. Haynes, whose scholarly work on the Senate contributed greatly to passage of the amendment. Connecticut's approval on April 8, 1913, gave the Seventeenth Amendment the required three-fourths majority needed for enactment. The following year marked the first time all Senatorial elections were held by popular vote.

The Seventeenth Amendment restates the first paragraph of Article I, section 3 of the Constitution and provides for the election of Senators by replacing the phrase "chosen by the Legislature thereof" with "elected by the people thereof." In addition, it allows the governor or executive authority of each state, if authorized by that state's legislature, to appoint a Senator in the event of a vacancy, until a general election occurs."

———

https://www.Senate.gov/artandhistory/history/common/briefing/
Direct_Election_Senators.htm

The Seventeenth Amendment to the U.S. Constitution:

> *The Senate of the United States shall be composed of two
> Senators from each State, elected by the people thereof, for six
> years; and each Senator shall have one vote. The electors in
> each State shall have the qualifications requisite for electors
> of the most numerous branch of the State legislatures.*

> *When vacancies happen in the representation of any State in
> the Senate, the executive authority of such State shall issue
> writs of election to fill such vacancies: Provided, That the*

legislature of any State may empower the executive thereof to make temporary appointments until the people fill the vacancies by election as the legislature may direct.

This amendment shall not be so construed as to affect the election or term of any Senator chosen before it becomes valid as part of the Constitution.

Untitled cartoon, February 4, 1911

https://www.archives.gov/legislative/features/17th-amendment/dead-locks.html

This Clifford Berryman cartoon illustrates the recurring problem of state legislatures that could not agree on who to elect to the Senate. Party differences and machine politics often prevented a state from deciding on a Senator for months or even years. Berryman shows four States which left an empty Senate seat because they could not agree on a candidate.

RESULTS OF THE POORLY DESIGNED ELECTION ACT
OF 1866
(Not the results of a defective Constitution as alleged by
supporters of A17)
Title added by MJG, 2020
[This cartoon, posted at the Center for Legislative Studies website,
was originally untitled]

TREASON OF THE SENATE? OR MISREPRESENTATION OF IT?
https://www.cop.Senate.gov/artandhistory/history/minute/
Treason_of_the_Senate.htm
(Author unknown or withheld, 1906)

[Note: This smear, taken from Senate archives, cuts to the heart of the questionable effort to replace State legislatures by the People in Senate elections: the greatly exaggerated hysterical certainty, that monied interests were everywhere colluding with Senators and State legislators to take economic advantage of the people. Two unnamed corrupt Senators were cited here to justify support for A17 as the means to cure Senate corruption. Too bad the author, whomever he or she was, didn't have access to the corruption rates of modern times, he or she might have concluded we were better off without A17. For it is true: corruption rates, used to leverage the need for A17, are worse now than they ever were. See, for one example: "More Than Two Dozen Members of Congress Have Been Indicted Since 1980," Schwarz, Hunter, The Washington Post, July 29, 2015]

TREASON OF THE SENATE
"In February 1906, readers of Cosmopolitan magazine opened its pages to this statement: "Treason is a strong word, but not too strong to characterize the situation in which the Senate is the eager, resourceful, and indefatigable agent of interests as hostile to the American people as any invading army could be." This indictment launched a nine-part series of articles entitled "Treason of the Senate."

This "Treason" series placed the Senate at the center of a major drive by Progressive Era reformers to weaken the influence of large corporations and other major financial interests on government policy making. Direct popular election of Senators fit perfectly with their campaign to bring government closer to the people.

As originally adopted, the Constitution provided for the election of Senators by individual state legislatures. In the years following the Civil War, that system became increasingly subject to bribery, fraud, and deadlock. As Congress took on a greater role in shaping an industrializing nation, those with a major business stake in that development believed they could best exert their influence on the U.S. Senate by offering financial incentives to the state legislators who selected its members.

The campaign for direct election of Senators took on new force in 1906, following conviction of two Senators on corruption charges. Each had taken fees for interceding with federal agencies on behalf of business clients. The resulting negative publicity inspired publisher William Randolph Hearst, then a U.S. House member and owner of Cosmopolitan magazine, to commission popular novelist David Graham Phillips to prepare a series of investigative articles.

Making the point that large corporations and corrupt state legislators played too large a role in selection of Senators, these articles doubled Cosmopolitan's circulation within two months. Yet, Phillips's obvious reliance on innuendo and exaggeration soon earned him the scorn of other reformers. President Theodore Roosevelt saw in these charges a politically motivated effort by Hearst to discredit his administration and coined the term "muckraker" to describe the Phillips brand of overstated and sensationalist journalism.

For several decades before publication of Phillips's series, certain southern Senators had blocked the direct election amendment out of fear that it would increase the influence of African American voters. By 1906, however, many southern States had enacted "Jim Crow" laws to undermine that influence. The Phillips series finally broke Senate resistance and opened the way for the Seventeenth Amendment's ratification in 1913."

———

Chapter 8

THE U S CONSTITUTION: A HILLSDALE COLLEGE READER

"The protection of our property, argues Franklin Roosevelt, requires that we surrender that property to the government freely. The defense of our rights, he argues, requires that we empower the government far beyond the limits permitted by the Constitution."
Arnn, Larry P., President, Hillsdale College;
Constitution *Reader*, Foreword, p xiii

While exploring the medieval walls of Rothenburg, Germany as a tourist many years ago, I fancied myself as one of those ancient watchmen who were long ago obliged to protect the town's valuables from plunderers by keeping a nightly watch on the horizon for their dreaded campfires. So, I might be in the possession of a few DNA molecules of a lesser form of animal in my system; a watchdog, if you will. For I am convinced I have detected signs of unrequited danger of another kind on our horizon.

I've arrived at a stage of this punishing yet worthwhile ordeal where I need help. Like a resolute hound dog on a quarry quest, I am determined to get to the heart of this mischief if only to expose the fact that that is just exactly what it was: a mischievous act of benevolence that, for precious few of us, more resembles a road to hell paved with good intentions.

I will get to the bottom of Amendment 17 - this threat of permanent damage to the former greatness of America - if it means enrolling in one of those tedious online politics courses offered by Hillsdale College. Surely that widely reputed defender and protector of the American Constitution, who refuses to be on the take for a single dime of government money, will know all about that constant 19th century drumbeat of amendment resolutions to change the way Senators were elected. Surely there exists at Hillsdale, or will soon exist, a scholarly treatment about the pros and cons of any such attempt to modify a document so important to the mission of Hillsdale – and to the rest of us. Can we imagine, even for a millisecond, that any of Hillsdale's course outlines would not include an impact statement of any change to that precious document deemed worthy of preserving "to the current day?" (Hillsdale President Larry Arnn quote from the *Reader's* foreword, p xi)

It gave me a measure of pride and relief - temporarily at least - to visualize Hillsdale as being a noble guardian of a Constitution worthy of defending to "its very last syllable forever" - assuming it's okay to translate "to the current day," as meaning forever.

But alas and alack, this might not be.

After enrolling and scanning course outlines, I could find nothing about Amendment 17 or any hints that might lead to a discussion of it in any of Hillsdale's literature – here on earth, or in cyberspace. Not one to give up easily, and being impatient about sitting through online lessons when what I really needed was immediate gratification on specifics about how Amendment 17 impacted what Hillsdale holds as sacrosanct, I order the supplement to the Politics 101 course: "*The U.S. Constitution: A Reader.*" Maybe I'll find something about this profound change to the Constitution most of us claim to love and cherish in 2 or 3 of its 790 pages.

Still, it was not to be.

There was adequate representation in the *Reader* from honorable gentlemen who influenced our founding. Many of their important works were rightfully reproduced there to be sure. And many significant speeches compatible with Hillsdale's mission to preserve and protect the Constitution were transcribed, as well. Such was the respectable nature of the *Reader's* first 614 pages.

The balance of the *Reader*, chapters X and XI (pp 615 – 790), however, proved somewhat discomforting. It took this dummy a while to digest the possibility that the *Reader's* editors might be practicing a form of devil's advocacy; presenting material that a seasoned veteran or a proctored student would immediately detect as contrary to founding principles; or reasons to stiffen friendly resolves against all opponents of the original United States Constitution whether foreign or domestic.

But to the uninitiated like me; to the newbie who might scan that *Reader* in a casual manner, virtually all of Chapter X and most of Chapter XI reads like a respectable who's who in the domestic Progressive movement, presenting a rather well-reasoned series of 10 eloquent and convincing essays in Chapter X alone. Had I been 18 years old with a virgin mind, yet unstudied in our founding principles in liberty, freedom and property rights, I might have been sold on Progressive benevolent philosophy with its prescription for big government, wealth transfers and a culture of dependency.

It therefore seems somewhat disingenuous that Hillsdale College, known far and wide for its staunch support of our founders, would sanction a *Reader* that provides such a high level of visibility and respect for Progressives holding positions contrary to those of the founders Hillsdale claims to support, protect and defend forever.

In the very first sentence of the *Reader's* foreword (p xi), President Arnn describes how it was "...made up of original source documents that bear upon the founding of the American republic, the making of its Constitution, and the struggle to preserve that document..." Well, no. That's not entirely true. Virtually all the essays in Chapter X and most of Chapter XI are source documents that bear, not "upon the founding of the American republic," but upon the growth of Progressivism with its deceptive desire to reduce the essence of that venerable document, proceeding then to obfuscate the history of the deception.

For those unfamiliar with FDR's inclination toward the Progressive or LBJ's Socialist leanings, chapters X and XI portray these American presidents as heroes for socialists and progressives alike. It suddenly seems that Hillsdale juggles two conflicting personalities: (1) a noble giant who rises like The Hulk to preserve and protect a cherished document while (2) that same noble giant looks the other way as Progressive counterparts vigorously support the partial dismantling of that precious document he assigned himself to preserve and protect "to its very last syllable forever."

It's one thing to amend the Constitution for legitimate reasons using legitimate means. Quite another, however, to amend the Constitution for legitimate reasons using illegitimate means. It smacks of the subversive.

For now, letters to Hillsdale College President Larry P. Arnn, the faculty, and Board of Trustees are being drafted in efforts to obtain (1) clarification on the Hillsdale mission and (2) a scholarly review and estimate of how A17 may, or may not, have damaged our once venerated Constitution of the United States.

Meanwhile, I will wonder, as we all should wonder, why Hillsdale College, in describing itself as "a trustee of...heritage finding its clearest expression in the American experiment of self-government under law," would give prominent exposure to Progressive essays in their *"U.S. Constitution: A Reader."*

> *"By studying the Constitution, students will understand*
> *better the nature of political justice and the serious*
> *challenges, especially those represented by the Civil War*
> *and the rise of progressivism, in preserving "the American*
> *experiment of self-government under law."*
> (Hillsdale Course Description, Social Sciences, U.S.
> Constitution, Politics 101)

Did Hillsdale College not notice the connection between the Populist or Progressive movement with its notable support for the controversial, 86-year effort to amend the Constitution of the United States? Did their trustees intend to ignore the possible effects a questionable amendment might have had on their fiduciary relationship with our mutual heritage?

Why would Hillsdale not mention that 86-year drumbeat in a *"Reader"* published for the purpose of detailed study of a magnificent political document – or any possible threat to the "American experiment" enabled by that mind-numbing drumbeat?

In the *"Reader's"* Foreword, Hillsdale College President Larry P. Arnn States:

> *"Progressivism, which has in modern times remade the*
> *federal government both in purpose and in scope, also arises*
> *from a historical view. In its early account, "the laws of*

nature and of nature's God" are themselves constructs of a particular time and set of circumstances and not the <u>abiding</u> things they purport to be. In a later Progressive account, these <u>eternal</u> laws are indeed <u>eternal</u>, but because they are <u>eternal</u>, the arrangements of the Constitution cannot be. In the nature of things, circumstances change radically. As they change, government must be able to adapt freely, without constraint. The protection of our property, argues Franklin Roosevelt, requires that we surrender that property to the government freely. The defense of our rights, he argues, requires that we empower the government far beyond the limits permitted by the Constitution."

It could be that my reading/comprehension skills aren't quite what I fancied for myself; and it's possible - as I was told by my less-than-diplomatic teenage friends growing up - that I'm "not the brightest bulb in the class." But, to better understand Arnn's statement above, I tried substituting a common synonym like "permanent" for the words "abiding," and "eternal," and I read it again. The drill didn't help me much, but hey, maybe my teen buddies had a valid point.

Or maybe I'm in denial; hoping against hope that I'm wrong to suspect that the institution I held as the final defender of the liberty and property rights given to us by Madison and company, may instead, at least in part, be a Progressive institution perfectly willing to echo socialist maxims like Roosevelt's requirement that we *"empower the government far beyond the limits permitted by the Constitution."*[20]

---

20 Arnn, Larry P., President, Hillsdale College; *The U.S. Constitution: A Reader,* Foreword, p xiii

Chapter 9

A DIALOGUE WITH HILLSDALE COLLEGE

*"The thesis of the state socialist is, that no line can be drawn
between private and public affairs which the State may not
cross at will..."*
(Woodrow Wilson, "Socialism and Democracy," 1887;
as reported in the *The US Constitution: A Reader*, p.
646; a Hillsdale College publication)

[The following 4 **Exhibits** are: (**A**) A letter directed to Mr. Arnn; to
each member of the faculty; and to each member of the Board of Trustees
which was never answered except as described in: (**B**) A respectful response from one Mr. Ronald J. Pestritto, Ph.D., Professor of Politics,
who was somewhat off point; (**C**) my answer to Mr. Pestritto explaining
why I thought he was off point; and (**D**) a copy of **A** to the Board of
Trustees. – these **Exhibits** should prove self-explanatory. I have never
received an answer of any kind from any of the addressees excepting one
respectful, unofficial response on the side (**B**) from Mr. Pestritto]

EXHIBIT A

———

Michael J. Geanoulis, Sr.
PO Box 45
New Castle, New Hampshire 03854
April, 2019

Larry P. Arnn, President, and
Hillsdale College Politics Faculty
Hillsdale College
Hillsdale, Michigan 49242

Dear Mr. Arnn and the Politics Faculty,

I am an 83-year-old concerned citizen and Hillsdale College student who boldly approaches with a deep sense of alarm about the way we stray from the original intent of our founding fathers. I look to you, as primary guardians of our constitutional values, for possible guidance and redress.

You are my last hope it seems. I am barely able to find anyone in my area capable, or even willing if they were, to help raise this complex issue to a higher level of visibility. This is about the apparently forgotten 17th amendment (effective 31 May 1913), which, under Populist, or Progressive influence, transferred U. S. Senate elections from state legislatures directly to the people; and the possibility that that transfer may have replaced one set of problems (real or imagined) with another having greater potential for long term, irreparable damage of the kind Madison and Tocqueville warned against.

It was with considerable disappointment to find little or no discussion about this weighty amendment in your reader, "The U. S. Constitution: A Reader." It was necessary to seek other, possibly hostile and inferior, sources for estimates about benefits or disadvantages of an amendment that may well prove, in the end, to have had a major negative impact on our general welfare. Some sources were friendly to my theme while calling prematurely for repeal. But one condescendingly referred to the Honorable James Madison as a "cutie pie" who owned slaves. Another claimed defensively that Amendment 17 had little or no impact.

One needs only to look at business cycles, debt and inflation before and after 1913 to get a flavor of the influence to which I speak. Boom/bust cycles were harrowing under a Madisonian Senate of the 19th century to be sure, but were relatively mild compared to the busts supervised by the Progressive Senate of later years. The severe depression of the 1930s and the real estate carnage during the Bush and Obama years provide glaring examples.

For approximately 100 years prior to 1913, our currency and inflation rates were relatively stable even as the population exploded. Need I dwell on inflation rates and the slow erosion of our currency after Amendment 17 was enacted?

For approximately 100 years prior to 1913, the national debt, under the supervision of a Madisonian Senate, rose only slightly. Under the Progressive Senate of Amendment 17, the debt, a new untouchable third rail of politics, soars out of control, aggravated by an unnecessary war we otherwise might have avoided. See "Understanding the Dollar Crisis." (Greaves, 1953).

Debt service costs last year alone totaled almost $400 billion, enough to repair our bridges and roads twice or build 400 VA hospitals. The Office of Management and Budget (OMB) predicts such costs will soon reach one trillion dollars and more each and every year!

Former Senator Moynihan, moreover, provides a graphic social example about which I speak. He spoke and wrote at length against some elements of President Johnson's "Great Society" with its war on poverty out of a conviction it would provide counterproductive incentives for traditional family formation. Motivated more by the need to get reelected, though, and less by his innate convictions, he supported Johnson's programs knowing that he would otherwise be rejected in the voting booth by the masses who supported those well-intentioned but factious and divisive programs.

I find it hard to imagine, having investigated the power of his writings and the support he demonstrated for the needs of children to have both a mother and father in the home, that Moynihan would have had to worry about being reelected while serving under the supervision and approval of his state legislature as originally provided for. He, and very possibly, most of his fellows in the Senate, furthermore, would have had higher standing and confidence to demand that the federal government has no business micromanaging matters "reserved for the state and its people" as provided for in the 10th amendment.

As a consequence, books like "Fatherless America: Confronting Our Most Urgent Social Problem (Blankenhorn), and "The Boy Crisis" (Farrell) must be written in fragile attempts to compensate for widespread, Moynihan-like deficiencies, and, by deduction, the questionable wisdom of Amendment 17. Please entertain the possibility that our present problems in fragile families, persistent poverty, fatherlessness, rudderless children, school shootings, opioid addictions, a culture of dependency, debt, and more, may be rooted, at least in part, with the enactment of that well-intentioned, but debilitating amendment.

I further charge that State's rights, in addition to the Senate itself, for all practical purposes, were neutered in large part by A17.

I was additionally frustrated that your recent Imprimis article, "America's Cold Civil War," with its insightful analysis of conflicting factions, needs and causes of every kind, never once mentioned the possibility that the roots of that "war" may lie, at least in part, with the 17th

Amendment. It degraded the higher wisdom of state legislative vetting for Senate seats by substituting popular control with less well informed people who are more inclined to support inferior candidates and unwise, emotionally driven, short-sighted, unaffordable, divisive decisions that have long term negative consequences of the kind you must, by now, be thoroughly familiar with; the kind of factious selective benevolence our founders sought to avoid.

I provide a copy of my op-ed, published locally, which further delineates my concerns.

I hereby request that you elevate the visibility of Amendment 17 somewhat as follows:

1. Include a summary or two in chapter 11 of your reader, "The U. S. Constitution," about how Amendment 17 may have damaged the original spirit and intent of our founders.

2. Solicit an essay or two for the Imprimis Newsletter from experts who have acknowledged the need to revisit the wisdom of Amendment 17. I would like to see such an essay include themes described herein and in my soon to be released, "Amendment Seventeen: A Blessing and a Curse." You may use this letter and op-ed (enclosed) for the purpose as you see fit under your own signature. I give them to you freely, giving up any or all copyright considerations. I do ask, however, that if you use my letter for that purpose, you run it by me for possible suggestions. I do harbor some concerns about what seems as excessive emphasis given to themes antagonistic to the intent of our founders in chapters 10 and 11. That said, I do understand the need to present all sides of differing positions.

3. Provide a bulleted item in your curriculum devoted specifically to Amendment 17 for higher visibility. Suggest "The pros and cons of Amendment 17."

A couple of relevant notes: As I understand the near century long effort to justify the need for Amendment 17, it was claimed (1) there were excessive big-money power brokering and untoward political struggling within state legislatures that occasionally left Senate seats vacant for extended periods; and (2) that in any event the people should be as close as possible to the lawmaking process, state's rights at the federal level notwithstanding.

In response I bring a compromise brought by State Representative Kingsbury of New Hampshire (deceased) who prescribed a short list of Senate candidates selected in a bipartisan manner by the legislature for the people to vote on. There is a different kind of power brokering and influence peddling happening now, the kind encouraged by dark money for political campaigns that might prove pointless under a Kingsbury-like compromise and/or a repeal/replace effort.

Thank you for being guardians of what some intellectuals rightfully refer to as the highest and best political document ever conceived. With your contribution to this effort, we will survive any/all assaults on it. Hoping to get a flavor of your thoughts by return.

Sincerely,
Michael J. Geanoulis, Sr.
PO Box 45
New Castle, N. H. 03854
Ph/txt: 603-436-8810
Email: geanoulis@comcast.net

Note to Mr. Arnn: It was not possible for me to get address information on your Politics Faculty. Would you be kind enough to distribute the twelve copies I provide herewith to them?

cc:
The Washington Post
The Portsmouth Herald
ConventionofStates.com

———

EXHIBIT B

———

Ronald J. Pestritto, Ph.D.
Graduate Dean and Professor of Politics
Kendall Hall, Hillsdale College
33 East College Street
Hillsdale, MI 49242

30 April 2019

Mr. Michael J. Geanoulis, Sr.
P.O. Box 45
New Castle, NH 03854

Dear Mr. Geanoulis:

Your letter regarding the 17th Amendment to the Constitution was passed on to me by our Trustee, Cleves Delp, and our Vice President for Institutional Advancement. John Cervini. While I'm not normally the person at the College who sees and responds to correspondence of this kind, John knows of my expertise on the American Progressive Era and thus knew that I would be interested in the issues raised by your letter.

Your kind words about the college are most appreciated, and I certainly agree with the general concerns you raise with respect to the current political environment—talk of packing the court, of abolishing the electoral college, and of the "unfairness" of equal suffrage of the States in the Senate is troubling, not least because it betrays an ignorance of both the republican and federal nature of our regime.

I also agree with you that the 17th Amendment was a significant change to our government, and that this change doesn't get as much attention as it deserves (even among conservatives, who are more likely to focus on the 16th Amendment). My own inclination, however, is to see the 17th Amendment more as a symptom of the transformation taking place in our government at that time, as opposed to its cause. It was a symptom of Progressive thought generally, and in particular reflected the Progressive attachment to direct democracy as a means of circumventing Madisonian republicanism. This is one reason why, in our Constitution Reader, while we do not say much explicitly about the Amendment itself, we do devote very considerable attention to Progressivism and to its argument for direct democracy. The topic also gets very considerable attention, I should add, in our online courses).

There is no question that, in today's environment, the federal balance represented in the Senate—where, through equal suffrage of the States, no one faction or region can gain inordinate power in the legislature, in spite of concentrations of population—is misunderstood and is the object of attack. Were this balance ever to be eliminated, either through a change in the structure of the Senate or in an abolition of the electoral college (which simply mirrors the compromise on state representation in the national legislature), I'm sure we would agree that the results would be disastrous. But the virtue we are talking about here—that equal suffrage of the States in the Senate requires that government majorities be constructed with due attention to diverse regional interests—is not affected by the 17th Amendment.

With respect to the change that is brought about by the 17th Amendment—the direct election of Senators instead of entrusting their appointment to state legislatures—my own understanding is that that would have been problematic to the founders for two principal reasons, though one of these would have been far more important to them than the other. One reason—the one most commonly supposed—is that the amendment deprives the state governments of their representation in the national government *qua* States. The framers would have been troubled by this, to be sure, though one must also acknowledge that Madison and Hamilton had little love for state governments, the evidence for this in the "Federalist" is overwhelming. Hamilton is quite blunt about this, for example, in "Federalist 33," where he points to that lesson that it had "been a principal aim of these papers to inculcate, that the danger which most threatens our political welfare, is, that the state governments will finally sap the foundations of the union."

This is why I think the great concern that the framers would have had with respect to the 17th Amendment is not so much that it undermines the power of state governments, but rather that it makes the House and the Senate more like one another. Bicameralism was understood as an essential institutional means of mitigating the effects of majority faction—a central aim of the American Constitution. And in order for bicameralism to work as intended, the House and the Senate not only had to be separate institutions, but very different institutions—different, especially, in their genius or in the sources from which they spring. This principle is captured by Madison in "Federalist 62," where he reasons: "As the improbability of sinister combinations will be in proportion to the dissimilarity in the genius of the two bodies, it must be politic to distinguish them from each other by every circumstance which will consist with a due harmony in all proper measures, and with the genuine principles of republican government."

The House and the Senate, in other words, since they are now both directly elected, are also much more likely to be effected by the same fits of democratic passions, instead of acting as effective checks on one another. I have to imagine that this erosion of robust bicameralism in the 20th century could have been a contributing factor to some of the imprudent policies you mention in your letter. It's also why equal suffrage of the States in the Senate—a principle unaffected by the 17th Amendment—now seems to be one of the most important remaining safeguards against rash and unjust legislation today.

I regret that lack of time deprives me of the opportunity to say more about this question, but those are my own thoughts on the matter (which, I should be clear, don't necessarily reflect those of Dr. Arnn or the college—I'm speaking here in my own capacity as a scholar). I am very pleased that your letter was passed on to me, and most grateful for your common cause with the mission of the college.

Sincerely,
[signature on file]
Ronald J. Pestritto, Ph.D.
Graduate Dean and Professor of Politics
Kendall Hall, 33 East College St., Hillsdale, MI 49242
(517) 607 2483

———

EXHIBIT C

—

Michael J. Geanoulis, Sr.
P.O. Box 45
New Castle, NH   03854

14 May 2019

Ronald J. Pestritto, Ph.D.
Graduate Dean and Professor of Politics
Kendall Hall, Hillsdale College
33 East College Street
Hillsdale, MI 49242

Dear Mr. Pestritto,

Thank you for your interest with my concerns about Amendment 17 and for being pleased to discover them. It's encouraging that you agree that this topic deserves more attention than it gets. With this abbreviated note, I pray you will consider my counter positions below with patience and understanding. But for the nagging to "do something" in my soul, I would pursue my gardening hobby where I can meditate on the damage being done to the legacy of our founding heroes while sowing cucumber seeds and simply let the country go where it will.

I never raised political concerns like "packing the court" or "abolishing the electoral college" as you implied. My stated concerns revolved mostly around the before and after 1913; things like family disintegration, the culture of dependency, persistent poverty, debt costs out of control, federal overreach, severe depressions, forever wars and the dollar crisis (Greaves, 1973).

That "considerable attention" is given in your Constitution Reader "to Progressivism and to its argument for direct democracy" was my prime mover and the cause of the above described nagging. It seemed as a sales job for a pure democracy that Madison described as deadly. After studying many imported books on such topics, Madison wrote: "Hence it is that such democracies have ever been spectacles of turbulence and contention; have ever been found incompatible with personal security or the rights of property; and have in general been as short in their lives as they have been violent in their deaths" (Federalist #10).

Madison and Hamilton may have been avowed federalists in the beginning. But in one of the two books entitled "What would Madison do" (I can't remember which) it was alleged that in his later years, after discovering the growing mischief of a populist movement, he switched his allegiance from the Federalist camp to the Anti-Federalists. And I wonder what Hamilton would now say, if he could be resurrected, about what most threatens the foundations of our modified government these days. I allege that both he and Madison would have blamed Amendment 17 for the neutering of the Senate and the new inability of States to preserve rights "reserved for the state and its people" (Article X).

Hoping respectfully, you will see our dialogue as a positive deviation from the routine.

Michael J. Geanoulis, Sr
PO Box 45
New Castle, New Hampshire 03854
Cc: Cleves Delp
John Cervini

—

EXHIBIT D (Essentially a copy of Exhibit A)

Chapter 10

STATEMENTS SUPPORTING THE POPULAR ELECTION OF U.S. SENATORS

Popular Election of United States Senators
Charles James Fox. May 1902.

The sentiment in favor of the popular election of United States Senators is gradually growing stronger and stronger. On February 13 the fourth resolution providing for the election of Senators by direct vote of the people was passed by the House of Representatives. This fact is significant, for whatever may have been the individual opinions of the representatives themselves they have given by their vote a positive demonstration of their interpretation of the public will on the question. A more conclusive proof that the people favor this change cannot under the circumstances be reasonably asked for; yet those who oppose this change, and the foremost among them, Senator Hoar, refuse to see in this action of the House any indication of a real public desire for this change.

The Senator just mentioned even went so far as to state on the floor of the Senate that in his opinion the House had passed this bill "as half a joke." There is little evidence, however, to show that one branch of our national legislature permitted a resolution advocating an amendment to the constitution to pass without any opposition "as half a joke."

There is no doubt that the people generally favor this new method of election, and when the people of the United States seriously advocate any political innovation it becomes the duty of all earnest public men to make this innovation the object of their thoughtful attention. There are many who claim that, since this proposition involves an amendment to the constitution, those who favor it have assumed a difficult burden of proof and must show beyond all reasonable doubt that the proposed change is positively better than the present system of selecting Senators.

This is true to a certain extent; yet it might be answered that, in a country whose political dogma is the sovereign will of the people, when the people unite in demanding a certain change it becomes the duty of all opposing them to show good reasons why they should not have it. The people want the popular election of United States Senators, and we hope to show clearly that there is today no sound reason why public opinion should not be followed in this instance. This argument of the popular desire will appeal to many; it is indifferent to very few, and will be opposed chiefly by those who have selfish interests to guard.

There are, however, several sound and positive arguments for the election of Senators by direct vote of the people. First among them is that this new method is the logical outcome of our political development and is quite in accord with our ideals of government today. To look upon this question historically we must go back to the time of the birth of our constitution.

This step is important and necessary, as our knowledge of the past and present aids us in our efforts to foresee the future. But this attempt to seek advice from the past is often dangerous.

Influenced by a natural and just regard for the sound opinions of the framers of our constitution, we are very apt to overlook the fact that these men drew many of their conclusions from premises that no longer exist and while they were influenced by conditions that we have great difficulty in thoroughly realizing to-day.

In wondering at the stability of the great document drawn up by these men, we too often forget that this stability is quite as much the result of the sound political sense of the American people as it is of any inherent qualities of the constitution itself. Few people familiar with the subject ignore the fact that our constitution today differs much in spirit if not in letter from that constitution which was the result of the mutual ideas and concessions of the members of the convention of 1787. And yet many of us fail to take this fact into due consideration when we quote freely the opinions of these men upon specific questions of the present day.

Many opinions quite rational in 1787 would be ridiculous in 1902. Because our forefathers believed in a certain method of selecting Senators over a hundred years ago is no reason for supposing that they would favor it to-day. Every student of history knows that the political development of the United States has been a gradual change from the aristocratic and conservative ideals of the framers of our government to the popular democratic ideas of today; that the doctrine of the sovereign will of the people has ceased to be our abstract philosophic theory of political resources, and has become a live, practical, every-day principle of the politician.

Newspapers, railroads, telegraphs, and accumulated political experi-ence have in the course of time become some of the main causes of this change. When communication between the States was difficult; when the average citizen had merely local interests, little knowledge of state affairs and less of national; when to many Americans a newspaper was a novelty and to all of them a railroad or a telegraph was a dream, we can see the wisdom of those men who wished to keep direct power from a people who for unavoidable reasons had not acquired that political knowledge which is essential to the proper exercise of sovereign power in politics. But today, under present conditions, these same Statesmen and patriots would undoubtedly be of another opinion.

Remembering the condition of affairs in 1787, we can easily understand how the state legislatures elected the governors and all other officers, civil and military, of the state (even the members of the constitutional convention themselves were chosen by the several state legislatures); how the president was intended to be selected by electors; how property and even religious qualifications were retained in several of the States as absolutely essential to the privilege of voting. But by today many changes have taken place. Our president is practically elected by popular vote; so are the governors of the States. Civil and military officers are no longer appointed by the legislatures, and property qualifications are generally abolished. And it is not an extravagant supposition to believe that the framers of our constitution would today applaud these changes in the great instrument of their own creation. But this change, great as it is, is not yet complete.

We have still the choice of United States Senators by the legislatures to remind us of the days when the people were not trusted, and to remind us also that there remains still something for us to do in order to make the doctrine of popular rights everywhere a practical proposition rather than an abstract idea. These several steps in this great change have been gradual, and therein lies the stability of our institutions; but we claim, and we believe not rashly, that the time has now come to make this change, and that it follows in logical sequence with the others. To hold otherwise is to claim that a people that has made such wonderful advances in commerce, industry, and in civilization has remained at a standstill in politics. This argument of the historic necessity of this change gains in strength the longer and more attentively we consider it.

Another argument in favor of the change we propose is that the present method of choosing Senators is quite inconsistent with our political ideals of to-day. A republican form of government should avoid all inconsistencies in its composition. They form a great element of weakness, not only from the fact that they destroy the harmony of the system on which the government is based, but because they expose the government to the frequent natural and adverse criticism of the people and thereby lessen that popular respect which is so essential to the strength of any institution founded on the will of the people.

Political anomalies can be supported only by selfish class interests, by narrow bigotry, or by that timid and senseless conservatism which, forgetting that progress is an irresistible law, looks with dread upon all changes. We claim that the present method of choosing our national Senators has grown to be one of these dangerous political anomalies. It fitted logically into the scheme of our government when it was framed, but it is not in keeping with its spirit in the year 1902. When the people are considered capable of directly electing every four years a president who represents the entire nation, why should it be considered dangerous to allow them to choose directly two men who represent their state? Are not these two contradictory principles an excellent example of that dangerous inconsistency just referred to?

This question is all the more difficult to answer negatively when we remember that the president is nearly always a man of another state, and that the people know far less about him personally than about their own Senators. It may be claimed that in voting for the president the people are voting for a party; but this is quite as true of the Senators. It may also be argued that the people of one state alone do not elect a president; but it is quite as true that the people of one state cannot control the Senate.

Again, the position of chief executive may be filled by the people acting all at one time under the predominating influence of one agitated question, while the people can fill the Senate only after expressing their will in three separate parts and under the influence of three successive periods.

Perhaps it will be said that periods of two or six years are nothing in politics. This may be true, but the effects of a continued popular excitement of a longer period would invade the Senate even if the state legislatures shield them from the terrible influences of popular enthusiasm.

Furthermore, it is far from being the mere assertion of a demagogue to insist that to hold the people incapable of electing Senators is an insidious reflection upon the dignity of a nation whose political creed is the sovereignty of the people; and this the more so as these same people elect directly every four years the executive branch of the government whose hasty or foolish acts entail quite as great disaster as the similar action of one-half of the legislature. Surely these two principles of election are quite inconsistent. Again, our national legislature does not elect representatives of the nation, and why should the state legislature elect those of the state?

Every state in the union has a Senate, and its members are chosen by direct vote of the people. In fact, all the agents of the people with the single exception of the national Senators are practically selected either by popular vote or by executive appointment. It is true that the legislatures exercise a certain control over executive appointments, but that does not alter the fact that the present method of selecting Senators is inconsistent with our ideals and our practice.

Another consideration in favor of popular election is that it would not impair the efficiency of the Senate in any way, and would be beneficial to the Senators themselves. Our opponents usually put forward the claim that the Senate is a check upon the House, and then imply that this would not be the case under the system we propose. The Senate should no doubt exercise a certain restraining influence over the House. Many different opinions have existed on this subject, but today the only sound principle is that the Senate being elected for a longer term than the House, and being composed of older and usually more prominent men, represents the more permanent interests of the nation which at certain moments are apt to be disregarded; while the House is more responsive to the momentary impulses of the people.

To disregard the longer term, the more advanced age, and the greater prominence of the Senators, and then to claim that their acknowledged conservatism and dignity are based solely or even principally upon their manner of election is ridiculous. To say that the Senate would be under the new method of election, a second house of representatives is to declare that every state in the union has two houses of representatives.

It has often been said that the popular election of Senators will shorten the average time during which the Senators will remain in office. There is doubtless some truth in this statement, but its force is greatly diminished when we think of the large number of representatives who have spent a great part of their lives in the lower house even though the people had every two years a chance of changing them.

Then, again, it is not positively demonstrated that it is very essential for the Senators generally to remain several terms. If after an opportunity of six years a Senator cannot publicly demonstrate his worth it is perhaps just as well to give another an opportunity. The upper branch of our legislature is not a school where the Senators are supposed to remain several terms before becoming capable Statesmen.

Furthermore, a Senator must watch his constituents and should under ordinary conditions strive to be honestly reelected. It is far more dignified as well as more profitable for a Senator to sound the people at different times than it is for him to watch the state legislatures. Since he ought to know the wishes of his people, is it not better for him to find them out directly? A Senator can well afford to strive to remain in touch with the people, but to keep in communication with a certain section of every third legislature is undignified to say the least.

This new method of electing Senators would be very beneficial to the state legislatures. These are elected primarily to consider local and state affairs, and it is better that they should not be hampered with national obligations. This is all the more true when we remember that the choice of a Senator has many times occupied the entire session of a legislature; that Senatorial deadlocks are not of infrequent occurrence; that the election of a Senator has often divided the legislature into two hostile sections; that it has sometimes split the party in power and thereby disrupted its working harmony; that the question as to how a person will vote for Senators has become an important but illegitimate factor in his qualification for the state legislature, and furthermore, that this personal question relative to the selection of Senators is something foreign to our ideals of the deliberations of a legislative assembly.

It may be claimed that depriving the state legislatures of the right they now possess will be injuring rather than aiding them. But we are relieving them of a duty which is inconsistent with their other duties, and which is often disastrous in its results, as has just been shown. Again, the choice of the state governors and of all civil and military officers has been removed from the state legislatures, and why should we stop when we reach the Senators? Why should we hesitate to make this change in order to continue our gradual progress toward the absolute rule of the people? It is the growth from which we derive strength, and one which it is dangerous to attempt to prevent.

Finally, one important argument in favor of popular election is that it would be of great political value to the people themselves. The great store of political learning and experience which the railroads, telegraphs, and newspapers have aided in placing before the people is not always readily absorbed. There is no doubt that the people do not take entire advantage of their opportunities in this respect, and it is equally undeniable that the government should do all in its power to encourage either directly or indirectly the acquisition of political knowledge and experience by the people, because on the political foresight and ability of the people depends absolutely the welfare of all democratic governments. During times of political excitement and when called upon to choose by election their representatives the people acquire almost involuntarily a certain lesson in practical politics.

The election of the representatives is often a comparatively local affair and brings up usually but the discussion of local issues. All the other elections with one notable exception in which the people take a direct part are state elections, and the issues discussed are semi-local. But then every four years the people are called upon to choose the chief executive of the entire nation. There is no real medium step between the popular election of a state officer and that of the president of the United States. From the discussion of state issues and the consideration of state interests the people are suddenly called upon to give their opinion on the greatest questions of political category on questions that involve the vital interests of the nation as a whole.

Now, the popular election of Senators would supply that salutary and essential medium step. By this act the people would be instructed to a certain extent in national politics before being called upon to voice their opinions on a national issue. It is true that the people elect only two Senators every six years, but the very fact that they are elected by the people and that they are directly responsible to the people would naturally bring them in closer touch with the people to the great benefit of the latter.

Today a Senator does not fear popular criticism to so great an extent, but under the proposed method he would feel a more direct and immediate although not necessarily a greater responsibility and would therefore see to it that the people understood his actions in order to approve them.

—

U. S. Representative William Jennings Bryan, 1894.

We all recognize that there is a reason for the election of Senators by a direct vote today that did not exist at the time the constitution was adopted. We know that today great corporations exist in our States, and that these great corporations, different from what they used to be one hundred years ago, are able to compass the election of their tools and their agents through the instrumentality of legislatures, as they could not if Senators were elected directly by the people.

We are told that we must not change the constitution because it is a sacred instrument. He who would make such alterations as changed conditions necessitate is a better friend to the constitution and to good government than he who defends faults and is blind to defects.

Our state constitutions are frequently changed, and necessarily so, since circumstances change from year to year. Pennsylvania has had four constitutions, Missouri four, Texas three, Virginia five, etc. Each generation is capable of self-government, and must suit to its peculiar needs the machinery of government and the laws.

—

U. S. Senator David Battle Turpie, 1896.

An examination of our internal political history will show that ever since the organization of parties, at the close of the second administration of Washington, there has always been a third party. It has a right to be there, but it is owing to our present imperfect mode of choosing Senators that its presence becomes so potential, and that its power becomes vital, crucial, out of all proportion to the small number of voters who at the polls are known as its adherents.

Whether the state of political equilibrium in our legislatures, now so frequent, arises from the presence and action of a third party or from the personal divisions and private discussions in one or the other of the principal parties there represented, the result is the same the failure to choose, or the compulsory choice of someone not preferred by and not representative of

the wishes and opinions of the greater number. The election of United States Senators by a plurality vote of the people would instantly remove this growing evil, and would immediately re-store and perpetuate the legitimate rule of the majority voting.

———

U. S. Senator David Battle Turpie, 1897.

The pending amendment is in strict accordance with the great precedent of growth and advancement set forth in the preamble of the constitution. Our purpose is to form a more perfect union by bringing the national legislature in complete accordance with the legislative assemblies of the States; to establish justice by granting to the voters of the States that equality

of suffrage which the present system denies; to perpetuate the blessings of liberty to ourselves and our posterity by a further and nobler recognition of duties and rights inherent in all citizens, so that the supremacy of the people, never gainsaid, so often with the lips confessed, with the tongue asserted and maintained, shall at last be and become a vital force, a living presence, a fact accomplished, in the government of the republic.

———

Election of United States Senators.
Edwin Maxey. November 1908

We will mention the more prominent inconveniences and evils which the actual working of this method has developed. These may be fairly well classified under three heads, according to their effects (1) upon the Senate, (2) upon the state legislatures, and (3) upon the people.

As a result of this method the Senate is congested with men whose purse and political trickery is out of all proportion to their ability as Statesmen. For it is a matter which cannot be gainsaid that the political machine can be used far more effectively in electing a legislature favorable to a boss or his political creations than in securing their own election at the polls. And the further fact is well known that money can be used to better advantage in lobbying a legislature than in buying an election, where the money must needs be distributed over a larger surface and the safeguards against corruption are much more numerous. A Pennsylvania politician formulated this with more frankness than self-respect in the following statement: "I can use my money to better advantage in buying a legislature than in buying the people of the state."

Senators do not feel their responsibility to the people of the state to the extent they would if elected directly by the people. If a Senator is unscrupulous it is a matter of indifference to him what the people think of him so long as he can retain his hold upon their legislatures. It is a fundamental principle of representative government that power should be coupled with responsibility. While this in theory holds with reference to our United States Senators, as a matter of fact responsibility becomes considerably attenuated when the body to whom one is responsible is not a permanent body, and this is the case with our state legislatures. Few members of our legislatures continue in office more than six years, so that a Senator may disregard the wishes of his state legislature with comparative impunity. Not so when his responsibility is to the people; they are a relatively permanent body and the same constituency which elected him once will have an opportunity to elect or defeat him again. The fact that they are elected for a six years' term which is three times as long as that of a congressman removes sufficiently their sense of responsibility without having this insulating pad in the way of a legislature placed between them and the people. Responsibility is always most effective when direct and certain.

The effect upon our state legislatures is equally marked and all too often is equally demoralizing. The members of the legislature are chosen too frequently, not with a view to their fitness to serve their state in the capacity of legislators, but because they favor this or the other candidate for the United States Senate. Here, then, is a mixing of issues in state elections, the effect of which is too easily understood to need comment.

The next effect is to invite corruption; for there are always some members uninstructed by their constituents with reference to candidates for the United States Senate who can be influenced, and some more who are willing to disregard their instructions, providing the monetary arguments of the candidate or his friends are insufficiently eloquent; or, to put it in a balder form, they can be induced to set a price upon themselves.

There is the further objection that it frequently uses a large portion of their time. A direct election by the people would thus save the legislature considerable time and if this be not needed for legislation they could adjourn and go home so much earlier, and by so doing save the state considerable expense as well as suspense.

If the contest is fierce, the forces of the dominant party divided, and factional feeling bitter, we have a "deadlock." And of late "deadlocks" are by no means infrequent. If the case is an aggravated one, the whole session is sometimes consumed without getting anything done. This is a two-fold injury to the state first, in that the time which should have been spent in legislating for the interests of the state has been uselessly squandered; and second, in that the state loses a part of its representation in the United States Senate. The "deadlocks" in Delaware, Pennsylvania, Kentucky, Montana and California are too recent to need more than a passing mention in order to renew in our minds of the disgraceful incidents connected therewith.

Upon the people the effect is certainly not such as to commend the present method. It increases their distrust of their state legislatures; because if the contest is at all close there are seldom wanting charges, too often well founded, of treachery and bribery. It is in part responsible for a lack of confidence in and respect for the United States Senate.

It is a lamentable fact that the American people have, to a considerable degree, lost confidence in this body to which a half-century ago they looked with pride; and justly so, for during the early half of the nineteenth century it compared favorably with any legislative body in the world. True they had the same method of electing Senators then as now; but circumstances have changed.

The political machine exerted but a fraction of the effect upon the legislatures then than it does now; nor was lobbying practiced to anything like the same extent. Corporate influence, which now dominates the Senate, was then a relatively unimportant factor.

———

THE ELECTION OF SENATORS BY POPULAR VOTE
Walter McKenzie Clark, Associate Justice of the North Carolina Supreme Court.
September 1894.

At the date of the formation of the federal constitution in 1787, the governor in all but one or two of the States was elected by the legislature. In determining, therefore, the manner of selecting the two Senators who were to represent each of the several States in the federal Senate, the utmost the popular element could obtain was their election by the legislatures of the several States.

Some of the members of the convention, like Alexander Hamilton, insisted on their being chosen for life, others on their election by the lower house of Congress, and some on their appointment for each state by the governor thereof.

George Mason of Virginia and Mr. Wilson of Pennsylvania (afterwards on the United States supreme bench) alone advocated their election by the people. A measure so far in advance of the times received the vote of one state only Pennsylvania. The election was, as a compromise, devolved on the state legislatures in analogy to the mode then in vogue of electing governors.

One by one the several state constitutions were amended to place the election of governors in the hands of the people. The very same reasons which caused this change should long since have made a similar change in the mode of electing Senators. Doubtless the greater difficulty of amending the federal constitution, and the opposition of the Senate itself and of the strong element which finds its benefit in the present mode of election, have prevented an amendment which each state has shown to be desired and desirable by amending its own constitution as to the manner of electing its governor.

The facility with which the present mode of election lends itself to the control of the choice of Senators by the money power, the selection of a large proportion, probably a majority of the Senators, at the dictation of the accumulated wealth of the country, and the consequent indifference with which the average Senator is tempted to regard the people's interest, or the people's will, are reasons enough why the mode of election should be changed. These reasons are patent to all and require no argument.

But there are many other reasons which do not lie so apparent and on the very surface of things, but which nevertheless should be sufficient if fairly considered, to justify the change to an election by the people. Among them are these:

The present mode of election virtually disfranchises all the counties in which the party, which is dominant in the legislature, does not control. Take a state in which either party has only a small majority in the legislature on joint ballot. In such a state half the counties, containing possibly one half the voters of the dominant party, are completely disfranchised. Nay, more; as the choice is usually by caucus, one half of the dominant majority, coming from one fourth of the counties, select the Senator.

The parties being usually nearly equal at the polls, the members of the legislature who cast the votes of those counties may thus represent less than one eighth of the voters of the state. Such a system is not democratic. That it readily lends itself to manipulation and to the influence of corporate and plutocratic influences would be apparent, even if the world was not advertised of the fact by that unanswerable teacher experience.

But it is argued that the legislature represents the state. But so do the governor and the judiciary, and even more fully, since they must be chosen by a majority of the voters of the whole state, while not unfrequently the majority of the legislature is chosen by a minority of the voters of the state. Yet who would be content to have the Senators appointed by the governor or elected by the judges of the state? Why should they be chosen by the legislative department, when the people themselves are competent to express their own wishes at first hand, and not leave their choice to be determined, as often happens, by men who receive, as above stated, less than one eighth of the vote of the state?

Each of those members of the caucus majority may have been the choice in the nominating convention of his party in his county of a small majority only, making it thus in fact possible and not very unusual for one sixteenth of the voters of the state to control the choice of the Senator; and, by means familiar to all men, he may be selected, not even by the will of that one sixteenth, but by the infinitesimal fraction of the voters of the state who happen to fill one fourth of the seats in the legislature, and thus constitute a majority of the caucus of the party dominant in that body; such things have happened.

To be clear, take a state which casts 400,000 votes. A majority of the legislature is elected from counties having 200,000 voters, or often less when there is a gerrymander. A majority in the caucus may, therefore, have been elected from counties having 100,000 voters. But nearly half of these were of the opposite party, leaving the majority of the caucus elected by 50,000 voters. These members were nominated in their respective conventions usually by a majority only of their party in their respective counties, or say 25,000 which is one sixteenth of the 400,000 voters of the state; whereas if elected by popular vote of the whole state, as he should be, a Senator must be the expressed choice at the ballot box of more voters than have cast their ballots for any other man, and his nomination must be made by the wish of at least one fourth of the voters, subject to approval of a majority at the ballot box.

Can there really be any difference of opinion as to which is the fairest and most American mode of selection, or as to which is least open to corruption, or is most likely to represent faithfully the wishes of the people? It is true States are not always so close; but many are, and any state may at any election become so. What particular sixteenth of the whole vote shall decide the result is rarely left to chance. Skillful manipulation and the adroit use of money for political machinery (not necessarily for bribery) decide the matter and not the people's will. That is evil enough.

The change to election by the people would greatly lessen the chances for corruption. The members of the party convention of the state, brought together directly from the people and so soon dispersed again among them, are not so subject to the subtle arts of the lobbyist and the professional wirepuller which are brought to bear on the member of the legislature as soon as his nomination is probable, and continued till after the election of Senator is over, when, like a squeezed lemon, he can be thrown aside. Besides, the party convention acts with open doors, subject to public sentiment and conscious that its choice, if not wisely made, is liable to rejection at the polls. Do such safeguards surround the deliberations of a caucus?

A Senator who is tempted while in office to disregard the wishes and the interest of the people, is emboldened by the knowledge that if by certain influences he can control the sixteenth more or less who compose a majority in the nominating conventions of those counties which send a majority of the legislators of the dominant party, he is safe for a reelection; and knows further that without being the choice of any perceptible element among the people it is sufficient if he can secure a majority of the caucus. But he will pause if he knows his renomination must command the approval of a majority of his party convention and an endorsement of a majority of the voters of the whole state at the ballot-box. Is there any reason why the people should not have this potent assurance of the fidelity of their servant in his office?

One of the disgraces of our institutions is what is known as gerrymandering. It is a disgrace because its purpose and object is to defeat the will of the majority, which is the corner-stone upon which a republican form of government is based. One of the commonest instances of gerrymandering is the apportionment of legislative districts, and sometimes even the creation of new counties, with a view to securing a majority of the legislature to the party which is in the minority in the state on a popular vote. The greatest inducing cause to commit this crime against popular sovereignty is the selection of United States Senators. It is well to remove the inducement.

It is well, also, at this stage to call attention to the point that the constitutional amendment which shall place the election of Senators with the people instead of with the legislature, should contain the provision that such election should be "from the state at large"; else there will be attempts at a modified gerrymander by dividing the state into two Senatorial districts of unequal size or dividing it by lines drawn to give party advantage.

At every great political crisis during the last twenty years, instead of proving itself the more conservative and deliberate branch of Congress, the Senate has in fact, been held in check by the House.

If the two [houses] were elected for the same period and by the same electors, they would amount in practice to little more than two committees of the same house. All foreign critics have found in the method of choosing the members of our Senate a sufficient if not the sole cause of its excellence as a legislative and executive authority. It is their opinion that the mode of electing that body constitutes its functions, one of the effectual checks, one of the real balances of our system.

The Senate is less democratic than the House, and consequently less sensible to transient phases of public opinion; but it is not less sensible than the House of its ultimate accountability to the people, and is quite as obedient to the more permanent and imperative judgments of the public mind.

—

U. S. Representative Stephen A. Northway, 1894.

It is expected that we shall get abler men in the Senate under the proposed system of election than now. I should like to know how any improvement can be expected in that respect, because at present three-fourths of the Senators are graduated from this body [the House] and were the election made by the people, the other portion of the Senators might be supplied by members of this House if they should have their ambitions fulfilled. I should like to know why the Senate would be stronger in ability if Senators were chosen directly by the people than it is to-day.

Unless my memory misleads me, I have seen as many newspaper charges in regard to members of Congress having bought their way into this body (House of Representatives) as I have seen of such charges affecting Senators, I mean as many in proportion to the greater number of members in the House.

Do you suppose that if they are Republicans, they would be able to hold their seats by fraud with Democrats ready to attack them? Do you suppose that Senators guilty of this charge would, if Democrats, be permitted to hold their seats there with the Republicans ready to attack them? Such charges may be made for political purposes, but they are difficult to be proved.

———

Congressional Record. 23: 6060-6. July 12, 1892.
Henry St. George Tucker.

The use of money in the election of Senators has a most vicious effect in another respect. The legislatures, under the present system, possess the electoral function in the selection of Senators. The money which corrupts, by purchase, the member of the legislature for Senatorial elections has debauched him as a servant of the people he is sworn to serve in local legislation.

The corporation that can enter the halls of a legislature and lay its unholy hands upon the members, claiming them as its own in the selection of a Senator, has already destroyed the hope of a pure administration of the local affairs of the people of that state by polluting the source from which such administration is derived. Under the specious guise of interest merely in the Senatorial election, legislatures are debauched and the purchased member in the Senatorial election can hardly pose as the unbought and unpurchaseable tribune of the people's local rights.

If the charges of corruption in Senatorial elections are true, the reflex action on the legislation in the States, incident to such corruption, must be immeasurable in its destruction of the rights and liberties of the people of the States.

We find also the Senate of the United States, under the treaty- making power of the constitution, is arrogating to itself the power to lay taxes. That power has been given by the constitution of this land to the Congress, but we find now that, under this power, the president and the Senate are not only making treaties, which they have a right to make, but they are making the treaties

which, in effect, levy taxes upon the people without the consent of this House, a co-ordinate branch of Congress, and which alone under the constitution has the power to originate tax bills.

It marks the gradual absorption of the taxing power of the government by the Senate, without responsibility to the people for "its exercise.

Don't Repeal the 17th Amendment
Joshua Spivak, for Forbes Magazine, April 2, 2010

—

Seemingly embittered by the passage of the health care reform, Congressman Louie Gohmert, R-Texas, has proposed a radical action to help his party: repealing the 17th Amendment - which mandates the direct election of Senators. Instead, Gohmert would have state legislatures once again elect U.S. Senators.

This isn't a new idea--over the last few years it has been gaining popularity with conservative proponents of federalism. The theory behind this revision is that it would increase the power of the States in the political process, and have elected officials who, presumably, would care primarily about the state's interest. Perhaps not coincidentally, the plan would probably benefit the Republican Party, adding a handful of Senators to its total number of representatives.

While Gohmert and others may like the short-term political benefit, it does beg a basic question: Have any of its proponents looked at the state of state legislatures? The "laboratories of democracy" have not exactly been the source of national pride, as they are frequently in the news for some new leadership indictment. For example, over the last few years current and former legislative leaders in New York, Massachusetts, Alaska and Florida were indicted on corruption-based charges. It is rare that a state doesn't have prominent legislative leaders facing investigation and indictment.

But what would be the practical effect if the state legislatures were tasked with choosing Senators? Currently, Senatorial hopefuls have to raise and spend a huge amount of money to have a chance at winning election. The money is needed to woo voters--as it is spent on ads, get-out-the-vote campaigns and others basics tool of electoral democracy.

Repealing the 17th Amendment would not remove this pervasive influence of money in the process. Candidates would still spend a ton of it (both personal and fundraised) to win office--only this time it would be directed at one specific interest group: state legislators. The Senators and assembly representatives would be showered with campaign funds and other potential benefits (after all, many of the part-time legislators hold outside jobs). Avoiding bribery and corruption in the selection process was one of the stated impetuses for the 17th Amendment in the first place. Despite a century of campaign finance reform debates and better investigative techniques, nothing has really changed with the state legislature. We may quickly find that enough legislators are still susceptible to financial inducements.

But that is not the only problem. State legislative elections would be instantly nationalized. We would quickly see massive amounts of campaign money spent to influence key local races. The issues that state legislators ran on would be further nationalized, turning local races on local issues into a national fever pitch environment, with the election decided on topics that have nothing to do with an average legislator's job. This already happens, of course, but it will become the norm. We can also expect recall elections run specifically to try and gain the majority in a closely divided legislature. This has also already happened, but may be a regular occurrence under the new system.

Maybe the worst result is one that is already being threatened--the growth in importance of gerrymandering. Redistricting is already overwhelmingly important. After the census is taken each decade, state legislatures redraw district lines. The law requires that each district contain an equal population. But even with this limitation, political leaders are able to slice the maps to maximize political benefit. Elected officials are aware that, with careful crafting skills, they can give themselves and nearly everybody in their party virtually unbeatable districts. The value is so great that former House Majority Leader Tom DeLay basically gambled his career on doing a controversial mid-term redistricting to score a few more seats for the Republicans in Texas.

This year both parties are raising and spending money specifically to elect state legislators to help win the gerrymandering war. Imagine how much more intense this battle will become, and how much more the parties will lean on abusive redistricting practices, if the U.S. Senate itself is actually at stake.

The argument to get rid of the direct election of Senators is a tough sell. It goes against the strong current in America favor of increased democracy. Though they claim it would benefit the populace by restoring the federal-state balance and presumably limit government, proponents would have to overcome the argument that they, in effect, do not trust the American people to properly select their own officials.

These are high hurdles to jump. Just as bad, though, is if voters are asked to take a look at the modern record of state legislatures throughout the country. While they may decide that repealing the 17th Amendment is not the worst idea in the world, they'll certainly realize it's up there.

—

Joshua Spivak is a senior fellow at the Hugh L. Carey Institute for Government Reform at Wagner College. Republished with author's permission.

Chapter 11

STATEMENTS AGAINST THE POPULAR ELECTION OF U. S. SENATORS

But the will so declared was to be mature, deliberate, well-considered—its sober second thought. They were building for centuries, not for hours. They were prescribing the laws of health and growth for a mighty national life, compared with whose duration years, terms of Presidential office, generations of men are but as the pulsation of an artery.
Senator George F. Hoar, 1890

Wendell P. Garrison, Journalist, Editor; *Reform of the Senate* (1840-1907)
Atlantic Monthly. 68: 227-34. August 1891

[Note: Mr. Garrison would rather revisit the ACT of 1866]

It might plausibly be maintained that the United States Senate is the most corrupting element in our national political system. This is not because it has become, as is sometimes alleged, a club of millionaires. Such a consummation would not have displeased certain of the framers of the constitution. General Pinckney opposed the payment of salaries to Senators, on the ground that their branch "was meant to represent the wealth of the country," and that, in the absence of salaries, "the wealthy alone would undertake the service." Franklin seconded his motion. George Mason would have annexed a property qualification, since "one important object in constituting the Senate was to secure the rights of property."

Their views did not prevail, but the millionaires have arrived, and make no scruple about drawing their salaries. They are a consequence of the mode of electing Senators established by the Constitution, and a part of the general demoralization ascribable to the same cause.

Notoriously, the Senate was the great stumbling block-almost the crux in the constitutional settlement. Edmund Randolph's plan provided for its election by the House "out of a proper number of persons nominated by the individual legislatures." George Read's substituted the president for the House. Dickinson, following Spaight, of North Carolina, moved that the legislatures elect. Wilson, of Pennsylvania, on the other hand, advocated direct popular election; arguing that a choice by the legislatures would "introduce and cherish local interests and local prejudices."

Any of the rejected schemes, we can see, would have had its own dangers and abuses; but who can say whether the result would have been more disastrous than that of Dickinson's, under which we have worked for a century?

Read thought he foresaw, from a general character of the constitution, an end of the federal system by absorption, so that the state governments would "soon be reduced to the mere office of electing the national Senate"; and this fear found an echo in the ratifying conventions. Thus, in Pennsylvania, John Smilie, speaking for the minority in opposition, said the state legislature would "necessarily degenerate into a mere name, or at most settle in a formal board of electors, periodically assembled to exhibit the servile farce of filling up the federal representation." In New York, again, it was objected that the Senate would tend to perpetuate itself, and Chancellor Livingston retorted: "Can they make interest with their legislatures, who are themselves varying every year, sufficient for such a purpose? Can we suppose two Senators will be able to corrupt the whole legislature of this state? The idea, I say, is chimerical. The thing is impossible."

No contemporary, so far as I can discover, anticipated the precise evil which has brought us to our present pass, and which is touched upon, all too lightly, by Mr. Bryce in the chapter on UK- Senate in his American Commonwealth. After quoting Hamilton, in The Federalist, as saying that the Senate would furnish "a convenient link" between the federal and state systems, Mr. Bryce remarks (the italics are mine):

"In one respect this connection is no unmixed benefit, for it has helped to make the national parties powerful and their strife intense, in these last-named bodies. Every vote in the Senate

is so important to the great parties that they are forced to struggle for ascension in each of the state legislatures by the way the Senators are elected."

In other words, the constitution from the beginning insured the coincidence of state with federal party lines. This, it may be admitted, tended irresistibly to the consolidation of the country, but it had also the effect of mischievously prolonging the term of party existence; producing artificial divisions in local matters; making party fealty, and not competence or honesty or patriotism, the credential of office-holding at every degree of the scale, whether state or federal; and so leading to the steady deterioration of the personnel of state legislatures, the growth of machine rule, the purchasability of Senatorships, and the decline of the federal Senate to what we now see it, in large measure a medley of millionaires, "bosses," and the representatives of selfish interests.

If we must have parties, it is highly desirable that they should arise spontaneously, on clearly formulated principles and with definite objects;

that they should cease to exist as soon as possible after these objects have been attained; that they should be easily attacked when the love of power becomes the real motive for existence, and when insincere professions take the place of genuine beliefs and aspirations; that honest members should be free to withdraw, and cooperate patriotically with others of like mind; that we should not go on stupidly transmitting from sire to son the antipathy begotten by obsolete party differences which have been outlasted by party names.

To such flexibility the Constitution has erected a formidable barrier in the provision which forces state politics to turn upon the national complexion of the legislature, and makes the arbitrary control of that body by the managing spirits of the great parties the key to the political game.

That a governor, again, in ordinary times, or a mayor, a town collector, an overseer of the poor, a constable, should be selected for his national party badge, and not for fitness and probity, is of course destructive of the idea that public office is a public trust, derived from the people and answerable to the people.

Have we not here the germ of the most of our civic corruption? The very existence of the machine and the boss is involved in keeping up this vicious confusion of things entirely distinct, and in hindering the subservient partisan from voting upon the real local (state or municipal) issue, or upon the character of the candidate, by making his concern for the success of the national party paramount.

So long as this state of things continues, it seems hopeless to look for any such purification of our politics as will tempt men of refinement, honor, training, and public spirit to seek a Statesman's career. The federal Senate, which should be the assured goal of the class competent to govern, and a model of legislative dignity, capacity, and behavior, cannot be expected to fulfill these functions while the state legislatures remain vulgar, petty, and sordid; and the state legislatures, in their turn, cannot avoid these vices so long as their excuse for being is primarily to elect Senators, and only secondarily to attend to the affairs of their respective commonwealths.

One who examines the subject closely, in search of a remedy short of an amendment of the constitution, will fix upon the abrogation of the existing statute regulating the election of Senators, and propose either the substitution of a new law, or the relegation to the several States of the control of the whole matter. The statute in question was approved on July 25, 1866, by President Johnson. It was introduced by Senator Clark, of New Hampshire, pursuant to instructions to the Judiciary Committee, on motion of Senator Williams, of Oregon, to inquire into the expediency of providing a uniform and effective mode of securing the election of Senators in Congress by the legislatures of the several States.

It was reported as Senate Bill 414, "to regulate the times and manner of holding elections for Senators of Congress" and read and passed to a second reading on July 9, 1866. It excited no partisan opposition, and was passed two days later, after a short debate. On July 12 it was ordered printed by the House; on July 23 it was read three times without debate, and passed by a large majority. It was intended, in the language of Senator Clark, "to avoid the questions and differences that have sometimes existed." In this it has only partially succeeded, while it has tended steadily to impair the quality of the Senators returnable under it.

The law provides that the two houses of the legislature shall meet and vote separately for Senator on the first ballot, afterwards in joint convention; that voting shall be *viva voce*, and election by majority; and that at least one vote daily shall be taken till election (by majority) is arrived at.

All these provisions encountered weighty objections. Senator Sherman, who voted in the negative, and who, from past experience, saw little need of Congress availing itself of its constitutional right to interfere, preferred a joint convention at once, *advocated election by plurality*, and was indisposed to interrupt the legislature's proper work till the Senatorial election was got out of the way. He also pointed out the awkward effect of the law in the case of States holding biennial elections, that a vote for Senator might have to be taken fifteen or eighteen months in advance.

Senator Fessenden made a strong but ineffectual stand against the *viva voce* vote, as not being the usage in his state of Maine for one thing, and because "it is generally understood that the ballot is a more free and unembarrassed mode of voting." Moreover, he said, the *viva voce* vote was liable to put men "under restraints from party discipline which would lead them to act against their conscientious convictions of what was right and proper in the individual case, and which might bring a sort of compulsory pressure upon them which might be objectionable." Against this, Western usage was held up by Senators Trumbull and Williams: Trumbull saying that constituents had a right to know how members voted, and that there would be no chance to cheat by false or double ballots; and Williams, that members were frequently instructed by constituents how to vote, and the latter had a right to know if their mandate was obeyed as it should be.

Senator Anthony, of the pocket borough of Rhode Island, even advocated open voting by the people at the polls as the only true way; alleging, "It prevents corruption, it prevents deception, and cultivates a manly spirit everywhere." Senator Sumner was of the contrary opinion as regarded popular elections, but held that in the legislature the votes belonged to the constituents. Mr. Edmunds and Mr. Sherman voted with Mr. Fessenden, and there were three others of like mind; but twenty-eight held to *viva voce*.

It cannot be doubted that the overruling of these objections played admirably into the hands of the machine, insuring its control of the nominations and its marshaling of supporters by party pressure and by purchase. The open vote does not "prevent corruption"; it favors it by putting an obstacle in the way of treachery on the part of the bribed. It "prevents deception" of a certain kind, while fostering the grave deception that the legislator is voting according to his "conscientious convictions," and not from "compulsory pressure." It "cultivates a manly spirit," such as rings and machines most delight in, or manufacturers who wish to coerce the vote of their employees. Happily there is no need to insist on this point, as we are in the midst of an extraordinary movement, state after state, to substitute everywhere the secret for the open ballot as a means of restoring a manly spirit to the voter, protecting him from the consequences of his vote, and, above all, enabling him to baffle the cut-and-dried schemes of the caucus and the machine with independent nominations, having a chance of success without great outlay or preliminary organization.

The Australian ballot, in fact, whose potency in purifying our politics cannot now be calculated, but which is certain to be very great, commends itself for adoption wherever the corruptionist or the boss finds a field for his devilish activity; and were the States once more free to elect Senators in their own fashion, this mode of voting might stand a chance of being prescribed for Senatorial elections.

To make it of the greatest utility for this purpose, however, it ought to operate on a greater number of nominations than are commonly presented to a legislature by the respective party machines or caucuses. To secure these we must look to the people, making an appeal to them in advance of the mischief which they are now powerless to stave off or to repair. For this we have the warrant of the supporters of the statute of 1866 themselves. Senator Williams, as we have seen, held that, despite the constitutional injunction that the legislature should choose Senators, constituents had a right to instruct members how to vote, and to be obeyed; and Senator Sumner quite as frankly took the same ground.

Both, in other words, acknowledged the rightful force of public opinion in shaping the legislature's action; and, as a matter of history, Senators have, in certain States, again and again owed their reelection to respect for the popular sentiment and tradition in favor of retaining faithful servants in office.

Let us, then, suppose the States free to give to the people the power of nominating, at the proper general election, candidates for the approaching Senatorial vacancy. Suppose that these nominations were reached as now under the ballot-reform laws; the state printing on the official ballot the names of such as had a certain group of petitioners behind them (say three to five thousand). Then let the five to ten highest be the popular instruction to the legislature to choose from among these, and let the legislative voting take place in joint convention, again by the Australian system, each member to vote on the first ballot for three on the list ; on the second, for one (or two, as the case may be) out of the three highest as determined by the first ballot. In case of a tie let the decision be by lot.

From this method certain obvious benefits would accrue. The legislator's choice would no longer be as it too often is now, as the common voter's generally is merely a choice of two evils. The people of the state would scan eagerly their own list of candidates, and could not avoid the comparison between the most worthy and the least, especially if the latter were the party nominees. A man fit to be Senator would have a decided prestige when proposed in this manner as against the product of intrigue and jobbery. Such men would tend to multiply in the popular nominations, inasmuch as they could allow their names to be used without loss of self-respect, and with no obligation to work in their own behalf. Their appearance in the public view as ready to serve the state would recommend them for election to the legislature or to the lower house of Congress; in either of which positions they would demonstrate their fitness for promotion to the federal Senate, while meantime elevating the bodies to which they were elected. Moreover, if an abundance of good material were always in sight, the practice of nominating non-residents of the congressional districts, which is much to be desired, and which was signally exemplified last year in Massachusetts in the case of Dr. William Everett, would become common.

If a precedent be demanded for nominations in the manner just described, we can cite that recalled to mind by President Welling in a recent address on Connecticut federalism before the New York Historical Society. "I must add," he says, "that the old electoral system of Connecticut was ingeniously devised to promote the genesis of a natural aristocracy, the aristocracy of talents and virtues. Each freeman in the colony was required, in September of each year, to name twenty men whom he wished to have placed in nomination for the office of 'Assistant,' the so-called 'Assistants' being the dignitaries who composed the Council, or colonial Senate.

From the mass of nominations made at these primary assemblies of the townships, the General Assembly, six months before each election, selected and published the names of the twenty men who had received the highest number of nominating votes, and these men could be voted for on the day of the final election, when twelve out of the twenty were to be elected."

Nearer in point of time and to our present purpose is the Massachusetts practice during the first quarter of the century, by which each congressional district nominated three presidential electors, of whom the legislature chose one for each district, besides the two electors at large.

Still closer and more recent is the provision of the constitution of Nebraska (1875) noticed by Mr. Bryce. The electors, in voting for state legislators, are allowed to "express by ballot their preference for some person for the office of United States Senator. The votes cast for such candidates shall be canvassed and returned in the same manner as for state officers." The futility of this, however, is apparent, as the legislature is in no way constrained to pay any heed to public sentiment. In fact, in actual practice, this privilege has only once been availed of by the people of Nebraska, namely, in 1886, when General Van Wyck made an active canvass in his own behalf as an antimonopolist. The Republican and Democratic parties abstained from preliminary nominations, and General Van Wyck secured in November about a third as many votes as were cast for governor. In January, on the first two ballots, he received a plurality of the legislative vote, but was finally rejected.

To head off the machine, to give back to the people the right of nomination as well as of election, to restore to the state legislatures their state ward-looking character and duties, to divorce (so far as is possible) national from state politics, to fill the federal Senate with men whose prime qualifications are unpartisan and whose election is spontaneous, to pave the way for the re-entrance into politics of the cultivated classes to whom it has become abhorrent, all this may be accomplished by making the choice of United States Senator uncertain to such a degree that no political rewards can be promised or obtained in connection with it. Let the people nominate, let the legislature choose, within limits. Mr. Bryce remarks on the Nebraska provision that it is "an attempt to evade, and by a side wind defeat, the provision of the federal constitution which vests the choice in the legislature"; and of course, the same criticism would apply a *fortiori* to the scheme set forth in this paper. But is it certain that the courts would so pronounce?

The legislature would still choose, if under conditions prescribed by the state laws, supposing the statute of 1866 to have been abrogated. Moreover, in practice, its range of choice would be, not diminished, but enlarged. Nobody has challenged, or would venture to challenge, Mr. Bryce's own account of the existing procedure.

Senators, he observes, "are still nominally chosen, as under the letter of the Constitution they must be chosen, by the state legislatures. The state legislature means, of course, the party for the time dominant, which holds a party meeting (caucus) and decides on the candidate, who is thereupon elected, the party going solid for whomsoever the majority has approved. Now the determination of the caucus has almost always been arranged beforehand by the party managers.

Circumstances may change, compromises may be necessary; still it is now generally true that in most States little freedom of choice remains with the legislature. The people, or rather those wire-pullers who manage the people and act in their name, have practically settled the matter at the election of the state legislature."

But what if the wire-pullers find that electing the legislature is not the same as electing the Senator? They will lose the chief reason for interfering with these elections, which will tend more and more to be governed by local issues and personal merit. The men thus sent up will be more independent of party, and more free to choose wisely and patriotically from the list for Senator returned by their constituents.

The stability of the federal Senate is, no doubt, a wholesome feature of our constitution, but we must not forget that this branch became the bulwark of slavery, which measured its term of life by the preponderance of its supporters in the upper house. Two years ago, the promoters of our present tariff legislation were confident that their control of the Senate would prevent for years to come the undoing of the extremist measure they might carry in the short interval of their having a majority in the House of Representatives also. Certain accidents by which the engineer was hoist with his own petard have falsified this calculation; but the danger is a standing one, and the Senate ought never to be counted upon as the citadel of sectional or selfish combinations.

The law under which it is now renewed (ACT of 1866) favors such a perversion of it, and it has not prevented deadlocks. It is time that the States should ask to have their freedom restored to them, and take the penalty of going unrepresented so long as they cannot agree upon a candidate. We might then introduce by degrees the combination of popular nomination and secret balloting described above, and trust to a steady if slow amelioration of the whole tone of our politics, a decline in the persistence of parties and a falling off in party management, the emancipation of the state legislatures, the reformation of the federal Senate.

—

TIME TO REVISIT THE 17ᵀᴴ AMENDMENT
Op-Ed
The Portsmouth Herald, Portsmouth, NH, Dec 29, 2018
Michael J. Geanoulis, Sr.

Imagine, for the sake of argument, that our founding fathers could be resurrected long enough to give us a critical review about the way we fostered their vision for America. And imagine, if you are up to the challenge, what might have been in the absence of the 17th Amendment.

At the conclusion of the Constitutional Convention (1787) that gave us the laws thought best for us, Benjamin Franklin was asked by a little old lady as he left that venerable meeting hall in Philadelphia for the last time: "Well Mr. Franklin, what kind of government have you given us?"

"A Republic, ma'am, if you can keep it," he answered.

With that ominous clause "if you can keep it," Franklin expected trouble of the kind Madison warned against in his Federalist #10 which eloquently anticipated the "evil" influence of factions; and the "mischief" later evidenced by the passage of the 17th Amendment (Effective date, May 31, 1913).

After discovering the hazards and failures typical of democracies controlled directly by the people, our founders opted instead for a Constitutional Republic which included a Senate designed to check government overreach and to keep the people at arm's length from the legislative process. Tocqueville, who feared a "Tyranny of the Majority" for America, referred to that construct as a stroke of political genius.

Madison, who spent considerable of his intellect studying two crates of books on the topic sent to him from Europe by Jefferson, would not be happy about the 17th Amendment. Under his influence, a bicameral legislature was established to include a lower House of Representatives controlled directly by the people, and an upper Senate controlled by state legislatures. To qualify for a seat in the U. S. Senate (prior to 1913), a candidate had to be vetted by his or her respective state legislature, who were elected by the people. The House and Senate would have their factions, but each would have a modicum of balance with the other. Compare that to today, when both houses are influenced in common.

Emotionally charged legislation in the old days were more carefully and deliberately processed by Representatives and partially isolated Senators who could then inject higher caution and wisdom about such things as property rights, selective benevolence, debt, government overreach and individual freedoms.

The population at large, however, frustrated by their inability to get all the things they thought necessary for the common good, rebelled against the way the Senate was populated and so entered a near cen- tury - long campaign to get more direct control of it by way of the 17th Amendment.

As of May 31, 1913, Madison's magnificent effort to control mischie- vous factions was crippled. Both houses are lower now - elected and controlled directly by the people.

To be sure, the seating of the Senate by state legislatures was not with- out problems of its own. Influence peddling sometimes left Senate seats unoccupied for extended periods. An amendment was urgently needed so stated the prevailing populism of the times.

Too bad Madison wasn't around during those debates. He might have called attention to a curious coincidence between Progressive efforts to modify the United States Senate and the well-intentioned Marxist movement to bring down capitalist freedoms everywhere. He might have charged that it wasn't empty Senate seats that bothered populists; it was their benevolent ambition to elevate common control over Senate legislation in Washington, and the assets of others—even those not yet born.

Madison would have approved of a New Hampshire legislative effort (Rep Kingsbury) to nominate a short list of Senate candidates for the people to vote on; and temporary appointments for absent seats by the governor. But who cares about common sense where self - serving factions rule?

Both the House of Representatives and the Senate are lower houses now thanks to a forgotten amendment that more easily facilitated divisive income tax rates, family decay, debt-riddled entitlement programs of every description and money - dominated influence of another kind ("Is it Time to Repeal the 17th Amendment," Demaggio, J., 2018).

Madison and his colleagues underestimated the power of determined factions. If they knew in 1787 what we know now, they would have made it more difficult to reconstruct our Constitution; and included a clause providing that "Congress shall make no law respecting the establishment of selective benevolence," to boot. Matters of public health, education, poverty and welfare could, and should, be handled more resourcefully and responsibly by the state and its people as provided for in the 10th Amendment.

Given the deficit of integrity demonstrated by both sides of the aisle in Washington these days, and the courts for their casual regard of the 10th Amendment, the public should study what the founders said and did in

1787, and request a repeal or repair of the 17th Amendment using political initiatives of their own.

Mike Geanoulis of New Castle is author of "The Big Gorge: Fragile Families, Precious Memories and a Concerned Father's Prayers for our Future." You can email him at geanoulis@comcast.net

—

Views of Mr. Danforth
The undersigned, a member of the Committee on Election of President, Vice President, and Representatives in Congress, is opposed to the action of that committee, at its meeting held this morning, in approving the joint resolution (H. J. Res. 39) proposing an amendment to the Constitution providing that Senators shall be elected by the people of the several States. My objections are on the following grounds: That said proposed amendment is unwise; that the committee has not been afforded time nor opportunity for a careful consideration of the same, requisite for the decision of a question of so much importance. Henry G. Danforth. April 12, 1911.

Chapter 12

THE ELOQUENCE OF SENATOR GEORGE FRISBIE HOAR

Senate Testimony
Congressional Record. 25:101-110. April 6 and 7, 1893.
Senator George Frisbie Hoar
The resolution submitted by Mr. Hoar on the 3d instant was read as follows:

Resolved, that it is *inexpedient* that the resolution sent to the Senate by the House of Representatives during the last Congress, providing for an amendment of the constitution securing the election of Senators by the people of the several States, be adopted.

Such a method of election would essentially change the character of the Senate as conceived by the convention that framed the constitution and the people who adopted it.

It would transfer practically the selection of the members of this body from the legislatures, who are entrusted with all legislative powers of the States, to bodies having no other responsibilities, whose election cannot be regulated by law, whose members act by proxy, whose tenure of office is for a single day, whose votes and proceedings are not recorded, who act under no personal responsibility, whose mistakes, ordinarily, can only be corrected by the choice of Senators who do not represent the opinions concerning public measures and policies of the people who choose them.

It requires the substitution of pluralities for majorities in the election. It will transfer the seat of political power in the great States, now distributed evenly over their territory, to the great cities and masses of population.

It will create new temptations to fraud, corruption, and other illegal practices, and in close cases will give rise to numerous election contests, which must tend seriously to weaken the confidence of the people in the Senate.

It will absolve the larger States from the constitutional obligation which secures the equal representation of all the States in the Senate by providing that no state shall be deprived of that equality without its consent.

It implies what the whole current of our history shows to be untrue, that the Senate has during the past century failed to meet the just expectations of the people, and that the state legislatures have proved themselves unfit to be the depositaries of the power of electing Senators.

The reasons which require this change, if acted upon and carried to their logical result, will lead to the election by the direct popular vote, and by popular majorities, of the president and of the judiciary, and will compel the placing of these elections under complete national control.

It will result in the overthrow of the whole scheme of the Senate and, in the end, of the whole scheme of the national constitution as designed and established by the framers of the constitution and the people who adopted it.

Mr. President, I suppose that no thoughtful person will deem a discussion of this topic out of time or premature. Four important States have sent to us resolutions of their legislatures favoring such a change in the constitution. Three Senators have advocated it in elaborate speeches. The House of Representatives, without a debate, has passed resolutions for submitting the change to the States. The careless and thoughtless dealing with this subject is shown by the proposal to take from Congress all power over the manner of electing Senators a step which would go far, in my judgment, to change this country from a nation into a league or confederacy.

I am not sure whether it is the good fortune or the ill fortune of our American political system that our controversies so often relate to matters which are vital, not only to the well-being, but to the very existence of the republic. The English take their constitution for granted. They can change anything in their state by a simple act of legislation. But it has been rarely in their history that great constitutional changes have been brought about by the action of legislative bodies. They have never been brought about by the direct action of the people.

The abandonment of the influence of the sovereign in legislation, the abandonment of the veto power, the diminished authority of the House of Lords, the transfer of executive power from the immediate servants of the Crown to the ministers, who depend for their official existence upon the majority of the House of Commons all these things have come to pass so silently that it is difficult to discover when any of them took place.

Although our constitutions, state and national, are all in writing, there are constant attempts to make changes of the most radical and vital character, and to bring them about suddenly and without deliberation or discussion by popular action.

If the Senate as at present constituted is to be defended, it is to be defended here. If the great reasons which moved our fathers to establish this chamber, which they hoped would last to unbroken succession until time shall be no more, to give its members a tenure of office more enduring than that of any other department of the government save the judiciary alone, to re-move it from the operation of the fleeting passions of the hour, to lay its foundation below the frost, and to remove the appointment of the men who are to compose it, as far as may be, from the temporary excitements which so often move the people to their own harm, are understood anywhere, those reasons must, be understood by the men who fill these seats. If this great part of the structure of our body politic is to be maintained, it must be maintained by the confidence of the American people in the character of their Senators and by the strength of argument which those Senators must themselves at least help to furnish.

This is clearly, Mr. President, a question of centuries, and not of years. In determining it we must appeal to our experience of a hundred years, and not merely to that of yesterday or the day before. A present impatience is not only no good reason for making a change, but its existence seems to me an especial reason for postponing it. If we listen only to present complaints, we must make radical changes also in the manner of electing the president, in the constitution of the state legislatures, in our judiciary, in the House of Representatives, in the management of our great corporations, of our railroads, our schools, our universities, the church, the law, and the private habits of the people.

Complaint, impatience, uneasiness attend upon everything which depends upon human instrumentality for its administration. They are the sign of vigorous health, and if soberly and thoughtfully dealt with are the conditions of all life and growth.

We must judge the Senate, as I have said, by the experience of a century, and not by a few recent failures. Whatever there may be of existing evil may be corrected by the intelligence and good sense of the people, as other evils quite as great have been corrected in the past.

When I came into the national service in 1869, all avenues to this and the other chamber and to every executive department were swarming with a powerful and corrupt lobby. That lobby has disappeared before an aroused and vigorous public sentiment. Who hears now of great measures of legislation promoted or affected in Congress by corrupt instrumentalities?

When I came into public life in 1869, the Senate claimed almost entire control of the executive function of appointment to office. Every Senator, with hardly an exception, seemed to fancy that the national officers in his state were to be a band of political henchmen devoted to his personal fortunes. What was called "the courtesy of the Senate" was depended upon to enable a Senator to dictate to the executive all appointments and removals in his territory. That doctrine has disappeared as completely as the locusts that infested Egypt in the time of the Pharaohs.

When I entered public life in 1869, Tweed was the dominant power in New York City. He dictated alike all civic expenditures and the appointment and the judgment of the courts of the city. It became my duty, in representing the House of Representatives on the impeachment of a public officer before the Senate, to utter the following language of warning, the timeliness and necessity of which I think few men will now question:

My own public life has been a very brief and insignificant one, extending little beyond the duration of a single term of Senatorial office. But in that brief period, I have seen five judges of a high court of the United States driven from office by threats of impeachment for corruption or maladministration. I have heard the taunt, from friendliest lips, that when the United States presented herself in the East to take part with the civilized world in generous competition in the arts of life, the only product in her institutions in which she surpassed all others beyond question was her corruption.

I have seen in the state in the union foremost in power and wealth four judges of her courts impeached for corruption, and the political administration of her chief city become a disgrace and a byword throughout the world. I have seen the chairman of the Committee on Military Affairs in the House, now a distinguished member of this court, rise in his place and demand the expulsion of four of his associates for making sale of their official privilege of selecting the youths to be educated at our great military school.

When the greatest railroad in the world, binding together the continent and uniting the two seas which wash our shores, was finished, I have seen our national triumph and exultation turned to bitterness and shame by the unanimous reports of three committees of Congress two of the House and one here that every step of that mighty enterprise had been taken in fraud.

I have heard in highest places the shameless doctrine avowed by men grown old in public office that the true way by which power should be gained in the republic is to bribe the people with the offices created for their service, and the true end for which it should be used when gained is the promotion of selfish ambition and the gratification of personal revenge. I have heard that suspicion haunts the footsteps of the trusted companions of the President.

These things have passed into history. The Hallam or the Tacitus or the Sismondi or the Macaulay who writes the annals of our time will record them with his inexorable pen.

Will any man deny the truth of any of these charges? Will any man find occasion to repeat them to-day? These great evils, one and all, have been corrected by the American people with the abundant resources which, under their existing constitutions, were at their command. Other evils, as grave, but not graver, demand our attention to-day. These evils will in their turn disappear when brought into the daylight before the intelligence and the justice of the American people.

The sufferings of the people have been mostly from their apprehensions, never from any actual misgovernment. Even our civil war itself came through the apprehension of the people of one section of the country of which those who waged it against the government now think it was an unmixed good. Our political history seems to be almost made up of popular movements which are the result of the fears of the people of evils apprehended from legislation which, in fact, are never experienced.

The history of the United States for a hundred years has been the history of marvelous prosperity and growth, which reads, even in the pages of soberest historians, like an oriental tale. Yet our political journals have been constantly filled with prediction of disaster and ruin. If anybody needs confirmation of this statement, let him read the political platforms of the party conventions of the minority. It is marvelous to see how safe, conservative, and beneficent has been our national legislation in spite of all the violence and all the extreme utterances of the journals and the platforms. This quality in our legislation is derived largely, though not wholly, from the character of the Senate under the existing method of choosing its members.

The dangers of the country are the dangers to the elective franchise violence, fraudulent voting, fraudulent counting, intimidation, corruption, gerrymandering, the unseating of legislators with unquestioned title to their seats for the accomplishment of political objects by unscrupulous men, the use of weapons intended to protect our institutions, to subvert them. These things, not mistakes in finance, or an erroneous fiscal policy, or unwise laws of succession, or even rash and violent projects of social extremists are the things that menace the permanence of our institutions today.

Every generation since the dawning of civilization seems to have been gifted with its own peculiar capacity. The generation of Homer has left nothing behind but a great epic poem, which for thirty centuries remains without a rival. Italian art had its brief and brilliant day of glory which departed and never has returned. The time of Elizabeth was the time of dramatic poetry which has been alike the wonder and the despair of all succeeding ages. The generation which accomplished the American Revolution had a genius for framing constitutions which no generation before or since has been able to equal or to approach. The features of the state constitutions framed in that day have been retained with little changes in substance, and have been copied since by every new state.

The men of that day had many great advantages for this work. They had conducted a great revolution. To prepare for it, they had been engaged for a century in discussing the principles on which self-government is founded and by which constitutional liberty is secured. They were men of English stock, trained in the principles of English liberty. There was no admixture in their body politic of men who had been born under despotic governments, and who associated the idea of government inseparably with the idea of tyranny. At their fathers' fireside the great debate of constitutional liberty had been conducted from the earliest recollection of the oldest men then living. They had the other advantage, that in framing their constitutions they were free from all party bias and from the temptation to consult party advantage, or appeal to the party prejudices of the people.

I do not, of course, claim that the people cannot now amend, or that they cannot now improve, our constitution. That constitution itself would be a failure if the experience of a hundred years under its operation found the people unfitted to improve it. The lives of our fathers would have been of little worth if, under the constitution they framed, there had not grown up and flourished a people who were also fit to deal with the great and fundamental constitutional principles of the state.

The men who entered upon the untried field of providing by written enactment what were the boundaries and limits of constitutional power and constitutional authority in the state have left children who, after a hundred years of trial, need not fear to approach and to deal with the same great problems. But they must bring to them the same wisdom and courage and virtue.

They must dare to tell the people plain truths. They must possess the wisdom of deliberate action and arise to the austere virtue of self-restraint.

Mr. President, wherever there can be found an expression of admiration for the American constitution in the works of any great writer or thinker at home or abroad it will be found that the admiration is based upon that part of its mechanism which secures the deliberate and indirect action of the popular will instead of its immediate, rapid, inconsiderate, and direct action. The parts of it which were everywhere the most praised and by which its framers sought especially to commend it to the confidence of the people were the constitution of the Senate and the constitution of the Supreme Court.

The great function of the Supreme Court is not merely or chiefly to afford a learned, able, and impartial tribunal for the determination of controversies between private parties upon the principles of ordinary municipal law; but it is the function of keeping the national and state legislatures alike within the appointed limits of their authority. In other words, it is a restraint upon the people's will when expressed in the form of legislation by the people's representatives, whether that will undertake an encroachment upon the individual and natural rights of the citizens or upon the domain of other appointed constitutional authorities. "It is, indeed," said Daniel Webster, "a great achievement; it is the master work of the world, to establish governments entirely popular on lasting foundations."

MICHAEL JAMES GEANOULIS, SR.

I do not propose to take any time in commending the excellencies of the constitution of the United States. I do not think it worthwhile to cite to ears to which they are familiar the praise of foreign Statesmen or philosophers, of Gladstone, or of de Tocqueville, or of Bryce. These compliments are trifling and insignificant in comparison with the great fact that the American people are satisfied with it, and that they would reject with swift and unanimous indignation any proposition which they thought would change it in its essence.

I think it can be established to their satisfaction that the proposed change in the method of electing Senators is in itself a change in principle and essence of the most vital character, and that its logic will lead to other changes equally vital and essential. And for that reason I have no apprehension of the success of this scheme when deliberately considered and discussed.

I am not afraid to say to the American people that it is dangerous to trust any great power of government to their direct or inconsiderate control. I am not afraid to tell them not only that their sober second thought is better than their hasty action, but that a government which is exposed to the hasty action of a people is the worst and not the best government on earth.

No matter how excellent may be the individual, the direct, immediate, hasty action of any mass of individuals on earth is the pathway to ruin and not to safety. It is as true to-day as it was when James Madison, the great advocate of the rights of the people in his time, one of the foremost among the framers of our constitution, first said it, "That, although every Athenian citizen might be a Socrates, every Athenian assembly would still be a mob."

Our fathers were profound students of history. They found that no republic, although there had been many examples of other republics, ever lasted long without a Senate. *The term Senate implied to their minds, as to ours, a body of men of mature age and of a tenure of office which was removed from all temptation of being affected by temporary currents of public senti-ment. The word Senate is a misnomer when applied to any legislative body of whom these things are not true.*

My friend from Oregon said the other day that the framers of the con-stitution distrusted the people. He said that one of them who declared in the convention that legislation ought to be removed as far as possible from the immediate action of the people would be remanded to private life nowadays with a promptness that would be almost grotesque. Why, Mr. President, that Senator represents a state, one of the new States of the union, that has incorporated the doctrine of that utterance into ev-ery department and arrangement of her constitution more completely, I think, than any other state in the American union.

The Senator overlooks what the author of the utterance with which he finds fault had so profoundly studied the difference between the imme-diate action of the people upon legislation and administration and the expression of the sober and deliberate will of the people through instru-mentalities whose own sobriety and deliberation are thoroughly secured.

Does my friend really think that the authors of the opening sentences in the Declaration of Independence, who rested their cause on those sublime and eternal truths in their great controversy with the mother country, who placed those truths at the very foundation of their new government, who pledged their lives and fortunes and sacred honor to maintain them, distrusted the people?

They trusted the people when they made those great declarations of natural right. They trusted the people when they declared the equal right of every human being without exception of race or color or nation-ality or rank or fortune. But they trusted them also with as profound and implicit a trust when they submitted to them constitutions, both state and national, filled with restraints which alike secure minorities and individuals against injustice and oppression from majorities, and secure the whole people against their own hasty and inconsiderate action.

No, Mr. President, *it is not because the framers of our constitution distrusted the people; it is because they trusted the people that they confidently asked their adoption of a constitution which compelled them to deliberation, to sober thought, to delegated power, to action through selected agencies and instrumentalities, to thinking twice before acting once. It was not Madison or Hamilton; it was the people of the United States who ordained and established the constitution.*

I have no respect for the notion that the people of the United States need to be flattered or cajoled, or that they are impatient of the necessary restraints of constitutional liberty. Truth, frankness, and courage are the avenues to their confidence. There is but one way to discover what will be popular in this country, and that is to discover what is right. There is but one road to the enjoyment of the confidence of the people, and that is to counsel them to wise, honest, and safe policies. The public man who appeals to temporary opinion or who flatters temporary passion will find his hold upon power as temporary and short-lived as are the instrumentalities by which he seeks to obtain it.

It has been said in this discussion that the constitution needed amendment at once. This is true; but all amendments were in the direction of placing checks on the power of the people and declaring that there were certain things the people should not be permitted to do. The great Statesmen who framed the constitution placed in it certain checks and safeguards against the popular will. The greater people to whom they submitted it perfected it by inserting other safeguards still.

I stated just now that the term "Senate" implied to the apprehension of every studious man certain essential conditions; but the Senate of the United States, as established by our constitution, implied something more than this. First, our fathers wished to secure a dual legislative assembly. With the exception of Dr. Franklin and his associates in the Pennsylvania delegation, who are understood to have cast a formal vote out of deference to him, it was thought best to provide a dual representative assembly. Every act of the legislature was to be twice considered and have the approbation of two different, separate houses.

Second, these two houses were to have a different constituency. So every proposed law must run the gauntlet of two diverse interests and be judged from at least two points of view. Every state in the construction of its legislature has maintained these two principles. The American people, I suppose, are flow agreed upon them with substantial unanimity.

Third, the Senate is expected to represent the equality of the States. This is the one principle which would never have been yielded by a majority of the States when the constitution was made, and which has been made eternal as far as possible by the provision that it shall not be changed without the consent of every state. Fourth, the Senate was to represent deliberation in the expression of the popular will by the length of the term of office of Senators and by its removal from the direct popular vote in the method of choice. It is this point at which the Senate is now attacked.

The constitution of the Senate secures the applications of all these principles in the four great constitutional functions of the national government in legislation, in the making of treaties, in the appointment of the great executive officers, and in impeachment. The last of these powers has happily not often been resorted to in our history but was regarded by the framers of the constitution as essential for the security of the whole.

As James Monroe well said: The right of impeachment and of trial by the legislature is the mainspring of the great machine of government. It is the pivot on which it turns. If preserved in full vigor and exercised with perfect integrity, every branch will perform its duty.

Each of these the Senate shares with other departments of the government, and to each of them it contributes the great and conservative principle which our fathers thought essential to secure to all generations and amid all popular temptations and excitements the government they framed against the evils by which all former republics had perished.

The constitution also carefully provides in the case of the Senate, as in the case of the House, that the manner of the election shall be prescribed by the authority of the nation for whom the persons selected are to legislate.

It will be seen, I think, very clearly that the change proposed destroys the essential character of the Senate in each of these particulars.

It substitutes a direct election by the people for an election by the legislature. For a selection by public officers to whom the great public duty of state legislation is entrusted there is to be a selection and nomination by conventions composed of persons without other responsibility. This, in most cases, will be the mode in which the majority, practically, will make its choice.

For a selection by men who are themselves selected under strict legal provisions there is to be, therefore, practically a selection by men who are not chosen in pursuance of any law.

Instead of selection by men under oath of office there must be a choice by men upon whom no oath is imposed.

For a selection by men of whose action there is a record the choice is practically to be made by men of whom no record exists.

For a choice in a manner prescribed by national authority, selection will be made by men who may act by proxy.

For a choice by a permanent body there must be a choice by a body lasting but a day.

For a choice in a manner prescribed by national authority, there must be a choice in a manner prescribed in no authority whatever.

For a choice by a body acting by majorities, there must be substituted, in the end, a choice by a plurality.

For a choice by a body representing all localities in a state where different local interests are fairly represented, there must be a choice by sheer force of numbers, where the popular masses in great cities will have an undue and disproportionate weight.

Instead of representing different constituencies to secure the different interests in legislation, the Senate and the House are to represent constituencies of the same kind, differing only in size.

From the change in the manner of election will surely and inevitably, in my judgment, follow the destruction of the equality of the States in the Senate. It is true the constitution now provides that no state shall be deprived of its equal vote in the Senate without its consent. But this provision relates to a Senate to be constitutional and selected in the old constitutional manner, and will never be long tolerated, in my judgment, by the large States under the proposed arrangement.

The state legislatures are the depositories of the sovereignty of the States. They are, in theory, and I believe in general in fact, composed of the picked and chosen men of the communities from which they come. The men who make up the state legislatures are chosen by their neighbors. They are chosen by men who know them or can know them. There have been exceptions, but in general they have been honest, wise, faithful, and just. The pages of the statute books of the forty-four commonwealths are in general without a stain. They can be read by the patriot without a blush. I am not afraid to compare them with the two hundred and fifty Parliaments through which, for eight hundred years, the freedom of England has broadened slowly down from precedent to precedent.

There have been many things we might well wish were otherwise. In the chambers where all men are equally represented, what is worst as well as what is best of humanity will sometimes find its representative. The ambition, the love of power, the party spirit, the private greed, the popular passion, injustice, and tyranny will occasionally appear there as elsewhere. In what spot in human history are they not found? But I am willing to take the legislation of any American state which is a quarter of a century old and compare it with the legislation of any government possessing a legislature in any period of its history.

Why, in the British House of Commons, Disraeli said that long after the close of the American war, and within the memory of men who heard him, a member of the government stood below the gangway at the final adjournment of the Parliament and gave a 500 note to every member who had supported the administration.

You and I can well remember when bribery was a common and necessary method of getting a seat in the English House of Commons. But English constitutional liberty and English constitutional government have not proved a failure.

Do you propose to strip the state legislatures of any other function of their sovereignty? Can you not trust the men who make all the laws upon which the safety of property, the marriage relation, the security of the home, the administration of the schools, taxation, freedom of religion, the punishment of crime, and everything else which enters into the comfort and honor of private life are depending with the choice of Senators because my honorable friend from Illinois thinks that, in the experience of the people of that excellent state, the selection of Senators under existing conditions has been unsatisfactory?

What is the alternative, and what must be the alternative? What is the alternative proposed? What must be the necessary and only alternative that can be proposed for the exercise of this great function of local sovereignty? The state legislature is a failure, we are told, and is not fit to be trusted any longer. Who are to nominate our Senators? To whom is the practical selection to be entrusted?

Whatever may be the theory, the voting population of the state of New York, or of the 10 million who within the lifetime of some of us will dwell within the borders of that imperial commonwealth, are not expected to gather together and put in nomination a Senator by direct action. No one hall will quite hold them, even were it as flexible and expansive as the court room when naturalization is going on.

The practical choice of the Senator must be made by nominating conventions. Are not these bodies quite as likely to be susceptible to mistakes or to corrupt manipulation as a state legislature? They gather together at midday, chosen by no constituency whose action, or even the freedom or purity of whose choice can be regulated by law. The men who gather are to perform but a single function, to which there is attached ordinarily little responsibility. They cannot be instructed by their constituents. Their functions may be exercised by proxy. They are not amenable in their individual action to a sound public opinion.

There is no record of the individual vote, or any means of correcting a mistake or fraud. They gather in the morning and disperse when the mists of evening rise. And it is to these bodies that the choice of the men who are to compose what we are fond of calling the most august body on earth is practically and in the ordinary course of things to be committed. It is these bodies who are fitter to be trusted than the legislatures to whom all the dearest interests of the people of the States are committed.

Cicero, in his oration for Lucius Flaccus, attributes the decay of Roman and the destruction of the Grecian liberty to the substitution of the turbulent popular assembly for the deliberative chamber in wielding the political power of the state. He has left his terrible picture of the popular assemblies of his time as a pregnant lesson for all mankind.

It may be said that governors and state officers and representatives in Congress are selected in this way now. That is true. But have all nominations of governors and representatives in Congress been on the whole more satisfactory to the people than the selection of Senators for one hundred years? I think that when any one of us wishes to arouse the state pride of the people he represents by enumerating the great men who have adorned their history we find that the names of the men who have sat in these seats arise to our lips quite as naturally as the names of the governors or the representatives in Congress, however illustrious.

When my colleagues here or my colleagues in the other house wish to stir the hearts of a Massachusetts audience they are quite as likely to speak of Webster, and of John Quincy Adams, of Charles Sumner, of Rufus Choate, or George Cabot, and of Edward Everett and John Davis as of anyone in our list of governors, excellent as that list has been. Is there any other state of which the same is not true?

And nearly every one of the great men who have been elected to the House by the choice of the people has also sat in the Senate. The people who by any constitutional method of choice will in any generation send to this chamber an ignoble or unworthy Senator will, I will venture to say, be found to have at the same time no better timber in their executive chair or in the House of Representatives.

It is a little difficult for a member of this body, without some violation of good taste or self-assertion, to state what we all think of the character which the Senate has maintained from the beginning of the government and of its title to the confidence of the people. But I am not afraid or ashamed to invite a comparison of the men who have sat in these seats and represented my own commonwealth, down to the date when the present Senators took their places, with any line of dukes, barons, or princes, or emperors, or popes who have successively filled the seats of any legislature or the executive chair of any commonwealth, whether these persons held their titles by virtue of the noble descent or royal favor or of the favor of the people themselves.

I do not believe the people of Massachusetts and the same challenge may be given with confidence in behalf of any other American state that has a history will accept this invitation to change the method of choosing the Senators, which depends, as I have said, not only upon the claim that the legislatures are unfit to be trusted with this duty, which is one among the chiefest functions of sovereignty, but that the Senate of the United States has, upon the whole, been a failure.

I do not believe the people of Massachusetts are quite ready to discredit their own general court with its two hundred and sixty years of legislative history, and give their confidence instead to a political convention which gathers in the morning and disperses when the mists of evening arise, whose members are without an oath of office, without a record, without legal restraint upon their election, who have no accountability to their representatives, or to anybody, without even the requirement that they shall be citizens.

And I do not believe that they are quite prepared to say that, on the whole, they are ashamed of the Senators who, by the free choice of their legislatures, have for a hundred years represented them in this great national council.

It is a poor, cheap flattery of the people, this notion that suffrage is to be deified and that the results of suffrage are to be degraded; that the people have all wisdom and all honesty, but that their trusted agents are to be bought or cajoled. Will it not be the same people who choose the

Senators and who choose the legislatures? Is there any evil influence which will operate upon the legislature which will not operate with like effect upon the convention?

But it is said that the choice of a nominating convention is but the first step; any mistake it may make will be corrected by the people. But, Mr. President, except in most extreme cases, the correction must be worse than the evil which is to be cured.

At what cost are the people to vote down the nomination made by the convention of the party which is in the majority because of their dis-approval of a man who is its candidate for the Senate? Of course, the plurality system will be applied to this, as to every popular election. The people, then, must manifest their disapproval of an unworthy candidate regularly nominated only by transferring their support to the candidate of another party. It is not likely that any man who would get the nomi-nation of his party convention will be so unpopular that substantially the whole membership of his party will refuse to support him. What will happen will be the choice of the candidate of another party.

Now, what does this mean? It means that the people of a state are to give their support to doctrines, measures, policies, political principles of which they disapprove solely because of their opinion as to the indi-vidual character of the man who represents them. We have a party in Massachusetts who think a protective tariff, a monopoly, extortionate, robbery, and plunder of the many for the benefit of the few. They think it operates grievous and intolerable injustice in its application to the in-dividual citizen, and that its effect upon the national welfare is immoral, evil, disastrous.

And yet if any of them happen to think that a man nominated by their party to represent these opinions is not a good man, they are to send to Washington a man who supports all of these things simply because of their opinions as to an individual character. They must prefer a man who makes his country the instrument of robbers, monopolists, plunderers, and evil managers of finances, who is amiable and honest in private, over a dishonest and unamiable man who will put an end to all this iniquity.

In other words, the correction of the mistakes made by the political convention is only to be made at the cost of destroying the character of the country because of the character of the candidate. The amiable man who has no objection to dishonest and fraudulent elections is to be preferred to the unamiable man who wants honesty and fairness in elections. I have no doubt but that in extreme cases a man may be nominated by mistake, by deception, by public indifference, as a candidate of my party, whose personal character is such that it would be my duty to refuse him my support, whatever happened. But those cases will, I believe, be extremely rare, and if the disease to be remedied be wholly evil, the remedy itself is almost as bad.

Mr. President, the experience of our first century has, it seems to me, most amply vindicated the constitutional purpose, which resulted in the Senate. It is not expedient to have two houses both directly dependent on the popular will. I would not speak with disrespect of the House of Representatives. Every American who knows the history of his country must feel a just pride, in that great assembly, which has been and will hereafter be the direct representative of the people's will. The names of its great leaders of Clay, of John Quincy Adams, and of Thaddeus Stevens rise to the lips when we would stir in the hearts of any American assembly the emotion of national pride or the love of constitutional liberty.

If there be anything in its conduct which at any time impresses the thoughtful observer unpleasantly, I think he will admit that, on the whole, it bears comparison with the French Assembly, or the great representative body of Germany, or even with the British House of Commons. But the constitution of that House has compelled it to resort to many devices and to submit to many inconveniences. We should all be sorry if we are compelled to submit to them in the Senate. The freedom of debate in the House of Representatives is gone. What I sometimes think is even of more importance, the freedom of amendment is gone also.

Both these great essentials to wise and honest legislation exist only to a very limited extent, and then at the pleasure of the majority. It is here only that the freedom of debate is secure.

From all this has grown up the most pernicious of unconstitutional practices, that of filibustering, which was introduced originally to prevent hasty or arbitrary action by the majority, but is now used to prevent or overthrow the rule of the majority altogether. So that the course of legislation in that House today is this: A few great measures, to which the party in the majority is agreed, are carried through by special rules adapted for the purpose, the minority being deprived of all rights of reasonable debate or reasonable amendment.

All other measures, however important, however salutary, can and undemocratic, and if continued long must result in the overthrow of republican government itself.

Another evil of like character and of equal magnitude has grown up from the necessities, or the fancied necessities, in the transaction of business in the House of Representatives.

The question whether an important measure shall be submitted to the House for consideration has to be determined, not by individual members, not by chosen committees, not by the majority of the House itself, nor even by its unanimous consent in many instances, but by the will of the presiding officer alone. He determines, at his sole volition, what members shall be recognized and what measures the House shall be asked to consider.

It is notorious that many measures of vast importance, many measures of relief demanded by justice and by the national good faith, abide session after session and Congress after Congress, having received the support of this body, and which would have received the unanimous consent of the other if they could be taken up, which never can be heard in that House because of the refusal of its presiding officer to submit them.

Now, Mr. President, habits like this in the conduct of legislation do not grow up and keep their place without some grave public reason, or at least some grave public necessity. It may be that a body which represents, as does that House, a temporary and sometimes fleeting popular purpose requires such restraints and chains and fetters as these for the public safety. I think we may well pause before we give to this body a character which will require such obstacles to be placed in the path of its free action.

The time may come some of us thought that it was near at hand when it may be necessary to introduce even here a rule for a limited and carefully guarded cloture in debate. Every member of this body would regard that as a most painful necessity. If that time ever comes, it will be because rules established for the protection of freedom of action in the Senate have been abused to prevent and subvert it. But I hope and believe the time will never come when any question will be taken in this Senate in regard to which every Senator shall not have an opportunity to express fully and freely his opinion in debate, and in regard to which he shall not have the fullest opportunity to offer amendments as seems to him desirable.

I suppose there have been a few instances of corruption of state legislatures in the election of Senators. In a few cases such attempts have been exposed and failed in the legislatures themselves. In a few cases they have been detected here. In very few, indeed, they have probably been successful. I thought the Senate touched its low-water mark when a few years ago it refused to investigate one of them. It is a great mistake to suppose that nominating conventions will be much more easily dealt with, or that popular elections have been or will hereafter be any more exempt from such influences.

Have popular elections in ancient republics, or in England, or here been freer from corruption than elections through delegated and chosen assemblies? Mr. President, there will never, for any length of time, be venal legislatures without a corrupt people behind them.

Besides, there are, unhappily, other modes of destroying the freedom of elections, to which popular elections are exposed, from which legislative assemblies are free. The great prize of the office of Senator is, if this amendment be adopted, to be added to the temptations which, unless many a report in the other House be without foundation, have induced in very many instances in our history false counts, fraudulent naturalization, personation of voters, fraudulent residences, forged returns, intimidation, and mob violence. These attend elections in great cities and in States where race differences still add their bitterness to the struggle for political power.

There have been, it is estimated, more than three hundred and twenty contested election cases in the House of Representatives. They have been the scandal and reproach of our political history.

Excepting a very few creditable examples, they have been decided for partisan considerations, as like cases were decided in the British House of Commons until jurisdiction was transferred to the judges.

I suppose it is not intended to take from the Senate the power to judge of the election of its own members. Until now the contested election cases in the Senate have in general depended upon constitutional or legal questions, or upon facts easily ascertained and established. But if this change be made, the Senate, in every close election, must undertake investigations which will range over an entire state. A contest in New

York, or Pennsylvania, or Illinois, or Ohio may put in issue the legality of every vote cast in a state of three million, or five million, or perhaps, within a generation, of ten million people. There will never be a close election without a contest here. Unless human nature shall change, the result of these contests will depend on partisan considerations and will shake public confidence in the Senate to its very foundation.

Let no man deceive himself into the belief that if this change be made the Senate of the United States will long endure. Another legislative system will take the place of that which our fathers devised for us, and which for a hundred years has been the admiration of mankind. The method of election is indispensable to secure the peculiar quality of the body to be elected. The change will lead to an attempted overthrow of the equality of the Senate.

The States never consented to perpetual equality in a Senate made up in any other way or on any other principle of selection. They never agreed that there should be forever between New York and Maine an equality in a legislative chamber which is only a house of representatives made up of differently constituted districts. In twenty years, the state of New York will have ten millions of people, with a vote for every five persons.

Do you think they will long endure to submit to equality in legislation, in the making of treaties, in the appointment of great executive officers, in the power to punish and remove great offenders, in the making of war, and in the making of peace, with the 8,000 voters of dwindling Nevada, when the two States are simply two representative districts, whose only difference is that one is two hundred and fifty times as large as the other?

New York submits to this loyally today. She has pledged her eternal allegiance to the constitution. She cannot change it without the consent of every other state. It is so nominated in the bond, and is the price she pays for being the Empire State of an imperial nation. She cannot escape it without a revolution.

But open to her this door. Tell her that the Senate, as Hamilton and Jay conceived it, is gone. Tell her that it is no longer to be made up of chosen men, selected by chosen men, to be removed one degree from public impulse and passion, and representing the deliberate, sober, and instructed will of the people. She will tell you that her constitutional obligation has gone also and that the equality of the States in the Senate may henceforth be abolished or modified like other provisions of the instrument. "I never promised," she will tell you, "to submit to it forever under your new arrangement." "Non in haec foedera veni" or, as my great predecessor on this floor used to translate it: "I made no such bargain, and I stand for no such nonsense."

Various methods of electing Senators were proposed and thoroughly discussed in the convention, but the vote for the present method was at last unanimous. I think the suggestion of another method of choice is of quite recent origin and is more the outcome of circumstances that are not only recent but will be temporary.

Chancellor Kent, volume I, page 225, says: The election of the Senate by the state legislatures is also a recognition of their separate and independent existence, and renders them absolutely essential to the operation of the national government.

The Federalist, number 62, written by Hamilton, says: It is equally unnecessary to dilate on the appointment of Senators by the state legislatures. *Among the various modes which might have been devised for constituting this branch of the government, that which has been proposed by the convention is probably the most congenial with the public opinion. It is recommended by the double advantage of favoring a select appointment and of giving to the state government such an agency in the formation of the federal government as must secure the authority of the former and may form a convenient link between the two systems.*

Hamilton adds in the same number of the Federalist: In this spirit it may be remarked that the equal vote allowed to each state is at once a constitutional recognition of the portion of sovereignty remaining in the individual States and an instrument for preserving that residuary sovereignty. So far, the equality ought to be no less acceptable to the large than to the small States, since they are not less solicitous to guard by every possible expedient again an improper consolidation of the States into one simple republic.

The convention which framed the constitution, after some consideration, unanimously rejected the plan of choosing Senators by the people, and unanimously adopted the present system.

Judge Story (constitution, section 704) mentions as one of the reasons that this "would increase public confidence by securing the national government from any encroachments on the powers of the States."

This idea deserves to be dwelt upon. The state legislatures are the bodies of men most interested of all others to preserve state jurisdiction more than the governors, who may be expected to aspire to national employments. It is well that the members of one branch of the legislature should look to them for their re-election, and it is a great security for the rights of the States. The state legislatures will be made up of men whose duty will be the administration of the state authority of their several state interests and the framing of laws for the government of the state which they represent. The popular conventions, gathered for the political purpose of nominating Senators, may be quite otherwise composed or guided. Here, in the state legislature, is to be found the great security against the encroachment upon the rights of the States.

How many instances there have been in our history in which an immediate popular vote would have led to disastrous consequences, but the sober second thought of the people has led to the path of safety. Mr. Madison said in the constitutional convention (see Madison Papers, vol. 2, p. 847):

If the opinions of the people were to be our guide, it would be difficult to say what course we ought to take. No member of the convention could say what the opinions of his constituents were at this time, much less could he say what they would think if possessed of the information and lights possessed by the members here; and still less what would be their way of thinking six or twelve months hence.

Suppose that if, instead of action through a convention, the adoption of the constitution itself had been submitted to a direct popular vote, it would have been rejected by a majority of the States, certainly by the States of Connecticut, Massachusetts, New York and Virginia, the four great States without whose cooperation the establishment of national government would have been impossible. How many times great waves of delusion have swept over the land, whose force was broken by the sober discussions of deliberative assemblies. The great anti-Masonic movement of 1835, the Know-Nothing movement of 1854 and the years that followed are but two out of many examples.

Neither Charles Sumner nor Salmon P. Chase could have been elected by a popular vote when they were first chosen. Mr. Sumner certainly would have gone down before the Know- Nothing movement, which he so bravely breasted, if the question of his re-election had been submitted to a popular vote in Massachusetts in 1855. It is quite doubtful if Mr. Webster himself would have been chosen by a direct vote of the people of Massachusetts at any time after 1850.

It is the purpose and the effect of this constitutional amendment to overthrow state autonomy in two particulars, in regard to which the state is to be bound and fettered for all time unless two-thirds of the two Houses of Congress and three-fourths of the States shall hereafter consent to retrace their steps.

First, the States, in many instances, distribute their political power evenly. The people are represented in the state legislatures by their neighbors and associates, by men whom they know and whom they respect and who represent the local feeling.

This proposed amendment requires the voice of the state to be uttered by masses of its citizens, and removes political power to the great masses who are collected in our cities. Chicago is to cast the vote of Illinois, Baltimore of Maryland, New York City of the state of New York, and Cincinnati of Ohio. The farmer class, which now have their just weight, will be outweighed by the dwellers of the great towns where the two extremes meet great wealth and great poverty and combine to take possession of the affairs of the government.

Second, plurality must take the place of the majority. The opportunity for third parties to have a just and reasonable weight will be destroyed.

Besides, there will be larger opportunities for fraud and crime in elections. These will be easy to commit and hard to be inquired into.

Mr. President, a people has always a distinct individual character. A city, a state, a nation, is very human. It has its hopes, its fears, its passions, its tastes, its prejudices, its resentment, its affection, its hasty impulse, its sober judgment, its deliberate will. We attribute to it the moral qualities of patience, endurance, and self-sacrifice. These qualities are made up of the prevailing temper of the men and women who possess them, but they are of a higher standard than is attained by any individuals except the best.

The Spartan or the Swiss or the American quality is as well-known and as individual and distinct as that of the great heroes of history. It is this trait that causes the affection which we feel for our country. We love it with an individual love. We cherish it with a supreme affection. Men die for it as they would die for wife or parent or children.

It is therefore no dishonor to the American people that we demand that in the conduct of their great affairs they shall do what every wise man and every good man and every brave man is expected to do in the conduct of his own.

It is no affront to the American people to require that they shall be asked to secure that deliberation, that caution, that putting aside of hasty impulse and passion in their important affairs that every wise man practice in his own. The republic is no mushroom growth. It is an oak which adds ring to ring through many a summer's heat and winter's cold. Its glorious gains come slowly that they may come surely. The deliberate will of the people is, however, sure and certain of accomplishment.

Whatever the American people have thoughtfully, wisely, and patiently considered and designed and resolved upon, that result is sure to be accomplished. And our present constitutional forms and mechanisms have always proved abundantly sufficient for its accomplishment. And it is hardly too much to say that the great beginnings of popular movements for liberty have been in the Senate.

Mr. President, it is not true that the Senate, in the sober judgment of the American people, has failed to meet the just expectations of the generation who framed and adopted the constitution. It has responded quite as speedily and quite as directly to the sober conclusion of the popular judgment and to the settled desires of the popular heart as has the other House or as has any state legislature.

It has originated far more than its proportion of the great measures in our legislative history, for the benefit of the people, which are found in our statute books.

It has resisted what is evil, but it has also initiated and accomplished what is good. This was never more true than in recent years. It is not too much to say and I assert it without fear of successful contradiction that If any private citizen wants justice; If any executive officer wants to improve administration; If any man desire new and wholesome laws; If any man wants the public mind awakened by discussion, he seeks and he finds what he desires in the Senate. Why, even the friends of this amendment to the constitution come here for its first serious discussion.

It is said the recent elections of Senators in States lately admitted have been attended with some occurrences that tend to bring the present method of choosing them into disrepute. There has been no investigation into this matter. No man here can say how much truth there may be in these reports, in the charges of suspicions which appear in the columns of the newspapers. The fact that those elections have resulted in a way some of us do not like is of little importance.

The only questions are whether whatever evil may have attended them is likely to be permanent, and whether the same evils would not have existed if the choice had been by popular election, and have not existed to an equal degree in the choice of governors and representatives in Congress. When we consider the circumstances of these new communities, it is astonishing and gratifying that they have done so well. It seems to me that the inauguration of their governments was creditable to them.

Their population is spread over large spaces of territory. The people of the different parts of the new States are unknown to each other, and the representative or Senator in the state legislature is frequently little known to his constituents. Mingled with the honest and enterprising men who have chosen their residences in the honorable ambition to achieve fortune for themselves, to perform every duty of good citizenship, to build on sure foundations States of the best kind, are adventurers, criminals, men from all parts of this continent, and from Europe and Asia, some of whom have left that country for their country's good. They are not worse than other communities in this respect, but they have less opportunity to know each other. They will compare most favorably with the dense populations of some Eastern cities. But the people of this class are there.

These communities are called upon to take upon themselves the great function of government under circumstances which would have rendered success impossible to our ancestors at Plymouth or Boston or New Haven or Philadelphia. Suppose that, added to the chosen and venerable men who founded the old thirteen States, there had come across the sea adventurers from all Europe; suppose that on the first organization of their legislative bodies had depended the political ascendency of one or the other of the contending factions who were struggling for the political control of all Europe; suppose that every passion and ambition and jealousy and evil desire which entered into such a controversy had followed them into their new domains and had blazed even more fiercely among them; suppose men of large wealth were ready to corrupt them to the service of their own personal ambitions; suppose members or emissaries of the national committees of great parties had seated themselves with their money bags at their gates is it likely that the Puritans at Plymouth, or the Cavaliers of Jamestown, or the Quakers of Philadelphia would have succeeded any better in founding their States than our countrymen and brethren in the far west?

But all these things will pass by. The people will come to know each other. They will understand their permanent interests. Combinations of dishonest men will be powerless before the honesty and intelligence of the people. Property will increase. Every honest and industrious man will get his share, and the interests of property will have their due and just influence. The people will choose legislators whom they are willing to trust with their local concerns, and so fit to be trusted to select the men who are to wield their share of national power.

I do not think the American States that have come into the union within the last twenty-five years have any reason to shrink from a comparison with any others in respect to the honesty, the capacity, the industry, the fidelity, or the wisdom of the men who have represented them in the national councils. While I have differed with them, or with most of them, upon some very important questions, I believe that if we had had a Senate and a House composed wholly of the representatives of these new States our national legislation would have gone on well, and would have been, in general, acceptable to the people of the whole country.

The argument of the able Senator from Illinois, which I have read with much care, is summed up in three propositions:

First. That the people of Illinois believe that under existing conditions the election of Senators by their state legislatures has failed of satisfactory results.

Second. The framers of the constitution did not properly estimate the intelligence and capacity of the then people of the several States. Most of the members of the convention were themselves still under the influence of inherited aristocratic ideas, and were without experience of the successful workings of popular institutions.

Third. The legislature of Illinois before 1847 was omnipotent and abused its great powers. The constitution of 1847 deprived the legislature of its electoral powers and conferred the election of governor and judges upon the people. The names of the illustrious men who have since composed the supreme court of Illinois, elected by the people, have justified the highest hopes of those who favored the innovation.

I have stated these propositions in the Senator's own language. They contain his entire argument. Let us look at them. "The election of Senators in Illinois under existing conditions," says the Senator, "has failed of satisfactory results." He invites us to a contrast with the results obtained by popular elections since 1847, under which governors and illustrious judges have been chosen by the people.

The Senators of Illinois in 1847 were Stephen A. Douglas and Sidney Breese. Does the Senator doubt that Stephen A. Douglas would have been chosen by the people of Illinois, if the question had been submitted to them, on every occasion when he was chosen by the legislature?

Mr. PALMER. Will the Senator allow me to answer that question?

Mr. HOAR. Certainly.

Mr. PALMER. Judge Douglas would undoubtedly have been chosen by the people at any time except at his last election, when the popular vote was against him.

Mr. HOAR. I do not so understand it. Was not Sidney Breese, successively justice and chief justice, one of the most illustrious of the illustrious men whom the Senator says the people of Illinois elected to the bench? They were succeeded by James Shields, the gallant soldier of Irish birth, who represented three States in this body, and by William A. Richardson. Will it be claimed that either of these eminent men would not have been chosen if the people could have chosen them?

Next came Lyman Trumbull and Richard Yates. Trumbull was elected by the people to the supreme bench in 1848 and Yates was governor. Then came Richard Oglesby, three times chosen governor, and John A. Logan, the most illustrious volunteer soldier of the war and the favorite candidate of Illinois for the presidency. I do not think we have quite yet reached the "failure under existing conditions."

Next, we have David Davis, three times chosen judge by the people, who came at last to the Senate from the bench of the Supreme Court of the United States, where Abraham Lincoln had placed him. Can the Senator from Illinois place his finger upon one of this illustrious line, who did grace and honor to the Senate, who was not among the foremost citizens of his noble state or who would not have been chosen if the choice had been by the people?

Then comes Cullom, the friend and pupil of Abraham Lincoln, twice governor by the choice of his fellow citizens, as he has been twice Senator by the choice of the legislature. Has the Senator yet reached the period for his argument that the legislative selection of Senator is on a lower level than the choice of the people for governor or for judge?

There remains to be considered the case of the Senator himself. I might otherwise feel a delicacy in discussing it. But the facts strongly support my argument, and, as stated in his ample autobiography, are so highly creditable to him, that I must be pardoned for alluding to them. After a career of brilliant civil and military service, and after having been tried for four years in the office of governor, he was nominated for governor again in 1888. The ungrateful people of Illinois defeated him by a majority of 38,000 on a direct popular vote.

Mr. PALMER. I ask pardon. Will the Senator please state again the majority?

Mr. HOAR. Thirty-eight thousand in 1888.

Mr. PALMER. My colleague [Mr. CULLOM] will furnish different figures.

Mr. HOAR. I have taken the figures very carefully, taking the votes of all other parties.

Mr. CULLOM. As my colleague [Mr. PALMER] has referred to me, I will state that, so far as the two prominent candidates were concerned, my colleague and his opponent, Governor Fifer, my colleague was defeated for governor by about 12,500 votes, if I remember correctly.

Mr. HOAR. At any rate, it is enough. The people of Illinois defeated him by 12,500, without counting the third party or the fourth party vote; and then he was elected Senator by the legislature. The people of Illinois elected a legislature whose majority was originally opposed to him. But on conference and comparison of views he was finally selected.

Now, if the Senator from Illinois means to affirm that this, the latest result of choosing Senators in Illinois by the legislature, is unsatisfactory to the people, we who know the value of his service must be permitted respectfully to dissent.

The Senator from Oregon [Mr. MITCHELL] has brought to the discussion of this interesting question the great industry and the great ability which always characterize his contributions to our debates. I have carefully read his argument of April 22, 1890. I think he summed up in that all the chief reasons for this change. He begins with a history of the proceedings of the convention which framed the constitution, so far as they deal with this subject. As I have already observed, he imputes to that convention and to its members a distrust of the people. I differ from him in that opinion, as I do from the Senator from Illinois [Mr. PALMER], who utters the same opinion.

I think the members of the convention exhibited a sublimer trust in the people than any other body of men who have been gathered together in human history. They were, some of them, the same men who signed the Declaration of Independence in 1776. They were inspired by the same faith that inspired the Congress which, as its final act, ordained that great security of freedom, the Ordinance of 1787. They were laying the deep foundations of what was hoped would be an eternal structure.

Every stone, every beam, every rafter, was laid in confidence of the wisdom and the justice of the people and their eternal capacity for self-government. Trust in the people was with them an article of profoundest religious faith. They derived the great doctrine of human equality, which they placed in the forefront of the Declaration which made us a nation, from the word of the Creator of mankind himself, as they read and interpreted it.

But, as I have already said, their confidence in the people was like the confidence we feel in a wise, just, and righteous man, capable of self-government and understanding and self-restraint, who in the great actions of life exercises for himself deliberation, reflection, self-control. It was the immediate action of the people which they deprecated. It was final and absolute self-control and self-government which they ordained and secured.

The Senator from Oregon said that the constitution these men ordained has required amendment. He is amazed that the amendments were not understood and incorporated in the constitution by the men who originally framed it. But the Senator has failed to see that every one of these amendments, from the first to the fifteenth, is an amendment in the direction of putting new control upon the immediate and direct action of majorities.

Every one of them secures the rights of the people by a restraint upon their power. Every one, with a single exception in the change of the method of electing the president adopted after the election of Mr. Jefferson both the original twelve and the three that have been adopted in our time, are simply declarations of those things which, for the welfare of the whole people, no majority under our constitution shall be permitted to do.

The Senator goes on to announce, as the foundation of his argument, the principle that no system can be properly termed free or popular which deprives the individual voter of his right to cast his vote directly for the man of his choice for any office, whether it be a state officer, member of the national House of Representatives, United States Senator, or President. And the logic of his position compels him to avow this doctrine. So that, if the people go with him, this amendment must be followed by others, under which the United States judiciary and the president and the vice-president are to be chosen by the action of a direct popular majority. This may be sound policy; but when it is established, the constitution of the United States is gone.

The Senator further adds that in his judgment lodging this power in the state legislatures tends to the election to the legislature of a man solely because of his opinions as to election of a Senator, and the "question as to his qualifications for the business of the general legislature, or the views he entertains with reference to the great material interests of the state internal improvements, assessments, taxes, revenues, corporations, appropriations, trusts, municipal affairs, salaries and fees of officers, civil and criminal code, apportionment, and other like important subjects are wholly lost sight of."

I can only oppose to this opinion of my honorable friend my own opinion that this is a very important consideration in favor of the present system. I think that it is best to commit this great function of choosing the members of this body to the deliberate and careful judgment of men who are trusted with every other legislative function of sovereignty, and not to adopt a method which in practice will commit it to men whom the people trust with nothing else.

Mr. President, if you take from the men who now represent the sovereignty of the state in all its domestic relations the right to choose the men who are to exercise its share of national legislation, you will diminish their weight and character. You will get for the discharge of both duties men less fitted to be trusted with either.

The Senator from Oregon says that he finds, as a chief reason for promoting the change that he finds everywhere discontent and unrest. If he means that he finds everywhere discontent with the present method of choosing Senators, or with the existing constitution of the United States, or even among thoughtful men with the Senate itself, I must express my dissent from his opinion. On the contrary, I believe that any intelligent assemblage of American people will unite as readily and enthusiastically in praise of their national constitution as at any time since it went into operation. I believe, if called upon to declare what it is in the Constitution they especially value, they would now, as ever, state that among the chief titles to their regard are the Senate and the national judiciary.

If the Senator means that there is a general feeling of dissatisfaction with existing conditions, that our social life is disturbed, that the classes in society are getting into conflict with each other, that the people are in that frame of mind which precedes a great revolution while I think he exaggerates very much the state of feeling, so far as he is right I think he urges an especial reason for not changing the constitution today.

Certainly, such a change should be made soberly, quietly, deliberately, and by men who can look through the history of a century, and not look merely at the fleeting and passing evils.

I have read also with great attention the argument upon this subject by the accomplished and thoughtful Senator from Indiana [Mr. TURPIE]. He thinks that neither of the three departments of the national government is now controlled by the people. If he means that the choice of neither is directly controlled by the people, I would remind him that not only one of our two legislative branches is the direct popular choice according to numbers, but that action of the electoral colleges is, in fact, a direct expression of the popular will. So that the House of Representatives, which shares equally with the Senate in power of affirmative legislation, and the President, with his executive and treaty-making powers and his veto upon all legislative action, are the result of direct popular choice.

If he means that, when our three departments of government are chosen, their action should be the result, not of the individual conscience and judgment of the legislature, of the executive, or of the judge, but should respond to the present and instant pulsation of the popular heart, I answer that I think he is wrong in desiring a government so constructed or administered.

If the Senator's doctrine be sound, it seems to me it should be applied everywhere; that the people should, as far as possible, deliberate for the legislature, execute for the officer, and decide for the judge. If, as I believe, that be the worst and not the best theory of government on earth, the doctrine should be applied nowhere.

Mr. President, the Senator from New Hampshire [Mr. CHANDLER] well said that this is the first change ever seriously proposed in the framework of our national government. All the other amendments have been restraints upon the people's will to secure the people's rights. The amendment in the time of Mr. Jefferson only required the designation by the electoral college of the offices to be held by the persons for whom their votes were cast; a change shown to be necessary by the experience in the famous contest between Jefferson and Burr.

Never before has there been proposed, so far as I know, a change which is to affect the great balance of political power which our fathers adjusted with so much care. I quite agree with the Senator from Oregon that the principle of this change will lead to the choice of the President, the choice of the Senators, and in the end to the choice of the judges by the mere brutal force of numbers. I do not agree with him in thinking such a change is desired by the American people. When it shall be accomplished, the American constitution is gone.

Mr. President, I have no respect for the habit which has long since grown up of undervaluing the character of American legislative assemblies. Since our government went into action it has been the habit of thoughtless persons or of persons who in their own lives have had no experience in public responsibilities; the habit has even crept into grave histories to decry and disparage the Continental Congress. The men who made up that illustrious body began their services with the great state papers which commanded the admiration of Chatham, who declared that although he had read Thucydides and was familiar with the master minds of the past, in his judgment they equaled anything in antiquity.

These papers, the address to the King, the address to the British people, and the address to the people of Ireland were followed by the Declaration of Independence. It was the same Continental Congress whose wisdom selected Washington for the command of our armies and Franklin and John Adams for our diplomatic agents abroad. It was the same Continental Congress which stood faithfully by Washington during the seven years of the Revolutionary war, which ended its labors with the great Ordinance in 1787, and whose members composed in large part the body which framed the constitution itself.

Of the thirty-nine men who signed the constitution, eighteen signed the Declaration. Ellsworth, who signed the Declaration, was absent when the constitution was completed. Gerry, who signed the Declaration, refused to sign the constitution. The failure, if there were any failures in the conduct of the Revolutionary war, was the failure of the American States, who were too jealous to part with their own power or to establish and trust the necessary agencies for their own protection and safety.

The legislature of my own state has had two hundred and sixty years of illustrious history. During my life, while the legislature has been in session, it has been the target for the sneers of critics and of the press. But every session has ended its own term of laborious service, completing a record in which always is to be found some new and valuable legislation for humanity, for labor, for education, for administration of justice, which is alike beneficial to their own constituencies and an example to the people of other commonwealths.

I am neither afraid nor ashamed to compare the statute book in which is found the essence of the history of Massachusetts for nearly three centuries with any other body of laws which may be produced by any other commonwealth or by any nation. I believe the men who have done this work have performed also to the satisfaction of the people the important work of selecting their representatives in the national Senate.

Why, it is said the Senate has not responded to the popular will. When has it failed to respond to the popular will when the popular will itself had become settled? The gentlemen who make this complaint are impatient. They must remember that the Senate has to act for the interests of a people of 65 million and for a nation whose life is to be measured, not by years or by generations, but by centuries. Sessions of Congress, terms of presidential office, generations of men, count but as minutes, are but as the pulsation of an artery in this mighty national life.

But whenever the American people has made up its mind, when its judgment is formed, when its will is determined, that will is sure to be carried into effect. Whether through Senates or over Senates, through courts or over courts, through presidents or over presidents, through constitutions or over constitutions the irresistible current will make its way.

Mr. President, I have no patience with the spasms of dismay which seem now and then to affect some worthy philosophers, and the effects of which are occasionally seen in the Senate chamber. One day there is a fear that a few speculators in cotton or corn will diminish the price to the seller and raise it to the buyer; and so we are asked to overthrow and sweep away all of the rights of the States by a single legislative act, and a majority of this body and the other House lose their heads and are taken off their feet.

They think all our existing constitutional resources are powerless before a few speculators. So, because a few millionaires clink their money bags about our state legislative halls, it is proposed to overthrow the constitution of our fathers and build up a pure democracy in its place.

The American people have dealt with dangers that were serious before. They have put down rebellion, they have abolished slavery, they have thrown off the yoke of foreign tyranny by strictly constitutional processes, and with the weapons in their hands that have served them so well in the past they have no occasion for apprehension of these new dangers.

The people of the United States are proud of their history. It is a touching and noble story. The American youth knows something of the annals of other lands. His childhood has delighted in the half-fabulous legends by which they explain their origin. He is especially acquainted with the history of the older republics and of countries where constitutional liberty has in other years found its home. He can tell you something about Solon and Lycurgus, about Romulus and the she wolf, of Numa in his cavern, of Tell and Winkelried, of Alfred and Edward, of Agincourt and Cressy, and the barons who wrung Magna Charta from King John.

But he better loves the story, with which no romance or fable mingles, upon which history pours its full and blazing torchlight, of the men who founded these States of ours in Christian liberty and law. He likes better to hear of the Pilgrim of Plymouth, of the austere Puritan of Salem and New Haven, of the liberty-loving enthusiast of Rhode Island, of the Quaker of Pennsylvania, of the Catholic of Baltimore, of the adventurous Cavalier of Jamestown. He knows the quality of the woodsmen who, in the later generations, struck their axes into the forests of this continent; of the sailors who followed their prey from the Arctic to the Antarctic Sea.

He knows how his country has spread from a little space by the side of the Eastern sea, till in her westward march the gates of the East become visible again, and she has added to her dominion until, as my late colleague said, "before the sun sets upon Alaska he has risen upon Maine." He knows by heart the military achievements of the Revolution and the great sea fights of the war of 1812. He knows what this country has done in science and literature. He knows what her inventive genius has added to the world's wealth and how it has lifted the burden beneath which the back of humanity has so long been bowed and bent.

But he knows, also, something of that which makes these great achievements permanent and secure. He knows something of the great foundations upon which the structure of our constitution is reared. He knows something of the temperate restraints of American liberty. The figures of great judges and of great Senators command his admiration and stir his enthusiasm and excite his sober approbation quite as much as any achievement by sea or any military glory upon land.

The profound sagacity of Ellsworth, whose great fame in the beginning of the government reached the people even from within the closed doors of the Senate chamber; the unequaled wisdom of Marshall, without whose luminous exposition the mechanism of the constitution must have failed; the robust sense of Taney; the ripe learning and lofty patriotism of Bradley these will be as familiar to his instructed intelligence as the name of any great captain or admiral.

He comes of a race of political shipwrights, and he knows by heart below and aloft the whole structure of our ship of state. He knows to the fullest depths of its meaning what the flag stands for. He knows how to bend the sails and step the masts. He likes only too well the sound of the guns. But he has found out that it is not the colors, or the armament, or even the sail that makes the ship stanch and the voyage prosperous and secure. It is the tough resistance of the mast, the strength of the timbers, the fashion of the keel, the strength below the water line, the chain and the anchor to which the ship of state, with her precious freight, owes her safety.

He knows what master laid her keel; What workmen wrought her ribs of steel;

Who made each mast, and sail, and rope; Were shaped the anchors of her hope!

What anvils rang, what hammers beat, In what a forge and what a heat

He fears no sudden sound or shock, 'Tis of the wave, not of the rock;

'Tis but the flapping of the sail, And not a rent made by the gale!

I said in the beginning that this is a question of centuries and not of years. It is to the credit of the men who framed the constitution that they so understood it. If they had taken counsel of their own recent experience, they never would have ventured to appeal to the people of their own generation to establish the permanent securities of the constitution, and would never have ventured to trust them with the powers which the constitution creates.

The six years which followed the peace of 1783 present but a sorry story. It is a tale of feeble government, of disaster, of discontent, of broken faith, of depreciated currency, of stay laws, of suffering debtors, of cheated creditors, of lawlessness, of Shays' rebellion, and of popular commotions North and South. Some of our best friends abroad thought it was all over with us, and that the best thing we could do was to ask George III to take us back into favor.

But out of it came the Ordinance of 1787, the constitution of the United States, the design of the Supreme Court, the conception of the Senate, the great debate upon the adoption of the constitution, and the adoption of the constitution by the unanimous action of thirteen States.

We have had one great civil war. But yet it is our glory, as it is the glory of the country from which our ancestors came, that we determine the differences which cause revolutions elsewhere by debate and not by arms. We reason them out, and do not fight them out. This chamber has been the most conspicuous arena of these conflicts. Here the champions have encountered and measured their strength. There have been chieftains in the Senate chamber whose names and memory the American people cherish with pride and gratitude, as they cherish the names and memory of the men who marshaled the forces at Saratoga or Yorktown, or New Orleans, or Appomattox.

The great conquests which gave the union and constitution their empire over the reason and affection of our countrymen have been achieved here. Here Webster hurled the weighty projectiles of his irresistible argument. Here the voice of Clay taught his countrymen North and South the great lesson of reconciliation. Here Calhoun was borne in his dying hours, his great heart overcoming the weakness and infirmities of his sinking body, sitting, as his colleagues said, like "a wounded eagle, with his eyes turned to the heavens to which he had soared, but into which his wings could never carry him again."

Here the blood of Sumner was shed the baptismal water of our newer liberty. Here Seward summoned his countrymen to that irrepressible conflict from whose issue the vanquished gained even more than the victors. Victories in arms are common to all ages and to all nations. We do not excel, and it maybe we do not equal, other people in these things. But the greatest victories of constitutional liberty since the world began are those whose battle ground has been the American Senate and whose champions have been the Senators who for a hundred years, while they have resisted the popular passions of the hour, have led, represented, guided, obeyed, and made effective the deliberate will of a free people.

Chapter 13

THE ELOQUENCE OF SENATOR ÉLIHU ROOT

Senate Testimony in Opposition to A17
2242 CONGRESSIONAL RECORD-SENATE. FEBRUARY 10, 1911

(Mr. ROOT): Mr. President, the joint resolution now before the Senate contains two separate and distinct amendments of the Constitution of the United States.

The first amendment proposed is to change the third section of the first article relating to the election of Senators, so that it shall provide for the election of Senators by the people of the several States instead of their election by the legislatures of the States. That is accompanied by an appropriate provision regarding the filling of vacancies which occur at such time as that they cannot conveniently be immediately filled by an election.

The other amendment proposed by the joint resolution is to strike from the fourth section of the first article the provision that - The times, places, and manner of holding elections for Senators and representatives shall be prescribed in each State by the legislature thereof; but the Congress may at any time by law make or alter such regulations, except as to the places of choosing Senators. And to substitute therefor a provision that - The times, places, and manner of holding elections for Senators shall be as prescribed in each State by the legislature thereof.

That involves two changes in the existing provision. One is to abolish the peremptory command of the Constitution directed to the legislatures of the States, requiring them, as a matter of their duty under the Constitution, to prescribe the times, places, and manner of holding elections for Senators, and to substitute for that peremptory command for the performance of a duty under the Constitution a reference to action which the States may or may not take under their own authority. That change is accomplished by inserting the word " as" in the new provisions.

I hope I make it clear. The present section 4 of the first article of the Constitution provides that the times, places, and manner of holding elections for Senators and representatives shall be prescribed in each State by the legislature thereof. That is the command of the Nation by the sovereign authority of the Constitution to the legislature of each State, requiring it to prescribe the time, places, and manner of electing Senators; and when they act they act in the execution of a mandate from the Nation embodied in the National Constitution. Now read the proposed substitute: The times, places, and manner of holding elections for Senators shall be as prescribed in each State by the legislature thereof. If a State prescribes, well and good. It does it under its own authority. If a State does not prescribe, well and good.

There is no mandate of the Constitution of the United States requiring the State to do it. It is a clear, distinct, and unquestionable abandonment of the requirement of the Constitution for this fundamental and essential act under national authority for the preservation of the national life.

The second change in the fourth section of the first article of the Constitution is made by omitting from that section all authority in

Congress to make or alter the regulations which are prescribed. The present section reads: The times, places, and manner of holding elections for Senators and representatives shall be prescribed in each State by the legislature thereof; but the Congress may at any time by law make or alter such regulations, except as to the places of choosing Senators. The proposed substitute for the fourth section reads: The times, places, and manner of holding elections for Senators shall be as prescribed in each State by the legislature thereof. All vestige of national authority as the source of power to perform the act and of national control over the performance of it, or of national power to modify or supplement or compel conformity to national interests, disappears from the provision which is recommended to the Senate in the joint resolution now before us.

Mr. President, I am opposed to both of these amendments. I am opposed to changing the election of Senators from the legislatures to the people at the polls, and I am opposed to abandoning the authority of the National Government over the election and the constitution of the members of this branch of the Government.

Let me first state the reasons why I am opposed to the change in the manner of electing Senators. It is not wise that the people of the United States should contract the habit of amending the Constitution. Stability in our Government is a matter of vital concern. When America set forth in her great experiment, the almost universal opinion of the world was that she would speedily encounter the disasters that all attempts at popular government had met before that day.

The world knew well that the tendency of democratic government was toward frequent change; it knew well that; while all forms of government have weaknesses peculiar to themselves, the weakness of democratic government was its liability to change with the impulse and enthusiasm of the moment, and, through continual changes, *to vary from extreme democracy, which men called ochlocracy, on the one hand, to oligarchy and dictatorship on the other.*

And since the time when our fathers framed the Constitution, half a score of nations, seeking to follow the lines of our experiment, have, in varying degree, and some of them to the last degree of failure, justified such an apprehension. *But with us, Mr. President, there has been one great anchor.*

In our Constitution we have embodied the eternal principles of justice; we have set up a barrier against ourselves. As Ulysses required his followers to bind him to the mast that he might not yield to the song of the siren as he sailed by, so the American democracy has bound itself to the great rules of right conduct, which are essential to the protection of liberty and justice and property and order, and made it practically impossible that the impulse, the prejudice, the excitement, the frenzy of the moment shall carry our democracy into those excesses which have wrecked all our prototypes in history.

Mr. President, reverence for that great instrument, the belief of mankind in its perpetuity, the unwillingness of our people to tamper with it or to change it, the sentiments that are gathered around it - these, constituting the basis of stability in our Government, are the most valuable of all the possessions of the Nation that inhabits this rich and fertile land. Because the American people stand by their Constitution and are unwilling to yield to suggestions that it be tampered with and altered upon slight provocation, every acre of farm land, every farmhouse and barn, every stock of goods, and every manufactory in the country are of greater value.

No change in our Constitution should be permitted to cast a doubt upon its permanency and inviolability unless there be the weightiest and most commanding reasons. All presumptions are against it. The great public policy of a century is against it. A heavy burden rests upon those who wish to make the change. This is especially true, Mr. President, when a change is proposed which in any degree alters the delicate relations which exist between the National and the State Governments, or which in any degree affects or modifies any of those great compromises of the Constitution which enabled the 13 original Colonies, different in interests, in traditions, in size, in population, and in industries, to adjust their different views and to enter into a binding agreement.

Whenever a proposal is made to change the provisions that affect the relations between the States and the National Government, or to modify any of the terms of one of those great compromises upon which the institution rests, there are special reasons for rejecting it, and a double burden rests upon those who propose it. For more than 100 years the provisions of this instrument as they are, with every sentence weighed, with every word scanned and receiving its full meaning, have been considered and clarified and determined upon by the courts. Our people have become accustomed to statutes based upon these provisions as they are.

A great war has been fought to settle the most vital and important of the questions arising under this instrument as it is. The different parts have become adjusted to each other. We have come to understand what their relation is. The ship has found itself and we are free, after a century of discussion, from serious questions as to the relations of the General and State Governments. How the field of discussion has changed! Look at the old records of Congress, and you will find them filled with animated and excited controversies which have passed away. And now I say that for us to launch into a new era of changed provisions and new questions arising from them would be justified only by the most serious and weighty reasons.

Changes by amendment may seem to gentlemen who propose them simple, and their effect may seem to be unquestionable. *But, Mr. President, no one can foresee the far-reaching effect of changing the language of the Constitution in any manner which affects the relations of the States to the General Government. How little we know what any amendment would produce!*

One hundred and seven years ago we made an amendment relating to the election of the President and Vice President. Has that amendment produced the result which its authors expected? No; far from it. The results of action under that amendment are as different from those which were expected by its authors as our Government is different from the government of any oriental power. Forty-five years ago we made a series of amendments, following upon the great Civil War. Have those amendments worked out as their authors expected? No. No man can open to the fourteenth and fifteenth amendments of the Constitution and for a moment maintain that they have accomplished what the Congress of the United States expected them to accomplish when it passed the resolutions for their submission, or what the State legislatures expected when they approved them.

We enter upon a field of doubt, of new discussions, the end of which no man can foresee, when we begin to tamper with the delicately adjusted machinery to which we have been so long accustomed and which we now understand so well. *Mr. President, there has been but little attempt here to assign reasons for the proposed change in the election of Senators.* It has been left in the main to rest upon the proposition that the people of the country desire it; that there have been resolutions adopted by many legislatures; that planks have been put in many political platforms; and that as a whole the people of the country wish for the change.

I am convinced, sir, and I think I can anticipate a general agreement from the Members of this Chamber in the proposition, that the desire of the people for this change, if there be a desire, is not a very active and violent feeling. It is a rather mild assent to a proposition which is suggested to them as an appropriate remedy for certain ascertained and recognized evils. There is we all know, a general tendency in all democracies to favor propositions which look to the extension of power at the polls. Extension of suffrage, extension of the direct power of the voters at the polls, naturally receive assent at first blush.

There is another tendency which is natural and in which we all share and that is that when an evil is recognized, and someone suggests that such and such a provision of law will cure the evil, our interest is attracted and our support is conciliated for the proposed measure. I submit that what the people of the country really want is to have certain evils which they recognize in the present election of Senators cured, and that they are quite indifferent about this change except as it is certified to them to be a sure cure for the evils.

Whether it will be a cure or not has been little discussed and little considered by the people of the United States, and it has been little discussed and little considered by the Senate. *The evil which the people of the country wish to see cured, and which I wish to see cured with them, and we all do, consists of certain patent defects in the working of the system of election of Senators by the state legislatures. The first of those is a defect in the execution of the law which requires them to select.* It is the deadlock that exists so "frequently.

The inexplicable delay of the Legislature of Montana to return my friend, the Senator from Montana [Mr. CARTER] the obstinacy of all branches of the Democratic Party in the· Legislature of New York, the reluctance of the Legislature of Iowa to follow any of its great and gifted leaders - all these cause dissatisfaction on the part of the people, and, I believe, constitute the chief reason for the assent of the people to propositions to change the manner of election.

But, Mr. President, it is not our duty to say to the people of the United States that these deadlocks come not from the constitutional provision, that *they come from our statute of 1866. They can be ended forever on any day by this Congress through a simple amendment of the statute.* For the deadlocks arise from the fact that our statute requires a majority vote, and everywhere among people of independence and individual will it is a difficult thing to secure a majority vote.

If we chose today to amend our statute so that the legislatures of these States could elect by a plurality, they would elect tomorrow. If we chose to say that in any legislature where a majority vote should not be obtained within 30 days of the beginning of the Congress in which the successful candidate was to take his seat, there should be an election by plurality, in every one there would be an election the day after the period expired. And what is more, there would be majorities obtained in order to avoid those elections by pluralities.

But we have not chosen to do it. We have fallen upon times when it seems as if not the last thing, but the first thing, that is to be done to cure an evil is to amend the Constitution of the United States.

Mr. President, this very joint resolution proposing to amend the Constitution of the United States will force us to abandon the majority rule and to entrust the election of Senators to a plurality, for never can the Senate of the United States maintain a working force if a majority vote is required for the election of Senators by the people of the several States.

I appeal to a universal recognition of the fact that it will not be practicable to have Senators elected under a requirement of a majority vote in case this amendment to the Constitution is adopted. In every close State the outlying parties, the irreconcilables, not occasionally or accidentally, but as a rule, poll more votes than the difference between the two great parties, and that means that, as a rule, in the close States of the Union no one is elected by a majority vote. So, sir, we are proposing to cure this evil by an amendment of the Constitution which lands us in the same position as to the rule of majority or plurality that we would reach if we cured it as we can cure it absolutely by an amendment of our (1866) statute.

But there is another reason why the people are dissatisfied with the discharge of the functions of our state legislatures. From time to time there are rumors, suspicions, and occasionally proofs of corrupt conduct on the part of state legislatures, and from time to time a belief that state legislatures have been influenced by personal considerations or controlled by extraofficial influences in the performance of their duty.

Mr. President, we are too apt in having our attention fixed upon the exceptional to forget the usual. It is true that what have long been known in this Chamber as forbidden and abhorrent forces do sometimes affect the election of a Senator, but it is only occasional, and the great body of the Members of the Senate are, and always have been, elected as the free and intelligent judgment of their state legislatures dictate. There is no claim, sir, that I have heard, certainly there has been no ground suggested to sustain a claim, that an honest and intelligent legislature, fairly canvassing the abilities and the character of the men who can best serve their country as Senators for their States, cannot make as good a choice, if not a better choice, than the electorate at large. *There has been no claim, or certainly no ground stated to sustain a claim, that the wise men who framed our Constitution were mistaken in their belief that wise and intelligent and faithful State legislatures would make the best possible choice for Senators of the United States.*

No; the real ground is that, arguing from these exceptional and occasional cases, the people of the United States have been led to believe that the legislatures of their States are unfaithful to their trust in making their selections, and that they will continue unfaithful. Mr. President, what is the remedy the people of the United States should seek, if this be true? Are they to abandon the performance of their duty in the election of their State legislatures? Are they to abandon the system, rather than reform the system? *This whole proposition rests upon the postulate of the incapacity of the people of the United States to elect honest and faithful legis-latures.* If the framers of the resolution had made it read so that it would express the true principle on which they base it, they would have made it read like this: Whereas the people of the several States have proved Incompetent to select honest and faithful legislators in their own States:

Resolved, That the Constitution of the United States be so amended as to re-lieve the people from the consequences of their incompetency by taking from the State legislatures the power to choose Senators of the United States and vesting that power in the same incompetent hands.

But Mr. President, if the people of our States are to abandon the attempt and be faithless to the duty to elect honest and faithful legislatures what becomes of the governments of our States? The growing complication of life, the daily increasing interdependence of all men under our highly developed social system under which for food, for clothing, for shelter, for fuel, for health, for opportunities for business and for transportation, and at every side and on every occasion in life we are dependent on each other. In this highly developed interdependent condition day by day we grow more and more to rely on the government that is regulating all the agencies that are necessary to our lives. What government shall perform that function? If the State government is abandoned, if we recognize the fact that we cannot have honest legislatures, sir, the tide that now sets toward the Federal Government will swell in volume and in power. Here is a power that can answer the demands of life.

Let me tell gentlemen who are solicitous for the preservation of the sovereignty of their States that there is but one way in which they can preserve that sov-ereignty, and that is by repudiating absolutely and forever the fundamental doctrine upon which this resolution proceeds. Let them go home to their States when this session ends and invoke the patriotism of their people to make the government of their States worthy of the great duties that rest upon them and competent to preserve the autoimmunity of their States against that incursion of federal power which is being continually urged, urged, urged by those who fail to find satisfaction from the governments of the States.

In my humble judgement, sir, the most vital thing to be done in the United States today is to strengthen the legislators of the States. I fear the breaking down of the government of the United States by the accumulation of demands upon it, through the gradual weakening of the state governments, through the failure to keep pace with the continually increasing demands of our social and business life.

We have come very near the limit, sir, of what we can competently do, very near the limit of what we can do as well as it ought to be done. Our executive offices are overburdened. The business of this Congress is conducted with less and less knowledge on the part of the members of the body in general as to what the committees have been doing. We are forced session by session to more complete reliance upon the reports of the committees, with less and less consideration from the Members of the Congress at large. Our judicial is being overburdened and our calendars clogged, and we are looking about for ways to relieve this court and that from too heavy a burden and to prevent the law's delay.

Let us continue upon the theory that State governments are corrupt and incompetent. The time will come when the government of the United States will be driven to the exercise of more arbitrary and unconsidered power, will be driven to greater concentration, will be driven to extend its functions and to the internal affairs of the States; and then sooner or later the people of the country will reject a government that has subjected their personal and intimate neighborhood affairs to the control of a central power in Washington, and then in the place of competent States governing their own affairs we shall go through the cycle of concentration of power at the center while the States dwindle into insignificance, and ultimately the breaking up of the great Republic upon new lines of separation.

Mr. President, there is another view of the fundamental proposition on which this resolution rests. It is an expression of distrust for representative government. It does not stand alone. It is a part of the great movement which has been going on now in these recent years throughout the country and in which our people have been drifting away from their trust in representative government. These modern constitutions which are filled with specific provisions, limiting and directing the legislature in every direction, furnishing such startling contrasts to the simplicity of the Constitution of the United States, are an expression of distrust in representative government. The initiative is an expression of distrust in representative government. The referendum is an expression of distrust in representative government.

This resolution is an expression of the same sentiment. And strangely sir, this movement comes at the very time when the development of our country in its business and social and political life makes it all the more necessary that we should depend upon representative government. We have gone far, far away from the days of the old New England town meetings. I doubt if some of the Senators coming from the States of small population realize how far we have gone in the great industrial communities of the east and the middle west from that condition in which direct democratic government is possible.

Mr. President, this whole series of expressions of distrust, the detailed limiting constitutions, the initiative, the referendum, the amendment of the constitution, which is now before us, are all an expression of that weakness of democracies of which it is the function of the constitution to guard democracies themselves against.

Mr. President, what is to become of the State legislatures if we follow the principles of this resolution? If you rob them of power, of dignity, of consequence, what will be the personnel of the state legislatures? We have had illustrations. The board of aldermen in some of our American cities, originally bodies of high consideration, filled by citizens of consequence and of high standing among their fellows, have dwindled and sunk to insignificance and worthlessness, as power after power has been taken away from them. Once begin the progress in that direction by taking the first step based upon the principal of this resolution and you will find the members of our State legislatures growing less and less competent, less and less worthy of trust, and less and less efficient in the performance of their duties.

You can never develop competent and trusted bodies of public servants by expressing distrust of them, by taking power away from them, by holding them up to the world as being unworthy of confidence. Honest men, good men, self-respecting men, men whose standing in their community makes it desirable for the public service that they shall go into our state legislatures, will never subject themselves to be ranked in bodies suspected and discredited and deprived of power.

Mr. President, this resolution providing for an amendment is not an expression of confidence in the people: it is an expression of distrust in the people. It is not progress; it is a slipping back. *It is not an improvement on our system of government; it is an abandonment of our system of government.*

The true remedy for the evils that we see is not to abandon our duty, but to perform it. Sir, there is no weaker course for men to take then to endeavor to make up for the failure to do their duty by changing the form of the duty. This is a proposition that the people of the several States who have stayed away from the polls, who have been deaf to the considerations of public interest, who have allowed personal favoritism to supplant their desire to select the best public servants, who have been bought to cast their franchises, as the people of Adams county, Ohio, were bought, instead of curing themselves and performing their duty in the election of their State legislatures, shall try another way to select Senators of the United States. *It is a proposition that the people who cannot not elect honest men from their own neighbors can elect honest men in the Senate of the United States.*

Sir, what vote ever cast by an American citizen can be cast with a stronger probability that it is well informed than a vote for a member of his legislature? He is a neighbor: he is a man whom he has known all his life: he knows all about him. How can the men who are unable or unwilling to perform the duty of making a selection of an honest and faithful legislature from their own vicinage and improve upon their performance in the selection of a candidate in a state-wide election of candidates who most of them know very little or nothing about, except what they get from the newspapers?

Sir, apart from that, it is never possible to cure neglect of duty by changing the form. There is but one safety for a popular government. No matter what constitutions you have or what statutes you enact, sooner or later you come to the polls; and if you do not have virtue and public spirit there, your government goes down.

I press upon the Senate now the duty of saying that it will not give its assent to any attempt at an evasion of that duty by the people of the United States. The pathway lies clear before them under the constitution. If they will do their duty, the Constitution needs no amendment. If they do not do their duty, you can amend the Constitution a thousand times without any utility. Here, if anywhere, the truth ought to be told: here, if anywhere, should be found men with the courage to say to their own constituents: "the trouble in the election of Senators of the United States is not in the constitution; it is with you: it is because you are not doing your duty." If there be no voice found in this land with authority and power to reach the minds of our people with such a message, then we are caucusing over idle words when we talk of an amendment to the Constitution.

Mr. President, it is wholly unnecessary to abandon the attempt to elect honest legislatures. The whole purpose of relieving and remedying the evil which has led to this agitation for an amendment to the Constitution can be accomplished, and it is in process of being accomplished, without an amendment.

We are today in a condition of affairs political, social, and business which is but temporary. The enormous increase in the productive capacity of mankind, followed by an enormous increase of wealth, an increase which always in the beginning is congested before the processes of distribution are fully at work, is in active operation. The necessity for a readjustment of the relations of government to the great properties that constitute and continually create wealth, to the great enterprises through which that wealth is gained and is continued the necessity for a readjustment of the relations of government to these new conditions has led to a control over our State legislatures in many cases which is abnormal, which is to be condemned, and which has been the cause of practically and substantially all of the evils that underlie the desire for a reform.

That control has been exercised in part through a form of political organization which grew up under simpler conditions and is in many respects outgrown by our people, and in part by the direct application of the wealth which was 'seeking to save itself from destruction in the readjustment of conditions to influence the action of legislators. I say that condition is temporary. I say the process of relieving it is going on, and is going on all over this land. I think it has been proceeding longer in the Southern States, and then in the Western States, and now in the Eastern States.

With many of the expedients for the readjustment I do not agree; with many of them I do agree. Of this I am certain, that, altogether, they exhibit the strivings of a great democracy adjusting itself to new conditions, and they are bound to result in a successful accomplishment. The pendulum will swing to and fro. Experiments will be tried and abandoned. Experiments will be tried and found successful here, and needing modification there; but ultimately, we shall come back to a new

adjustment under the new relations, having all the competency of popular government that existed before the great increase of wealth in our
generation.

Mr. President, the proposers of this joint resolution ask that we shall
make one of the first steps in this great experimental process, the irrevocable step, of amending the Constitution of the United States. Ah,
Mr. President, that is an inconsiderate proposal. It is hardly worthy of
grave and experienced legislators. The time may come, after all these
experiments have been worked out, when it will be found necessary to
amend the Constitution. I do not believe it will; I am confident that under the broad terms of that instrument, which has been sufficient for all
the growth and change of a century and a quarter, the process of reform
which has now begun will go on to a successful end in conformity to the
Constitution as it is. But, if I am wrong, *if at some time or other it becomes
needful to amend the Constitution for the purpose of remedying evils, let us
amend it after the experiment, and not at the beginning;* let us do it as the
result of that experience which brings wisdom, and not as the result of
those conjectures which lead to continual change.

Mr. President, there are specific reasons against this change. The first
and great reason in my mind is that it is inconsistent with the fundamental design of the Senate. *The purpose of the Constitution was to create
in the Senate a body which would be as unlike as possible to the other House.*
It was to be a body more secure in tenure, different in the manner of
its election, different in its responsibility, more conservative, more deliberate than the other House, which responds year by year to every
movement of the public mind and the public feeling. As the limitations
of the Constitution were set up by the American democracy to protect
them against themselves in every impulse to violate the fundamental
rules of justice, *so the Senate was established by the Constitution to protect
the American democracy against itself* in the legislation which was required
under the Constitution. The framers of the Constitution realized that
the weakness of democracy is the liability to continual change; *they*

realized that there needed to be some guardian of the sober second thought, and so they created the Senate to fulfill that high and vitally important duty.

Mr. President, this change tends to decrease the difference between the Senate and the lower House. It tends to make the two more alike; it tends to make the function of the Senate less distinctive, and to reduce the benefit which the Senate can render to the public service. There has been a restiveness in the country at times, Mr. President, over the delay of the Senate; but when you examine the statutes and when you talk with your fellow citizens wherever you may go throughout the country, of whatever calling or condition in life, you will find that America has suffered not from too little but from too much legislation; not from too much consideration, but from too hasty and inconsiderate action; and if you will probe down into that universal consciousness of the people that is never wrong, you will find that there rests a conviction which proves beyond the possibility of doubt that in the delay, in the long-drawn discussion, in the deliberate and unhurried action of the Senate, it has during all its existence performed its duty to the Government and to the people of the United States.

This change would tend to decrease the peculiar quality and character of the Senate which has enabled it to perform its duty. The change proposed would interfere with one of the great compromises of the Constitution and would lead the minds of our people up to the point where they look over into the constitution of the Senate - and let me say to the gentlemen who are here as Senators for States with but a few thousand or few hundred thousand people, States with 84,000, with 124,000, with 300,000, which have the same representation as Illinois, with her five millions and nearly six, Pennsylvania, with six millions and nearly seven, and New York, with nine millions, that they cannot afford to put these great industrial communities in an attitude where they feel that the honorable obligation of the great compromise of the Constitution has been taken away.

This change, sir, would prevent the Senate from having the benefit of the service of a large class of citizens who are specially qualified by character and training to render a peculiar kind of service specially needed for the purposes of the Senate, men who by lives of experience and effort have attained the respect of their fellow citizens and who are willing to undertake the burdens of public office, but are unwilling to seek it; men who will accept the burden as a patriotic duty, accept it doubtless with mingled feelings of satisfaction at the honor and dissatisfaction with the burden, the disturbance of life, the abuse of the press, the controversies about performance of duty, but who never would subject themselves to the disagreeable incidents, the labor, the strife, the personalities of a political campaign.

Mr. President, I do not mean to say I beg that no one who hears me will for a moment think that I consider that such men as I have described are any better or more useful to the public than the men who are younger and full of the energy of life and the willingness for strife. No; if we can have but one class, then let us have the young and the vigorous; but, Mr. President, we are not confined to the choice of one. We can have both, and it was the purpose of the creation of the Senate that it should contain men who should be the elder Statesmen and who should answer to the universal appreciation of the dignity and deliberate judgment involved in the title, Senator.

This change will exile from the floor of the Senate men who answer closely to many of the greatest names in the glorious history of this body. Still you approach nearer and nearer to identity with the lower House, to identity with those functions that it is necessary the lower House should perform, identity with those characteristics that it is necessary the lower House should have and which ought not to be duplicated here, else our usefulness will greatly disappear.

Mr. President, this change would take the direct responsibility of Senators for their actions from the State's legislatures to the people at the polls. The members of the State legislature - I am talking about an honest and faithful State legislature, such as I know our people can have if they do their duty - are familiar with the incidents and the difficulties of legislation. They know how necessary it is that in order to accomplish beneficent results mutual concession shall be made. They know how impossible it is that any one man, or any one locality, or any one State can have all of its own way.

When Members of this body have to explain to the State legislature the reasons for their action, they meet minds that are competent and trained for the appreciation of their explanation. The people at large have far less understanding upon the subject that I am now speaking of than their legislature, and the inevitable result of such a change as this will be to increase the unyielding opposition of the position of one State and its Senators to the position of other States and their Senators. It will largely do away with the benefit of discussion and comparison of views and mutual concessions and that fair and open-minded yielding to the argument of our fellows, which is the essential of good legislation. *This will cease to be a deliberative body if every Senator has to convince, to explain to the great body of the people of his State every act he performs and every concession he makes.*

Mr. President, it is unnecessary to demand or to provide for a reform in the constitution of the Senate upon the theory that the existing system has failed. I grant you that occasionally bad men are sent to the Senate; occasionally a man is sent here who would not have been chosen by a fair and honest choice of the people of his State; but, sir, they find their level and they find it in innocuous insignificance here. I undertake to say I am so young a Member of this body that I can say it - the basis of my experience and my ostentation has been so largely formed while holding executive positions and not as a Member of this body - I undertake to say and to maintain here or anywhere *that never in this world has any institution of government wrought out more successful results than the provision of the American Constitution for the selection of Senators of the United States.*

Exercising a power more varied than any other deliberative body in the world; sharing in the legislative and executive and judicial functions; with control over the laws providing for the raising and the expenditure of revenue, through its constitutional power of amendment; with control over the appointments to offices by the necessity for its confirmation; with control over foreign affairs, through the necessity of its consent to the ratification of treaties; with the function, that highest of all judicial functions, constituting it the court for the trial of impeachments, after a century and a quarter of life, I declare to you and to my countrymen that the Senate of the United States has performed its duty loyally, faithfully, and competently, and has furnished to the history of its country a line of illustrious names and a record of great achievement which furnish one of the most convincing proofs the world has yet had that popular government through representative institutions is a possibility among men.

Mr. President, when we consider the multitude of failures that line the pathway of history, when we consider the multitude of difficulties that stand in the way of successful government, let us pause before we abandon the character and the constitution of a body which has proved itself and been proven as has the Senate of the United States.

Mr. President, *one of the illustrations of the dangers of intermeddling with this delicate relation between the States and the National Government established in our Constitution is found in this joint resolution.* The gentlemen who fathered this joint resolution have found that they could not make this change without going on and proposing another amendment striking at the relation between the States and the National Government at a vital point. The interdependence of these provisions of the Constitution is well illustrated by this joint resolution. The danger of tampering with one cog, one spring, one lever, one wheel of this delicate machinery is well illustrated by the fact that *in the same breath that the committee reports a resolution for a change in the manner of electing Senators it reports a resolution to revolutionize the relation between the National Government and the States.*

I say "revolutionize " advisedly, sir. The theory of our Constitution was that regarding all matters within the limit of the Constitution the relation of the National Government should be a direct relation between the Government and the people; that it should operate upon the people. It was that these Senators who are about me are not ambassadors from a foreign State, but they are officers of the United States; that their primary obligation is not to any one State, but it is to the common good of the commonwealth of the United States. And the theory of the Constitution was that the National Government should be invested with all the powers necessary for the presentation of its national life and the execution of its national powers and the performance of its national duties, so that it would not be dependent in any respect upon the will or pleasure of any State. That was the fundamental change from the Confederation to the Union under the Constitution.

So the Constitution, after providing that the Members of the House of Representatives should be elected by the people and that the Members of the Senate should be elected by the legislatures, provided that the times and places and manner of holding elections shall be prescribed. As I have already said, it is a peremptory command so that the duty is performed as a duty under the Constitution of the United States and not at the will or pleasure of the State itself. They provided that when the times, places, and manner of holding elections for Senators and representatives have been prescribed by the legislature of a State, in performance of that duty under the National Constitution, the Congress itself may at any time by law make or alter such regulations. Now, I submit that the proposed substitute, which takes out of the Constitution the peremptory command resting upon the legislatures of the States, and which takes out of the Constitution the right of the National Government to make or alter regulations for the selection of the Members of the Senate, revolutionizes the relations between the Government of the United States and the government of the States.

We no longer have, if this amendment is adopted, the power of self-preservation and self-perpetuation. James Madison, of Virginia, was the great advocate of the provision which gave to the Government of the United States the power, in the last resort, and, if ever need be, to control and direct and require the elections which were to determine the constitution of both bodies of its National Legislature.

Now, sir, we are about to abandon it, if this resolution is adopted. Mr. President, the provision which is now to be wiped out of the Constitution was the basis of the Federal election law.

(Mr. BORAH): Mr. President – (The PRESIDING OFFICER, Mr. CARTER in the chair). Does the Senator from New York yield to the Senator from Idaho?

(Mr. ROOT): I will yield; but I shall conclude in a very few minutes, and I shall prefer that the Senator would wait. My memory goes back far enough to remember the condition of affairs in the State of New York when the Federal election law of 1868 was first applied. For several years while it was in force, I happened to be the district attorney of the United States for the southern district of New York and to be charged with the enforcement of it. I beg to assure my colleagues in the Senate that the application of that Federal election law broke up a condition of corruptions in the elections in the city of New York which made the election of Senators and presidential electors a mere matter of the dictation of one man. Ballot box stuffing, false counting, repeating in large parts of that city were the rule rather than the exception, and it was only the application of the Federal election law of 1868 which made possible a reform in those conditions and led the way which the State of New York itself followed by its own enactments designed to continue the honesty of elections produced by the application of the Federal law. I do not know, sir, that the time will ever come - I hope it never will - when it will be necessary to apply another Federal election law to prevent the creation of members of this body from being a shame and a disgrace, but I protest against robbing our Nation of the power to exercise such control over the selection of the men who are to constitute its Government.

I am deeply sympathetic, Mr. President, with our friends from the South, who are dealing with the difficult problem of adjusting the relations between the white and the black populations of their States. I look back over our history and realize that mistakes have been made in the attitude of that part of the country where I was born and bred and where I received my first ideas of the political policy of our country. I would not now like to see an attempt to stretch out the hand of Federal power and interfere with the progress of our friends in the South toward the solution of that difficult and embarrassing problem. But, Mr. President, I must protest with all the energy of which I am capable against our country's robbing itself of the power to do it if it need be. Freely conceding to our friends of the South the manifold shortcomings of my own people in the North, they must not think hardly of me if I say that from time to time things are done in some parts of the South that the States ought to prevent, and if they do not that the country must prevent the moment they touch the Constitution of our Government.

It is true that in the State of New York we cannot afford to be without the safeguard always standing back of our political procedure of power in the Nation to compel purity, fairness, honesty. No State can afford it; no State, North or South, can afford it; and, above all, loyalty to the Nation cannot afford it.

Mr. President, it is true that this resolution would leave in the Constitution that provision which makes each House the judge of the elections and qualifications of its Members; but, sir, it would rob this House of the power to require the regulations regarding the elections of Members to be such that we could exercise the power of judging of the elections. Sir, we found it necessary in 1842 to change the method of electing Congressmen. We found it necessary in 1866 to reach out our hand and change the methods by which the State legislatures were electing members of the Senate. With that experience before us, will gentlemen tell us that never in the long process of time is it possible that it will be requisite for the National Government to reach out its hand and in order that the election of Senators shall be so conducted as to make it possible to perform the duties of government in judging of their election to control and direct and modify the regulations under which they are elected?

—

"Elihu Root's Correct Instinct," By Daniel De Leon
Daily People, March 10, 1911
www.deleonism.org/text/19110310.htm
www.deleonism.org/people.htm

[Note: This article by Daniel De Leon appeared in response to Senator Root's speech. The *"Daily People"* is a newsletter of the Socialist Labor Party (SLP). The SLP was reorganized on a Marxist basis in 1890 and claims to be the original socialist party in America. The article demonstrates the likelihood that amendment resolution proceedings were closely observed by the SLP. It had, and continues to have, strong links with the philosophy of Marx and Engels.]

(www.slp.org; see also www.deleonism.org)

—

Among the debates, recently held in the Federal Senate, that every militant in the movement should read, was the debate on the proposed amendment to the Constitution whereby the election of Senators shall be by direct, by a general vote in each state. Valuable as historic flashlights though most of the speeches were, the speech of the New York Senator, Elihu Root, easily ranks highest.

Senator Root opposed the amendment. Long was his speech and yet short. Its lengthy part was "fillings"; its short portion was of the essence. It consisted in a short "text" of not more than twenty words, prominently placed, and tersely supported. The text was:

"It is not wise that the people of the United States should contract the habit of amending the Constitution."

Whether Senator Root did so consciously or not, he drew the sap for his text from a philosophy that both ancient wisdom and modern wit have illumined.

Tacitus, the profound Roman historian, condenses in a short observation the significance of the election to the Caesarship of Galba, then at the head of an army in Spain, whereas thitherto the election of the Caesar had been attended to by the army or armies which happened to be bivouacked in Rome. Tacitus observes, "the secret being out" that the Caesar could be elected outside of Rome, as well as inside, every army, wherever located, thenceforth assumed the privilege thitherto supposed to be vested in the armies at Rome only.

Artemus Ward, the glory of American humor, tells the tale of a man who was fifteen years in prison when one day a bright thought struck him: He opened the door and walked out. The point made by the two writers is the same; and Senator Root either "took the hint" or his own instinct supplied it.

Superstitious reverence is the cornerstone of despotism, on the one hand, and of its supplement, slavery, on the other. The superstition that presence in Rome invested an army with a political privilege not shared by others palsied, so long as the superstition prevailed, the political power of the other armies; the superstitious notion that the unlocked door of his cell was locked unbrained, so long as the notion held sway, the prisoner of Artemus Ward. The instant the superstition regarding the special political privilege of the armies in Rome dropped, the equal political power of all the other armies leaped into existence; the instant the superstitious notion concerning the state of the door of his cell came to an end, the imprisonment of the fifteen years' prisoner came to an end with it. In the one instance and the other, the "secret was out." Correctly do the Interests, whose apprehensions Senator Root voiced, desire to keep from getting out the secret that the Constitution can be amended.

Sacred things are of all time and for all time. They are not tinkered with; they may not be tinkered with. For the purposes of despotism, it is all one whether a thing is sacred, or whether it is held sacred. The policy, accordingly, is to promote the superstition, in behalf of a principle useful to usurpation, that it is sacred. No better means to that end than the one outlined by Senator Root-to avoid allowing the people to "contract the habit" of tinkering with the principle.

The Constitution of the United States -- ample for its purposes at the time of its enactment, and expected to guarantee the people's aspirations to life, liberty and the pursuit of happiness -- is, due to the progressive economic revolution that has since taken place, proving itself more and more inadequate to its original purpose. To speak, not irreverently of a great document, but with historic accuracy, the Constitution of the United States has become a misfit. The body social has outgrown it. Yet, such is the exceptional merit of that document, that, first of its kind, it proclaimed the mutability of social conditions, and foremost of all of its kind, it incorporated in itself the people's right and duty to change it, and adapt it to the altered conditions, according as to them may seem fit. The amendment clause in the Constitution is the legalizing of Revolution. (emphasis added).

Nothing more alarmful to the top capitalist than just that. The amendment clause in the Constitution makes powerfully against all attempt at turning the Constitution into a thing sacrosanct. It has been tinkered with in the past; alack the day! All the more strenuous the effort to prevent all modern tinkering. What is done once may be done again. The habit once contracted, there is no telling where the thing may end.

It matters not that Senator Root's instinct is at fault in believing that by preventing an amendment to the Constitution he is "taking a stitch in time." His warning to his fellows that "it is not wise that the people of the United States should contract the habit of amending the Constitution" - that bespeaks an alert instinct, backed by a full grasp of the fact that the element, whom the Interests he represents are at war with, is none other than "the people of the United States."

———

Chapter 14

MEET ATTORNEY JOHN RODERIGO DOS PASSOS

"I have not seen a solitary ground based upon principle,
reason or fact to sustain this proposition."
J. R. Dos Passos, Esq.

Some Observations on the Proposition to elect United States Senators
by the People
By John Roderigo Dos Passos, Esq.
Of the New York Bar, 1911

The Constitution of the United States provides (Art 1, Section 3):

"The Senate of the United States shall be composed of two Senators
from each State chosen by the legislature thereof for six years and each
Senator shall have one vote."

The debate in the Constitutional Convention upon this clause was thorough. It was necessarily entwined with the debate upon the method of
electing the members of the House of Representatives. From the report
that exists, it is significant that the proposition to elect the Senators by
the people was distinctly presented, fully considered and overwhelmingly

negatived. One must judge of the painstaking care given to this question not so much from the debate upon it, as by the character of the men who composed the Convention, and who brought to the work as the result of years of study the most varied and profound knowledge of the origin and purposes of government. *Any suggestion that this clause of the Constitution did not receive full thought is therefore foundless.* And Hamilton in his many explanatory and defensive essays of the Constitution did not feel it necessary to say more upon the method of electing Senators than the following:

> *"It is equally unnecessary to dilate on the appointment*
> *of Senators by the State legislatures. Among the various*
> *modes which might have been devised for constituting this*
> *branch of the government, that which has been proposed by*
> *the convention is probably the most congenial with public*
> *opinion. It is recommended by the double advantage of*
> *favoring a select appointment, and of giving to the State*
> *governments such an agency in the formation on the federal*
> *government as must secure the authority of the former and*
> *may form a convenient link between the two systems.*
> (Federalist #62, Alexander Hamilton or James
> Madison)

After an existence of nearly a century and a quarter as part of the organic law, we are confronted with the most serious attempt ever made to change this clause, and place in the hands of the people, instead of the legislature, the power of electing Senators. A majority of the Judiciary Committee of the United States Senate through its distinguished and brilliant sub-Chairman, has submitted a report advocating this Amendment to the Constitution.

The time has arrived when the question should be taken to heart and studied and disposed of with intelligence and patriotism. In my humble opinion unanswerable arguments have been made against changing the method of electing Senators by many members of that body, notably by Senator Hoar, since deceased, and ex-Senator Edmunds. But they have been forgotten and long since interred in that vast mausoleum of parliamentary literature into whose deep and musty caverns none ever penetrate except the student who seeks to enforce his statements and principles by the authority of great names.

Unfortunately, many prominent men on both sides of politics have thoughtlessly or hastily given their assent to the proposition to change the Constitution, and unless it be demonstrated that the substitution of the people for (the state) legislature(s) is fraught with actual danger to our institutions; that it involves an alteration of the whole machinery of the Constitution by removing the checks and balances therein so exquisitely adjusted, a step may be taken without the people realizing the grave consequences it involves. I respectfully dissent from the view that this move to change the manner of electing Senators is a popular one, or that there is any clamor of public opinion demanding it.

On the contrary, notwithstanding many States have pronounced in favor of it, I believe that the people at large have taken very little interest in the question. Certainly, as a separate national issue it has never been seriously discussed. *In the last Presidential campaign Mr. (William Jennings) Bryan distinctly tendered it and the people distinctly voted against it.* It has been largely engineered by a class of reformers which overlooking the lurking dangers involved in the change, has blown the infectious doctrine throughout the land upon the wings of a false *vox populi.

After examining with more than superficial attention the small library of official and academic literature accumulated upon the subject, I have not seen a solitary ground based upon principle, reason or fact to sustain this proposition.

On the contrary, in my humble judgment, history reason and principle unite in an emphatic and deep protest against it. In unfolding my views,

I shall in the proper places endeavor to fully answer the several grounds urged by the advocates of the amendment.

Any change of any kind in the organic law is a serious event and unless there be plain and very substantial reasons demanding an amendment it should not be encouraged. Constitutions are not like laws, which closely follow the temper, customs and present tendencies of the people. These can always be changed by legislation to suit existing conditions. They are not unlike fashions of dress which are often altered to meet the whims and caprices of the people, and if they do not suit, they can promptly be modified or abandoned.

Constitutions are bodies of permanent rules, general and wide in their language and application, and intended to meet every condition and phase of national life. These monuments of wisdom comprehending in their text and spirit, the humanity, justice and freedom of a people, are made to endure, and like the magnificent architectural structures of the world, have been erected to withstand the storms, changes and ravages of centuries. Unhappily, this important distinction has been frequently overlooked, and many State Constitutions are unnecessarily loaded with provisions whose subjects should be dealt with by the legislatures. This has encouraged a looseness of thought among many of our public men, and propositions to change the organic law are often treated as if only ordinary legislation were involved.

A change in the method of election of United States Senators will eventually result in the absorption of the two houses of legislation as now constituted by one large popular Assembly. *For, it may be asked, of what efficacy are two houses of legislation chosen in the same manner? Two legislative bodies popularly elected?* And a resolution has already been introduced in the Michigan Legislature asking for the abolition of the Senate. The Thane of Cawdor had but one bloody step to take and he would be King.

This legislator of Michigan, gifted with the prophetic vision of the witches, would hasten the course of evolution and precipitate a result which must inevitably follow a change in the method of electing Senators--the abolition of the Senate.

The Articles of Confederation provided simply for a House of Delegates sent by the respective States to represent them—one legislative body—but the nature of our present Constitution, recognizing the necessity of proper checks and balances, created two—to act as one when wisdom prevailed, but to operate separately when the folly or passion of the lower house would result in injury to the people.

The proposition now is practically to make the two one; one body listening to, and inspired solely by the voice of the people. *The question preliminarily arises why such a radical change in our government is required? What are the defects of the present system? What are the mischiefs which arise from the Senate as now constituted?* Has the United States Senate made such an unenviable record that we must resort to the serious step of amending the Constitution?

There are two propositions which must be demonstrated before such a change can fairly be demanded; first, that the method of selecting Senators by the legislatures has proven a failure; second, that the remedy proposed will give the people a better class of Senators than we now have by (state) legislative selection. The former is incapable of being affirmatively answered by facts; and the latter is a pure dream or speculation utterly insufficient to justify a change in the organic law.

Naturally these questions must be squarely answered before the people of this country should move; naturally there must be some demonstration of existing evils before we apply a knife to the Constitution which will cut away root and branch a function so important as the Senate.

It affords me infinite satisfaction and pride as a citizen of this Republic to make this statement: That since its creation, looking at it as a whole, the Senate of the United States compares very favorably with any legislative body of ancient or modern times. It has fairly fulfilled all of the predictions of its authors and friends. Its usefulness as a check has been illustrated on many occasions, memorably when a few Republican Senators rising high above party and partisan political motives repulsed the scandalous attempt to remove Andrew Johnson from the Presidency by impeachment.

In point of intelligence, patriotism, wisdom, and of the political and moral honesty of its members it is a legislative body which the people should be proud to sustain in its entirety. Surely it has at times been the subject of just criticism; I grant that at times some of its members have been partial, ignorant and even corrupt, but it is as near an approach to political fitness as any other branch of the government. Hold it up to the mirror of comparison with the Executive, the Judicial—or the popular body—the House of Representatives—go back through all the mutations of party and political strife—and it does not suffer by the view.

It may be true that a few men have obtained seats in that body by the use of money; it may also be true that some have been returned through the worse influence of partisan politics; and it is true that some of its members have been ignoramuses, demagogues, and blatherskites, but neither of these classes have had any appreciable influence upon legislation.

One thing is sure that in no legislative body do men find their true level so quickly as in the upper House of Congress. He who has been returned by corruption; he who, being a pure demagogue, has obtained the Senatorial toga; he who has mere tongue and no brains; the first, the second and third, the men of these classes may cut sensational and dramatic fantastics in that body, but they will soon sink into oblivion and contempt—derided and despised by their associates and finally condemned by their constituents and countrymen.

The American people are not slow to mark their public men and where political crimes or personal defects are discovered the finger of scorn is soon raised to point them out as unworthy public servants. That a few demagogues; that some bad and ignorant men have made their way to the Senate; or that even the Senate as a body has on occasions been derelict in its duty to the people, is no reason whatever for a change in the method of electing its members.

Compare its members and the history of the Senate with the members and acts of the House of Representatives, and then let anyone conscientiously, if he can, say that the method of direct election by the people would be better for the interests of this country, or would produce a higher class of representatives than those elected by the legislatures of the different States.

It will be a sad sight to this country when the Senators of the United States shall, as a body, make a confession to the American people that they are unworthy of the trust committed to them and no longer fit to represent the sacred interests which the States have confided to their hands [Ed note: written in 1911, prior to effective date of Amendment 17].

The nature of our two Houses of Congress renders it most dangerous to the true interests of the people to alter the method of election of Senators. In every free government there must be two houses of legislation chosen by different methods, and distinctly examining proposed legislation from different standpoints. The popular house has its hands constantly on the pulse of the people and knows its immediate desires and wants; the upper house determines how far these desires and wants are consistent with the settled and fixed happiness and prosperity of the people. As Plato substantially puts it: forecast should direct improvidence; reason control passion and wisdom command folly.

Our political system is based upon checks and balances, each function or branch as delicately arranged, as nicely adjusted, as the works of a watch. Any change like the one contemplated will throw out of gear the whole machinery of the Constitution. The three departments of our government are separate from each other but they are all contiguously connected. We enter from one branch into another as one walks from one room to another in a symmetrically arranged house; yet each branch is an entirety and independent of the other. The Senate is a check upon the House, and the Executive a check upon both, and each of the houses severally a check upon the Executive and upon each other.

John Adams, in a letter to John Taylor, gives the following description of the United States Government:

> *"First, the States are balanced against the general government. Second, the House of Representatives is balanced against the Senate, and the Senate against the House. Third, the executive authority is in some degree balanced against the legislature. Fourth, the judiciary is balanced against the legislature, the executive and the State governments. Fifth, the Senate is balanced against the President in all appointments to office, and in all treaties. Sixth, the people hold in their hands the balance against their own representatives by periodical elections. Seventh, the legislatures of the several States are balanced against the Senate by sextennial elections. Eighth, the electors are balanced against the people in choice of President and Vice-President."*

In fact, we have more checks upon each department than in any government ever instituted. To wantonly remove one or more of these when there is no semblance of weakness or sign of decay, with great respect to its advocates, would be an act of sublime folly.

The Senate is peculiarly a representative of the States; the House photographs the present feelings of the people. The House ebbs and flows according to the caprices of popular vote, the Senate is the permanent agent of the States—it is unchangeable without the consent of all of the States as such. No popular current, no matter how strong, can sweep a State out of the Senate without its own consent.

So, if we look beyond the surface of things into the causes for the creation of the Senate, we can hardly fail to be convinced that the different method of choosing the members of each house of Congress is based upon the profoundest study of the workings of governments. *To maintain the checks and balances each must be fed from a different political breast. If not, their inspirations of duty and the result of their labors would always be the same.* It is impossible to get a full conception of the theory and spirit of our Confederation by reading the sometimes-jejune reports of the debates and proceedings of the Constitutional Convention of 1787 or of the State Conventions which ratified the Constitution. These must be supplemented by historical and political research, which light up the meaning of the remarks of the distinguished Statesmen who created it, and which show why, and of what material, the different branches of the government were created.

The members of the Convention had both ancient and contemporaneous precedents for electing the Senate and House of Representatives by different methods. The State of New York, for example, had adopted a Constitution at Kingston on April 20, 1877, ten years before the Constitutional Convention assembled, in which it was provided that the electors of the Assembly should possess a freehold of the value of twenty pounds but that the Senators should be chosen by the freeholders possessing freeholds of the value of one hundred pounds over and above all debts charged thereon. This discrimination between those voting for members of the Assembly and for the Senate was not a capricious one but based upon sound and substantial grounds to which I shall hereafter refer.

I could quote very extensively from the greatest constitutional, philosophical and historical, writers to show that the distinction is fundamental, but I do not deem it essential. Perhaps at some stage of the discussion it would be interesting to do so. *But at present when the advocates for change show no defects in the existing system, and in fact make no criticism of its work, and where their whole argument for a change rests upon speculation and guess, a recourse to general principles is sufficient.*

The Senate has as its prototype the English House of Lords, but, with three profound differences: First, the members of the one are in substance hereditary peers, the members of the other are selected by the legislatures of the different States. The former has its origin in birth or appointment by the King—the latter owes its selection to the people through their legislative bodies. As the people choose the members of these legislatures with special reference to electing United States Senators, it is after all the people themselves, considered this time as citizens of the State, who choose their Senators. But as to one main purpose, the House of Lords and the Senate of the United States are substantially identical. *They both represent the maturity, the wisdom, and as has been well said, the second thought of the nation. They protect the wealth, the property and substantial rights and interests of the people; they are a breakwater against the seas of passion and prejudice of the excited masses which sometimes roll in against the vested interests and rights of the people. At times the people must be protected against themselves.* Willoughby well expresses the thought:

> *"The people even when acting in their most direct manner cannot always be trusted to act wisely and according to their own best interests; that passion and prejudices of the moment will urge an electorate or assembly to measures   destructive as well to the welfare of the State as to its stability, and that at times the despotism of the multitude can far exceed in severity that possible of exercise by the most autocratic of*

monarchs."
(Willoughby, W., *The Nature of the State*, 1869, P. 399.)

On such occasions, happily rare in our history, the Senate checks attempted encroachments upon the rights of persons or things urged by the other house, it balances the scales—and maintains the equilibrium of the Constitution. A select council or an upper House of Legislation exists for the twofold protection of minority interests and of property.

A nation with one house chosen by popular vote cannot live long, and it would not alter the result that there were two parliamentary bodies chosen by popular vote instead of one; or that the term of one was two and the other six years. The same breath would blow them into a two-fold rage, and the eventual consequences would be the destruction of the form of government.

Some public men seem to think that in discussing political questions, property and the minority interests must be considered secondarily. Indeed, they are often not referred to at all. *The class of which I speak regard it as a quick road to public favor to frame an issue of the people against wealth. But personal rights and private property are so entwined that in fundamental legislation it is impossible to separate them.* Indeed, nothing is more superficial and evanescent than to ignore these interests, in any class of legislation, for, when such political issues reach the final stage of adjustment—when the chaff is separated from the wheat, when a true analysis is made, it is found, especially in this country, that *all classes of the people are property owners*—they have their farms; their small houses in the city; their deposits in the savings banks; their various business-es, and interests in industries; and in many different ways the working classes (in which I include all men who employ or are employed) the merchant, farmers, professional men, clerks and laborers, are the substantial owners of the property of the country.

These interests—of incalculable value—the result of years of toil and suffering, are entitled to the same protection as the purely personal rights of the proletariat —a word again coming into use but which in this country is yet happily limited to the individual who can pack his belongings in a satchel and segregate himself from society. *Let us not be chary or timid in asserting and upholding the rights of property, not only to a full protection of the law, but to a distinctive participation in legislation. The true and ultimate interests <u>of all of the people</u> require it.* This phrase "the people" is a very popular one—but it is frequently misunderstood or misapplied. In all discussion respecting the organization of governments what is meant is the people massed and acting as a body. Such a body becomes a distinct department, call it what you please—an assembly, a legislature, a witenagemote, a council of wise men, House of Commons, or what not. As a department of government, it must be subject to the same checks as the Executive. *The tyranny of "the people" thus concentrated is as far reaching as that of a monarch or despot.* The general people recognize this fact for in making constitutions they expressly create check reins against their own impulses. No government could be operated unless the people subjected themselves to checks.

There are three elements in every organized government; first, the State; second, the magistrates (which includes legislative and judicial officers); and third, the people. All internal disturbances come from a lack of adjustment between these three. It is conceded the State must have absolute power within the sphere of her operation, hence the real difficulties lie in a proper division of power—too much to the executive or magistrates or too much to the people, or too little to one or the other produce discord. *The success of a government reaches its climax when by an adjustment of the different parts all work harmoniously.*

I confess I am amazed at the argument used by the advocates for this amendment: that a changed condition of the country from that which existed when provision was made for electing the Senate by the legislature, demands that the people be now substituted in place of the latter. On the contrary it is the strongest reason in favor of retaining our present system. A republic with thirteen million inhabitants presents an entirely different question from one with one hundred million of individuals. I respectfully maintain that contemporaneous history shows that the natural political trend of our country as our population increases is towards a representative government; that each day we drift farther away from a pure democracy; and that the necessity of the people in all of the affairs of the government to be represented by political agents has increased almost tenfold since its formation. *He who advocates the application of pure democratic principles to existing conditions it seems to me but poorly comprehends our real political, commercial and social status.*

Convinced of the absolute impracticability of governing directly, the voters have committed their interests to representatives, whom they choose at stated intervals, either voting directly for the nominees of party conventions, or, in the case of Senators, through legislators, duly chosen by them.

It is a physical and political impossibility that any but a representative government can exist here, unless forsooth we agree to a despotism, or divide the country into hundreds of States, each so small in the number of its inhabitants that every member thereof could directly exercise a voice in it— another remote possibility—and one reaching into the confines of a political millennium. At the bottom, however, of this representative government, we find the people. They are its movers and its inspiration. They choose freely their representatives to political conventions, and govern by exercising a perpetual control over their political agents, having always in their hands the power to correct the evils, mistakes or shortcomings of the former.

The spirit of democracy breathes through and vitalizes all our political forms. Now many of the potential reasons which prevent the establishment of a pure democracy in this country, operate to render impracticable the proposed movement to vest in the people the power to nominate directly their officers. The people in such instances cannot act spontaneously or work harmoniously together. If it be a question of national

MICHAEL JAMES GEANOULIS, SR.

charity or national insult all hearts beat as one—all eyes are turned in one direction, and all hands work together; but in the multiplicity of ordinary national concerns the people must delegate their power. *Our population has become so dense and numerous that it is utterly impossible for the masses to nominate competent candidates; they cannot know whom to choose; they cannot put their finger upon the proper men.*

An excessive number of voters was the primary motive for the original creation of a representative government. It now has an additional cause growing out of the complications of modern commercial, economic, and political questions. The selection of candidates is a particular business, requiring special knowledge. The people must, therefore, from the necessity of things, act second-hand, through political agents and conventions. The members of the legislature are known to the voters—a direct responsibility can be fixed upon them. It is true that in many instances the occupation of a political agent is sordid rather than patriotic.

We must, however, recognize that professional politicians are a necessity, and the more respectable we make the occupation, the better government we will have. I believe that wholesale and undiscriminating criticism of this class is unjustified. Here is a movement which involves a bitter criticism of forty-eight legislative bodies. All of the sessions of the legislature and of political conventions are held in the broad light of public opinion—all of its acts are reflected in a press, most powerful in number, most vigilant in scanning every movement, and spurred on by conflicting views and by competitive business interests. An existing investigation into an election for a Senator shows the utter hopelessness of legislative bribery.

On the other hand, out of a system of direct voting there must inevitably arise irresponsibility. No one can trace the movements of an unorganized body, each one insisting upon his own candidate or choice. For each office, instead of two or three candidates, we should have many. Political modesty, a quality already sufficiently rare, would soon disappear, and each citizen would feel that he was as good as another for a given office. *The demagogue would come to the surface—not disguised as a patriot, but in his real costume, and then the people would hear of nothing but political candidates who would swarm upon the rostrums to the detriment of all our business interests and the real good of the people.* Is the nation not already sick of the spectacle of self-nominated candidates who patrol the different States declaring their own political greatness and personal virtues? Mr. Hallam says:

> *"Numerous bodies are prone to excess both from the reciprocal influences of their passion and the consciousness of irresponsibility for which reasons a democracy; that is, the absolute government of the majority, is the most tyrannical of any."*
> (Hallam, Henry, Constitutional History of England, Chapter XVI, 1862)

Property, small or great, of one hundred dollars, or one hundred million dollars, is entitled upon all political and social principles to distinct representation; for the establishment of liberty, the encouragement of industry, and the protection of property are the underlying motives of all social organization. The guaranty of such protection is found in an upper, the creation and development of personal rights and property in a lower, House.

No matter how a select council is created, whether by appointment of the State executive, or selection by the State legislative authority, it must when necessary act as a check to popular encroachment upon fundamental or constitutional rights. Caesar, after he became dictator, exercised the particularly important right of nominating Senators, but, having the power of nomination the office of Senator became dead as to him, for it was conceded that its work did not apply to the Imperator—which meant the concentration and perpetuation of official power in his hands. I by no means assert that when Caesar absorbed the whole government, it was a bad step for the Roman people; but we are not yet ready for an Imperator, *although the present movement, if successful, will be a large advance in that direction.*

But whether we have a Caesar in the Executive, or whether we have a Caesar in the Congress separate or united, concentrating and perpetuating all power in its hands, either is equally distasteful to our political education and incongruous in our free institutions. *No government can exist where the people exercise capricious power any more than one can exist where the Executive is a despot.* Join a popular Executive with a popular legislative body, for that is precisely what is involved in the proposed amendment to the Constitution, and what remains of the government established by the Constitution? *The best government is that in which the checks and balances are properly and equally regulated*—so that when one branch leans it is instantly held up by another.

The Senate is endowed with wisdom and strength to resist all innovations of fundamental rights. *It is just and necessary, therefore, that the power of appointment of Senators should be lifted out of the chaos and tumult of popular election and lodged in a different body.* The member of the House represents the people of a small district, and of the Senate the whole State, and all of the people therein. If the people are neglectful or undiscriminating in the election of representatives to the legislatures, they will be equally so in their choice of Senators.

Cannot the people trust themselves to exercise the same care in choosing their State Legislators as they would in the selection of Senators? The alleged reform is then nothing less than a stab at the people themselves—at their intelligence and discrimination. This argument has never been, and never can be, answered.

Besides, the deprivation of the legislatures of the power to elect Senators would be a direct and powerful blow at the morale of these bodies. It would be in effect the destruction of their usefulness. It is an unfounded and undiscriminating assault upon fortyeight legislative bodies en bloc.

It is argued that the State Legislatures often have "deadlocks" and that their time is frequently misapplied or wasted in an effort to elect a Senator, and that in the interim the State loses representation in the United States Senate. With great respect, this is a matter for the individual States to settle. It is purely a question of internal policy. Political manhood, State politics, religion or economy may be involved and the internal strife may be carried on to settle a great principle.

It may be thoughtful and patriotic for the United States Senate to suggest to a State thus situated that it has none or only a half representation in that body, and while it might not be the best of good manners to make the reply, it would be logical for the State to say to the Senate: "Mind your own business." And I cannot see how a State Senatorial deadlock is any worse than a long drawn out contested election case, or that the former are as frequent as the latter.

In the light of history, one is safe in asserting that in the advancement of the doctrine of the rights of man and of protection of property, the upper House, in this country and England, has always been found reliable. It was the aristocrats of England—the Barons—who extorted the Magna Charta from King John. But the wars waged by the Barons, by Simon de Montfort, were waged not for the aristocrats alone, but for the whole people of England. Magna Charta is the instrument from which the people draw as from a perpetual reservoir all of their inspirations of justice—it is the Anglo-Saxon fountain head of the rights of man to free government. *In fact, at an extreme juncture, one would be more secure in entrusting his personal rights and property interests to a Senate as ours is constituted than to any popular body chosen directly by the people.*

The Senate receives its propositions second class, as it were; it has the advantage of the debates and thoughts of the popular assembly. When the latter is bubbling over with excitement; when its leaders are red hot with partisan prejudice, the Upper House is cool and wise. Their eyes not only see the present but they look into the future. *They distinguish between a mere temporary and evanescent policy and one which is stable and for the real and permanent good of the people.*

Moreover, if the Senate is elected by the people, whether the elections for members of both houses should be simultaneous or held at different times, or under Federal or State regulations, the theory and spirit of the Constitution that the Upper House should contain a class of men superior in experience, knowledge and wisdom would be lost sight of, and the same stamp of individuals will be candidates for the Senate or House of Representatives indiscriminately as circumstances may dictate. The fruit follows the seed. Pumpkin seed will not produce oranges.

But there is another and second profound distinction between the Senate of the United States and the English House of Lords—growing out of the difference between the two governments. The one is a limited monarchy—the other a Republic. The members of the House of Lords represent the whole nation; the members of the United States Senate represent the individual States of the Union and are in the Senate to maintain the sovereignty of their respective States—they are its agents. This government could not have been formed if a council had not been provided for so that there would be absolute equality of the States in that body.

And in this respect, I feel it important to say one word as to the nature of our government.

Our federation is a union of States for mutual protection and benefit. The States maintain their individuality but give to the general government as much power as is necessary to make the federation a real sovereign as to all external and sufficient though limited powers over internal affairs, but the States have not stripped themselves of all of their sovereignty. Very much to the contrary. Which creates this anomaly: A citizen of the United States has two sovereigns—the United States and the individual State of which he is a member.

After an experience of nearly a century and a quarter, we find that the tendency of the Federal Government is to usurp more power, either through the courts or national legislature by an unjustifiably broad construction of existing provisions of the Constitution. On the other hand, the States aggressively resist Federal encroachment and seek to uphold the integrity of State sovereignty in its historical and political conception, and to maintain a true federation by yielding to the central government only power enough to enable it to support itself well and vigorously within the four corners of the compact of association—the Constitution.

This tendency on the part of the Federal Government to draw to itself more power directly leads to centralization and the obvious effect of selecting Senators by the people is a blow at State sovereignty, *for when the Senate is elected by the people, it **eo instanti becomes a popular body and it does not adequately secure the rights and safety of the States, nor is it a citadel in which property holders and minority interests can seek refuge from the storms of unfounded popular attacks.* As Willoughby substantially puts it, the independence of the Senator is lessened, the temptation to subordinate the general to local interests is increased, and the pressure brought to bear to give immediate and complete expression to a popular will, that may be ignorant or misinformed, is proportionately enhanced. And de Tocqueville observes that the existence of democracies is threatened by two dangers, viz: The complete subjection of the legislative body to the caprices of the electoral body, and the concentration of all the powers of the government in the legislative authority.

The more we encroach upon State Sovereignty, the more the trend toward nationalism becomes visible, to the consequent destruction of our theory of a federation of States, and the advantages of that form of government are gradually lost sight of. The States bear the same relation to the central government that a domestic family bears to a municipality. The family looks after its own particular foyer in its own way—it eats, drinks, lives according to its own conceptions of health and propriety, without interference by the municipality. The latter supervises the public concerns, the highways, the streets, the schools; it intrudes not into the domestic affairs of its citizens.

The same relation should exist in practice as it does in theory between each individual State and the central government. In the performance of its State duties, it has no superior; its citizens understand its wants; they are alive to its interests and their State pride makes them ambitious to see their State thrive and advance. But in proportion to the weakening of State Sovereignty the interests of its citizens wane, and soon State independence and individuality disappear, all power becomes vested in a central government, the domestic interest of the citizen in his State eventually dies, and the people are governed by a National head.

The identity, equality and individuality of the States is peculiarly preserved in the Senate because each State has two Senators. In most Senates or select councils of ancient governments, the Senators enjoyed a life tenure and while this was discussed and advocated in the formation of our Constitution, a very wise and happy medium was adopted to have the Senate refreshed and reinvigorated as to one-third of its members every two years, so that the tide of public sentiment was always flowing through its deliberations.

But if the identity of the States is not preserved in the Senate, all State Sovereignty becomes a mere name and the legislative powers, we repeat, now concentrated in two, will gradually melt into one popularly chosen assembly. If the American lawyers cannot appreciate where this condition will lead, I am sadly mistaken in their knowledge. The French Revolution offers interesting study in this connection.

But one thing is sure, that centralization and State Sovereignty cannot exist together; they are incompatible. Where will the small States be; what will be their position under such circumstances?

As it is provided "that no State without its consent shall be deprived of its equal suffrage in the Senate," there is a very grave moral question whether any part of the clause in question should be altered without the unanimous consent of all the States, for if the effect of the election of Senators by popular vote be to destroy or decimate the sovereignty of the States in the Senate or to diminish their full and intended influence therein as States, then how can this suggested change be made without the consent of all of the States? I place this proposition not on any technical ground, but upon good faith between all of the States of the Union. If altered, it was the opinion of Senator Hoar, one of the best lawyers who ever graced the Senate, that it would absolve the larger States from the Constitutional obligation which secures the equal representation of all the States in the Senate. I am bound to admit that I do not clearly follow this view, but others may understand the argument better than I do.

It is said over and over again that in many States the people already dictate to the Legislature their choice of Senators, and that as a matter of common practice the Legislature would not venture to disobey the directions of the people in this respect. Unhappily for our country the postulate is true, but I do not admit the conclusion. The Constitution is still preserved and the choice is actually sanctioned by the Legislatures no matter at whose dictation they act. In some instances, not necessary to be discussed, it is quite obvious that a Legislature would be fully justified in disobeying the commands of the people.

But the real answer to this suggestion is that it is an experiment outside of the Constitution which may, and I believe, will, be quickly abandoned, for when the people exercise full intelligence and discrimination in selecting their legislators they will not wish, nor will it be necessary for them to dictate the names of the Senators. The Legislatures will always faithfully represent their constituents in the selection of Senators, when the constituents exercise care and discrimination in choosing the legislators. If the change in the method of choosing Senators be adopted and this important attribute of State legislative power be taken from the members, where will it end?

It will inevitably be followed by a change in the method of choosing the executive and the judiciary! And then will follow the crowning step of all—the people will dictate the particular laws which the State legislators shall make (they are already doing this in at least one Western State); confusion and chaos will follow the destitution of the legislators of all discretion and judgment, and then — ochlocracy (mob rule). To avoid this, educate the people, bring to their direct attention all political questions, give them time to study and understand them. But, most of all, elevate the profession of politics and do not force our citizens to apologize for following such a calling.

The third difference between the English House of Lords and the United States Senate is that the Senate acts as a court in cases of impeachment of the President by the House of Representatives. The King of England cannot be impeached. But the House of Lords tries other impeachments presented by the Commons. When the President of the United States is on trial the Chief Justice of the Supreme Court of the United States temporarily quits his high place and presides over the Court of Impeachment. But the House impeaches and the Senate decides. If both Houses are elected by the people, the same tribunal acts as accuser and judge. They both receive their inspirations and conceptions of the case from the people and the impartiality and independence of the Senate disappears. This is not the American conception of justice.

Moreover, the Senate is associated with the President in making treaties, and in this respect again it differs from the House of Lords; it is only with the advice and consent of two-thirds of the Senators present when the question arises that the President has power to conclude a treaty. The King of England can make treaties without the concurrence of either house of Parliament, but the people have seen fit to associate the Senate with the President in the exercise of this executive function.

Jay, in an article in the "Federalist" upon the provision relating to the making of treaties, said:

> "*The power of making treaties is an important one,*
> *especially as it relates to war, peace and commerce, and it*
> *should not be delegated but in such a mode and with such*
> *precautions as will afford the highest security that it will be*
> *exercised by men the best qualified for the purpose and in the*
> *manner most conducive to the public good. The convention*
> *appears to have been attentive to both these points; they*
> *have directed the President to be chosen by select bodies of*
> *electors to be deputed by the people for that express purpose;*
> *and they have committed the appointment of Senators to*
> *the State Legislatures. This mode has in such cases vastly*
> *the advantage of elections by the people in their collective*
> *capacity, where the activity of party seal, taking advantage*
> *of the supineness, the ignorance, and the hopes and fears of*
> *the unwary and interested, often places men in office by the*
> *votes of a small proportion of the electors*"

Has this logic lost its strength because our population has increased from thirteen to nearly one hundred million people?

> "*The influence which naturally results from these*
> *considerations is this—that the President and Senators*
> *so chosen will always be of the number of those who best*
> *understand our national interests, whether considered in*
> *relation to the several States, or to foreign nations, who are*
> *best able to promote those interests, and whose reputation for*
> *integrity inspires and merits confidence. With such men the*
> *power of making treaties may be safely lodged.*"

Finally, it is only with the advice and consent of the Senate that the President can appoint ambassadors, other public ministers and Consuls,

Judges of the Supreme Court and all other officers of the United States whose appointment are not otherwise provided for in the Constitution.

It thus will be seen that the Senate is not only a legislative body but it has coordinate judicial and executive functions and possesses much more power than the House of Lords which rarely acts as a check to the House of Commons, because of the peculiar character of the whole government. The Senate of the United States has an unbroken record since its establishment that no legislative department of any government ever excelled.

It is to be destroyed by ***ipse dixit, for no argument are made against the general capabilities, honesty or patriotism of its members, and *no arraignment of its usefulness is presented. It is to be brutally abolished because somebody thinks and someone believes that the people will be better served if they directly elect the Senators. One of the most firmly established branches of the government is to be torn up by the roots and sacrificed to a spirit of speculation. All the teachings of history and principle are to be cast aside to satisfy a most superficial spirit of Reform.*

The main argument put forth that there has been a change in conditions since the constitution was adopted is the strongest in favor of its retention. The Senate was organized to meet not the existing but a future history when the nation would have a greater population and be confronted with more complicated questions of politics and commerce. The framers of the Constitution did not entertain the silly opinion that this country was to stand still, and that the Constitution was to be adapted merely to the situation existing when it was promulgated. It was launched for a voyage into the future centuries; it was constructed and equipped to meet all the emergencies and vicissitudes which an increased population and a growing nation would develop.

Wherever the population of a country is so large that an absolute democracy cannot exist, a representative government is necessary and a Senate appointed or elected by some power at least a degree removed from the people is not a mere form but an essential to a permanent government. The conception of a Senate was not original with the creators of our Federation. Even the name and age of the Senators were borrowed.

A Senate existed in Athens, anterior to Solon and he organized this branch with 400 members above thirty years of age chosen by lot, among the four tribes from among the citizens of the three first classes. It deliberated upon all affairs before they were carried into the assembly of the people. Being mindful of the experience of ages we have reversed conditions. It was substantially the same with the Spartan Senate which was organized by Lycurgus.

The Senate of the United States was only new in the aspect of the federation, each State small or great having two Senators to represent it. But if a Confederation had not been formed and the individual States had dissolved themselves and coalesced into a Nation, a Senate independent of the people, and of the Executive would have still been essential.

In conclusion, I feel that the only strength of this movement is that it has secured the support of Senators and others whose names and opinions are entitled to respect and weight. I could have hoped that in an issue touching a fundamental alteration of the Constitution there would exist practical unanimity. Unhappily, the opponents of the proposition to change the method of election have allowed this movement to run unchecked without organization or serried opposition. Many have believed that there would come a time when it would check itself and that sober second thought would suffice to kill it.

Once started, however, it has gathered momentum from the inertia of the people until it has reached a point where the Senate of the United States is asked to declare itself incompetent to fulfil its mission, and to pronounce the work of Washington, Hamilton, Madison and the other illustrious framers and supporters of the Constitution, a failure.

It is time the whole country aroused itself. We are passing through an epoch so momentous that the American bar should organize to resist the most dangerous innovation ever attempted since the formation of the government. Secession aimed to deprive the Union of part of the States, but the present scheme obliterates their sovereignty and changes the federation into a nation with one popular assembly.

JOHN R. DOS PASSOS.
New York, February 4, 1911.
*vox populi: "The opinions or beliefs of the majority."
**eo instant: "At that very instant."

***Ipse dixit: "He said it himself." An assertion without proof; or a dogmatic expression of opinion. The fallacy of defending a proposition by baldly asserting that it is "just how it is" distorts the argument by opting out of it entirely: the claimant declares an issue to be intrinsic and not changeable.

Chapter 15

KARL MARX AND THE COMMUNIST MANIFESTO

To these who propose to substitute Communism for this intense Individualism The answer, therefore, is: The race has tried that. All progress from that Barbarous day to the present time has resulted from its displacement. Not evil, but good, has come to the race from the accumulation of wealth by those who have the ability and energy that produce it.
Andrew Carnegie, The Gospel of Wealth, 1889

In Marxist philosophy, the bourgeoisie is the social class that came to own the means of production during modern industrialization and whose societal concerns are the value of property and the preservation of capital to ensure the perpetuation of their economic supremacy in society.

Marxist theory considers the proletariat to be oppressed by capitalism and the wage system. This oppression gives the proletariat common economic and political interests that transcend national boundaries. These common interests put the proletariat in a position to unite and take power away from the capitalist class in order to create a communist society free from class distinctions.

Around 1840, a time curiously coincident with the congenital effort to enact the 17th Amendment, there began a rapid rise in interest for Marxism and its well-intentioned, world-wide movement for wealth re-distribution and equality for all. <u>Did the philosophy of Karl Marx in any way influence politics in the United States – or its amendment effort?</u>

Marx's influence in America began as early as 1850 when he was hired to write articles about Europe for Horace Greely's *New York Daily Tribune,* one of America's most influential newspapers of that era. Some of Marx's articles not published in the *Tribune* were posted, instead, in *The People's Paper.* <u>Many of those articles, written over a ten-year period from 1850 to 1860, were mysteriously purged from the record in both places.</u>

(Google: "Articles by Karl Marx")

Marx also wrote a letter to President Abraham Lincoln in 1865 on the subject of abolishing slavery. Marx's founding of the First International Workingman's Association in London in 1864 led to the founding of the National Labor Union in 1865 as its American version. This brought Karl Marx's formula for class warfare to America that eventually led to the Pennsylvania Coal Strike in 1877; the Railroad Strike of 1877, the Knights of Labor mobilization; the May Day Strike; and the Haymarket Square Riot in Chicago in 1886. Even the Boston Police Walkout; the National Steel Strike; the Women's Suffrage Campaign and race riots in 1919 can be attributed to Marx's influence. These revolutionary events from 1877 onward are chronicled by Neil Painter.[21]

---

21 Painter, Neil Irvin, *"Standing at Armageddon: The United States 1877-1919,* 1987

Progressivism is the support or advocacy for social reform. As a philosophy, it is based on the idea of progress, which asserts that advancements in science, technology, economic development and social organization are vital to the improvement of the human condition.

Progress depends very much on objectives. If equality is the goal — as many self-described Progressives say it is — then any progress toward equality should be considered as, well, progress. If that is the case, shouldn't communism be the most progressive cause of all? Communism was certainly considered as such by many notable intellectuals of the past.

Could the real fight for A17 have been motivated more by a popular desire for closer political influence on the U. S. Senate with its control of the purse strings? Was that long struggle for A17 an honest effort to fix exaggerated corruption rates that could have been repaired by ordinary means? Or were inflated gridlocks and corruption charges an unwitting, or even a deliberate ruse designed to give closer public access to the purse strings of the United States Senate and redistribution opportunities?

A competitor of Karl Marx, Mikhail Bakunin advocated an armed uprising and the forcible destruction of state power while Marx, on the other hand, saw _a long process of education and organization as a necessary precursor for a revolutionary overthrow of the ruling class, followed by a "withering away" of the coercive state in the new non-exploitative world._[22]

At the time of its establishment (1864), the International Workingmen's Association (IWA) in America was far from a revolutionary organization seeking rather to advance the cause of labor through international cooperation of organized workers around a general program based upon

22 Braunthal, Julius, *History of the International: Volume 1*, pg. 176

the notions of liberty and justice. This somewhat tender trade unionist perspective was not universal among its members, however, as from the outset it gained the participation of German émigrés Karl Marx and Frederick Engels and many of their co-thinkers, for whom the purpose of the IWA were not the modest goals of raising wages, lowering working hours, and liberalizing election law through international coopera-tion, *but rather the construction of an international organization as a tool for the winning of state power from the bourgeoisie.*

Karl Marx saw the future as a utopian shift from slavery, feudalism, mercantilism, and capitalism; to socialism, progressivism, egalitar-ianism, and finally to communism. These roots go back to the Age of Enlightenment and before. Even to the class struggles of primitive tribal societies described by Engels in the preface to *"The Communist Manifesto."*[23] Engels asserted that those struggles were preceded by prim-itive Teutonic tribal societies holding land in common ownership with-out explaining the evolution from common ownership to class struggles.

Marx and Engels were apparently unaware of early communal expe-riences in the "commonwealths" of Plymouth, Massachusetts and Jamestown, Virginia (early 17th century), where - but for a speedy con-version to capitalism and private ownership of land (including most of the produce derived therefrom) - settlers would have starved to death. They were afterwards better able to survive as they struggled with each other to acquire the highest possible level of wealth accumulation and, by deduction, higher living standards for all – including the poor.

Is it not somewhat ironic that Massachusetts and Virginia are proudly referred to as "Commonwealths" to this day; even though it was capi-talism that saved them from extinction? *Is it not even more ironic that untested philosophies might have influenced a benevolent but dangerously*

---

23 Marx, Karl and Engels, Frederick, *The Communist Manifesto,* 1848

speculative amendment to a constitution once regarded as a standard of excellence throughout the world?[1]

Now please don't think of this as overly critical of Mr. Marx or any of his disciples. They were, and are still, all decent people who meant well.

> *Landholders ought to have a share in the government to support these invaluable Interests and check the other many. They ought to be so constituted as to protect The Minority of the opulent against the majority."*
> James Madison; Max Farrand, ed., The Records of the Federal Convention of 1787, 3rd ed., vol. I, p. 422)

A Test Point
Editorial by Daniel De Leon, Aug. 11, 1895
From: The People, a Socialist Labor Party news outlet (http://www.slp.org/index.html)

Last Sunday, Senator William Alfred Peffer delivered a lecture at Prohibition park, Staten Island, in the course of which he stated: "It would be unjust to take away any property from people who own it." Much turns on the seemingly simple question here involved. It may even be considered a test point that reveals both the fiber of both mind and body, or the total absence thereof, in him who dares to approach the social question.

In the hands of two sorts of holders, and of no other, can property be found; either: 1. In the hands of those with just title; or 2. In the hands of those with none. Taking the first, and leaving here aside all inquiry into what constitutes "just title," but assuming that certain property is found in hands justly entitled thereto, the justice or injustice of taking it away is a practical one; no abstract theories need here be applied. Men gather and organize themselves into social bodies for their well-being. A practical purpose, redounding to the ultimate well-being of all, lies at the bottom and is the aim of all "government" or social systems.

MICHAEL JAMES GEANOULIS, SR.

This principle is no longer open to discussion; in granite letters it is engraven in the words: "Governments are instituted among Men" to secure "Life, Liberty, and the pursuit of Happiness"; and "whenever any Form of Government becomes destructive of these ends, it is the Right of the People to alter or to abolish it, and to institute new Government, laying its foundation on such principles and organizing its powers in such form, as to them shall seem most likely to effect their Safety and Happiness."

Upon this practical principle, even before it was so strikingly worded, have men ever proceeded in their organization of society, and their conception of what was "just" or "unjust" was ever controlled by that which their experience of facts pointed out. If, in their opinion, the doing of a certain thing would not redound to their happiness, it was undone; if, in their opinion, it would redound to their happiness, it was done. Facts, material conditions, experience, in short, has ever lighted the path of justice. Whether property, held by good title, should or should not be taken away - in other words, whether the social system of ownership should or should not be changed - is, accordingly, to be determined solely by the experience gathered upon the happiness or the unhappiness that flows from its continuance in private hands.

If its continuance brings on misery, it ceases to be just to leave it where it is; it becomes justice to take it away. This undeniable principle firmly kept in sight, there can be no doubt that the system of private holdings of what is needed for production has become injustice, and that justice now demands the taking it away. This fact experience had pointed out as early as 1829, when the great New Yorker, Thomas Skidmore, uttered the pregnant maxim:

> *"Inasmuch as great wealth is an instrument which is*
> *uniformly used to extort from others their property, it ought*
> *to be taken away from its possessor, on the same principle*
> *that a sword or a pistol may be wrested from a robber, who*

shall undertake to accomplish the same effect in a different
manner."

Thus stands the case even with regard to property held in private hands with just title. Can there be any question to stolen property? None whatsoever. Now, then, the property found today in the private hands of the capitalist class is none other than stolen property. Labor alone produces all wealth. The capitalist class does no manner of useful work, directly or indirectly. He is a sponge on the body social. The original wealth that his class turned into a pistol, wherewith to increase its hoard by robbing others, was itself stolen, by child of some fraud or other, some fire, some failure. perchance some blacker crime. And from that starting point, the pistol used as capital has been enlarged, improved and perfected to do its criminal work on larger and larger scales.

To take away the property of the capitalist class is to restore their own to the working class, to the overwhelming majority, and thereby reorganize society in such a form as may promote the happiness of its members. This course has become unquestionable justice. Neither do the abstract principles that underlie the law of property stand in the claim that the property now held by the capitalist class, and needed to produce the necessities of life with, should be transferred from its present to other holders. On this subject, the keen intellect of Benjamin Franklin shed valuable light, nor did his robust manliness recoil before the truth. He said:

> *"Private property is a creature of society, and is subject to the*
> *calls of that society, wherever its necessities shall require it,*
> *even to its last farthing."*
> Benjamin Franklin

When the Populist Senator William Alfred Peffer sweepingly pronounces unjust the taking of "any property from those who own it," he reflects the mental and physical fiberlessness of both himself and of the movement of which he is so ridiculous a secretion.

> *"The real destroyer of the liberties of the people is he who spreads among them bounties, donations and benefits."*
> Plutarch (c.45-125 A.D.)

AYN RAND, RUSSIAN COMMUNISM AND AMENDMENT SEVENTEEN

Her book appears as a low-level shock to me as I browse the shelves of my favorite used book store. Tom, the owner, has a detailed inventory list of his books and the memory of an elephant.

"Hey Tom," I asked, "what would compel anyone (assuming they weren't smoking anything that contaminated their sanity) to title their book 'The Virtue of Selfishness?'" "How the (%#@!) can selfishness be a virtue?"[24]

I had been made aware of Ayn Rand in my earlier years, but she was billed as a sassy nut job with off-the-wall dreams about some sort of shrugging economic utopia, and so, rejectionable. This book of hers grabbed me, though, because of cover descriptions radiating a favorable connection between self-interested (or selfish) businessmen and higher living standards. That last was right up my alley, and Tom, who knows how to sell books, knew it.

"You should check 'We the Living,' as well, Mike," he suggested, knowing my penchant for non-fiction books about economics, history and such. "It's a quasi-autobiography by Rand detailing her survival experiences with Soviet Russian Communism in Petrograd."[25] What a salesman Tom is. Nice guy, to boot.

---

24 Rand, Ayn, *The Virtue of Selfishness*, 1964
25 Rand, Ayn, *We the Living*, 1936

I often wonder these days, after digesting Ayn Rand's book about her horrific experience in Communist Russia, how she might have influenced the outcome of A17 had her story appeared alongside the yellow journalism used to reduce the Senate and nudge the Constitution closer to the ochlocracy (mob rule) feared by Senator Root.

I discovered that when this narrow survivor of Russian communism arrived in New York City on February 19, 1926, she was so impressed with the skyline of Manhattan that she wept what she later referred to as "tears of splendor." She would go on to study and heap great praise and respect for everything America stood for, giving special recognition to the founders and the Constitution, calling it the highest and best political document ever conceived. "How else could such a magnificent skyline have been achieved," she wondered openly as she proceeded to develop a philosophy that promoted the importance of the individual (vis-a-vis the state) as the best way of obtaining prosperity for the collective.

I became totally smitten with this critical-thinking woman and proceeded to get my hands on everything she ever wrote.

> *"'We the Living' is not a story about Soviet Russia in 1925. It's a story about dictatorship, any dictatorship, anywhere, at any time, whether it be Soviet Russia, Nazi Germany, or – which this novel might do its share in helping to prevent – a Socialist America."*
> Ayn Rand, 1936

———

> *To take from one, because it is thought his own industry and that of his fathers has acquired too much, in order to spare to others, who, or whose fathers, have not exercised equal industry and skill, is to violate arbitrarily the first principle*

of association, the guarantee to everyone the free exercise of his industry and the fruits acquired by it.

Thomas Jefferson, "Letter to Milligan," April 6, 1816, in *The Writings of Thomas Jefferson*, ed. Albert E. Bergh (Washington: Thomas Jefferson Memorial Association, 1904), Vol. 14, p. 466.

Chapter 16

THE ETERNAL
PROBLEM OF POVERTY

*"When you reap the harvest of your land, you must not
finish the edge of your field at your reaping, and you must
not glean the remnants of your harvest—you shall leave
them behind for the needy and for the alien; I am Yahweh
your God"*
(Leviticus 23:22).

No discussion about the evolution of Amendment Seventeen would be
complete without an inquiry into the problems of poverty and wealth
distribution. For this is the sum, substance and root of the entire debate
over A17, all of it – not election problems, election laws, Constitutional
Conventions, deadlocks, corruption allegations or common sense – but
stubborn poverty problems that trump all else.

In Biblical times the plight of the poor must have been pure misery.
Much advice and counselling has been lifted from the Bible over the
ages in timeless efforts to relieve that wretched condition – but to little
avail it seems – at least until a properly regulated form of Laissez-Faire
Capitalism came along. (https//biblereasons.com/poverty/)

Around 1000 A.D., people had a mental image of a society like the divinity who had created and would ultimately judge it. Given the divine origin of the social order, the poor were not held individually responsible for their condition. Prosperity and poverty alike were attributed to the grace of God, and all should accept their lot with humility. Nor were the poor stigmatized. They were actually useful to the rich and powerful as an outlet to atone for their sins through the Christian charity of alms-giving. (www.buildinghistory.org/articles/heritagemercy.shtml)

In the Middle Ages paupers were in need of protection and were given it by the King and his minions in France and England. Even as poverty later became associated with economic hardship, it was not viewed as a social weakness.

In 17th century England, the poor were thought more as the order of heaven and were treated with a level of generosity that was seemingly rejected by Benjamin Franklin. His experience in 18th century England contrasted sharply with the economic conditions of early America, where there was no shortage of forests to clear and work to do. This might explain the not-so-generous attitude of Mr. Franklin, who was living in England as an Ambassador from America when he wrote, with apparent irritation, about the price of corn and the apparently generous poor laws there. His essay could also have been driven by the possibility that he was on a tight budget. I include his piece in its entirety because of the connection between high prices, poverty, scarcity of money and because we could use a brief change of pace.

On the Price of Corn, and Management of the Poor
Posted by Benjamin Franklin on 29 November 1766

For the LONDON CHRONICLE.

To Messieurs the PUBLIC *and* CO. I am one of that class of people that feeds you all, and at present is abus'd by you all; — in short, I am a *Farmer.*

By your Newspapers we are told, that God had sent a very short harvest to some other countries of Europe. I thought this might be in favor to Old England; and that now we should get a good price for our grain, which would bring in millions among us, and make us flow in money, that to be sure is scarce enough.

But the wisdom of Government forbad the exportation. Well, says I, then we must be content with the market price at home. No, says my Lords the mob, you sha'n't have that. Bring your corn to market if you dare; — we'll sell it for you, for less money, or take it for nothing.

Being thus attack'd by both ends *of the Constitution,* the head and the tail *of Government,* what am I to do? Must I keep my corn in barn to feed and increase the breed of rats? — be it so; — they cannot be less thankful than those I have been used to feed.

Are we Farmers the only people to be grudged the profits of honest labor? — And why? — One of the late scribblers against us gives a bill of fare of the provisions at my daughter's wedding, and proclaims to all the world that we had the insolence to eat beef and pudding! — Has he never read that precept in the good book, *Thou shalt not muzzle the mouth of the ox that treadeth out the corn;* or does he think us less worthy of good living than our oxen? O, but the Manufacturers! the Manufacturers! they are to be favour'd, and they must have bread at a cheap rate! Hark-ye, Mr. Oaf; — The Farmers live splendidly, you say. And pray, would you have them hoard the money they get? — Their fine cloths and furniture, do they make them themselves, or for one another, and so keep the money among them? Or do they employ these your darling Manufacturers, and so scatter it again all over the nation?

My wool would produce me a better price if it were suffer'd to go to foreign markets. But that, Messieurs the Public, your laws will not permit. It must be kept all at home, that our *dear* Manufacturers may have it the cheaper. And then, having yourselves thus lessened our encouragement for raising sheep, you curse us for the scarcity of mutton!

I have heard my grandfather say, that the Farmers submitted to the prohibition on the exportation of wool, being made to expect and believe, that when the Manufacturer bought his wool cheaper, they should have their cloth cheaper. But the deuce a bit. It has been growing dearer and dearer from that day to this. How so? why truly the cloth is exported; and that keeps up the price.

Now if it be a good principle, that the exportation of a commodity is to be restrain'd, that so our own people at home may have it the cheaper, stick to that principle, and go thorough stitch with it. Prohibit the exportation of your cloth, your leather and shoes, your iron ware, and your manufactures of all sorts, to make them all cheaper at home. And cheap enough they will be, I'll warrant you — till people leave off making them.

Some folks seem to think they ought never to be easy, till *England* becomes another *Lubberland*, where 'tis fancied the streets are paved with penny rolls, the houses tiled with pancakes, and chickens ready roasted cry, come eat me.

I say, when you are sure you have got a good principle, stick to it, and carry it through. — I hear 'tis said, that though it was *necessary and right* for the M——y to advise a prohibition of the exportation of corn, yet it was *contrary to law*: And also, that though it was *contrary to law* for the mob to obstruct the wagons, yet it was *necessary and right*. — Just the same thing, to a tittle. Now they tell me, an act of indemnity ought to pass in favor of the M —— y, to secure them from the consequences of having acted illegally. — If so, pass another in favor of the mob. Others say, some of the mob ought to be hanged, by way of example. — If so, —— but I say no more than I have said before, *when you are sure that you have got a good principle, go through with it.*

You say, poor laborers cannot afford to buy bread at a high price, unless they had higher wages. — Possibly. — But how shall we Farmers be able to afford our laborers higher wages, if you will not allow us to get, when we might have it, a higher price for our corn?

By all I can learn, we should at least have had a guinea a quarter more if the exportation had been allowed. And this money England would have got from foreigners.

But, it seems, we Farmers must take so much less, that the poor may have it so much cheaper.

This operates then as a tax for the maintenance of the poor. — A very good thing, you will say. But I ask, Why a partial tax? Why laid on us Farmers only? — If it be a good thing, pray, Messrs. the Public, take your share of it, by indemnifying us a little out of your public treasury. In doing a good thing there is both honor and pleasure; — you are welcome to your part of both.

For my own part, I am not so well satisfied of the goodness of this thing. I am for doing good to the poor, but I differ in opinion of the means. — I think the best way of doing good to the poor, is not making them easy *in* poverty, but leading or driving them *out* of it. In my youth I travelled much, and I observed in different countries, that the more public provisions were made for the poor, the less they provided for themselves, and of course became poorer. And, on the contrary, the less was done for them, the more they did for themselves, and became richer. There is no country in the world where so many provisions are established for them; so many hospitals to receive them when they are sick or lame, founded and maintained by voluntary charities; so many alms-houses for the aged of both sexes, together with a solemn general law made by the rich to subject their eStates to a heavy tax for the support of the poor. Under all these obligations, are our poor modest, humble, and thankful; and do they use their best endeavors to maintain themselves, and lighten our shoulders of this burthen?

On the contrary, I affirm that there is no country in the world in which the poor are more idle, dissolute, drunken, and insolent. The day you passed that act, you took away from before their eyes the greatest of all inducements to industry, frugality, and sobriety, by giving them a dependence on somewhat else than a careful accumulation during youth and health, for support in age or sickness. In short, you offered a premium for the encouragement of idleness, and you should not now wonder that it has had its effect in the increase of poverty.

Repeal that law, and you will soon see a change in their manners. St. *Monday*, and St. *Tuesday*, will cease to be holidays. SIX *days shalt thou labor*, though one of the old commandments long treated as out of date, will again be looked upon as a respectable precept; industry will increase, and with it plenty among the lower people; their circumstances will mend, and more will be done for their happiness by inuring them to provide for themselves, than could be done by dividing all your eStates among them.

Excuse me, Messrs. the Public, if upon this *interesting* subject, I put you to the trouble of reading a little of *my* nonsense. I am sure I have lately read a great deal of *yours*; and therefore from you (at least from those of you who are writers) I deserve a little indulgence. I am, yours, &c. ARATOR.

———

In 1787 Philadelphia, Ben Franklin's home, two alms Houses, a debtor's prison and a work house were situated barely a stone's throw or two from Independence Hall and the Constitution Convention on Chestnut Street. In their daily comings and goings to and from that venerable meeting place, there is little doubt that the founding fathers would not have had constant reminders of the poor. The aging Franklin was using prisoners to carry him, seated on a sedan gifted to him by the King of France, to and from the convention every day. Not a word, however, was given to slavery or personal economic considerations of any kind in the final draft of the Constitution excepting, of course, provisions to protect personal liberty and property rights considered to be inviolable. Madison stated, moreover, that he "thought it wrong to admit in the Constitution the idea that there could be property in men."

There were, to be fair, external hints of concern for the economically disadvantaged such as Benjamin Franklin's booklet, *"The Way to Wealth,"* and his appraisal while living in Europe that "the more public provisions were made for the poor, the less they provided for themselves, and of course became poorer. And contrarily, the less was done for them, the less poor they became." He thus advised that "the poor should not be made comfortable in their poverty."

Considerable attention, expenditure and care were given to the poor throughout Philadelphia's history. The city truly deserves its reputation as a primary example of brotherly love. A thorough historical accounting of this theme by researcher Mara Kaktins can be seen at: (https://philadelphiaencyclopedia.org/archive/almshouses-poorhouses/)

It was also the case in colonial Virginia, that those who sought relief were provided for – albeit somewhat less than generously given the money supply and lack of respect for vagabonds and the printing press in those days.

Below are excerpts from a 1779 Virginia "Bill for Support of the Poor." Because Jefferson and Madison were referenced in the notes, they were likely involved in its editing and passage. Note the references to "stripes" and "whipping." Deleted in a revision, was a harsh clause which required all persons receiving relief to wear a badge "upon the shoulder of the right sleeve of his or her uppermost garment, in an open and visible manner … with the name of the parish to which he or she belongs, cut either in blue, red, or green cloth." The vestry had been empowered to punish violations of this requirement by curtailing or suspending the allowance to the person or imposing a whipping. (https://founders.archives.gov/documents/Jefferson/01-02-02-0132-0004-0032)

Little patience was shown for the able-bodied who were not pulling their weight in colonial America – even in the liberal city of brotherly love.

A BILL FOR SUPPORT OF THE POOR
Committee of the Virginia Assembly, 18 June, 1779, [Excerpts]
Be it enacted by the General Assembly, that the Aldermen of every county wherein such provision, as is herein after required for setting the poor of the county to work, shall not have been made, shall, so soon as conveniently may be, purchase the inheritance, or procure a lease, of one hundred acres of land, or any less quantity that is sufficient for the purpose intended, in the county, and thereon cause a house to be built, if a proper one be not there already, and kept in repair, and shall cause all persons in their county, who are maintained thereby, or who seek relief therefrom, to be put into such house, to be there maintained and employed in such work as they shall be able to perform; and may also, by their warrant, apprehend and send to the same place all persons found wandering and begging alms, in the county, other than seamen......

......and shall put such beggar to work for any time not exceeding twenty days. And the said Aldermen shall hire some discreet man to oversee those who shall come or be put into such work-house, and shall, from time to time, ordain rules for his conduct, and for the government, employment, and correction of the persons subject to him, restraining him from correcting any of them with more stripes than ten, at one time, or for one offence. And in order to keep them at work shall provide wool, cotton, flax, hemp and other materials, with the tools and implements necessary for the manufacture thereof......

And also for the putting out the poor children apprentices, as well as for defraying the expenses of putting so much of this act in execution as relates to setting the poor to work and keeping them so employed.....

A bastard child shall be deemed a settled inhabitant of that county in which, at the birth, the mother was settled.

All able bodied persons not having wherewithal to maintain themselves, who shall waste their time in idle and dissolute courses, or shall loiter or wander abroad, refusing to work for reasonable wages, or to betake themselves to some honest and lawful calling, or who shall desert wives or children, without so providing for them as that they shall not become chargeable to a county, shall be deemed vagabonds, and shall be sent, by order of an Alderman, to the poor house, there to be kept to labor during such time as shall be limited by the order, not exceeding thirty days; or if he be a settled inhabitant of another county, shall, by warrant of the said Alderman, be conveyed, by constable to constable, to some Alderman of such other county, who shall, by his order, send him to the proper poor house, to be there kept to labor as aforesaid; unless, in either of the cases, the vagabond shall give surety for his good behavior, and that he shall betake himself to some honest and lawful calling for twelve months; from which order the party thereby condemned may appeal to the county court, who, if the order be affirmed, shall award him to pay the costs....

———

PROSPERITY, POVERTY AND AMENDMENT
SEVENTEEN

> *"Not one instance of even a well-dressed infant having been picked up in the Streets is on record. They come in rags, a newspaper often the only wrap, semi-occasionally one in a clean slip with some evidence of loving care; a little slip of paper pinned on, perhaps, with some such message as this I once read, in a woman's trembling hand: 'Take care of Johnny, for God's sake. I cannot.'"*
> Riis, Jacob A., 1903

WARM SPOT NEAR GRATED VENT, JACOB RIIS, 1885

Around 1880, a bright young immigrant from Denmark by the name of Jacob August Riis survived a debilitating bout with hard times in a seedy area of New York City that, as he put it in so many words, nearly terminated him. After restoring himself, Mr. Riis found employment as a photo journalist and sallied forth, with a remedial glow in his demeanor, to document the crowding, squalor, immorality, crime, alcoholism, filth, disease and death in the New York City slums that nearly killed him. You might say Jacob had a justifiable axe to grind.

DENS OF DEATH, JACOB RIIS, 1903

A NICKEL A SPOT, JACOB RIIS, 1885

MICHAEL JAMES GEANOULIS, SR.

His 1903 book was an emotionally charged slum-buster that won the sympathy and support of millions[26]. As he intended for NYC and beyond, reforms soon became only a matter of time and the cooperation of tenement builders themselves which, according to Riis' own account, was easily gained. He won support from then NYC Police Commissioner and future Progressive candidate for U. S. President, Theodore "Teddy" Roosevelt, who said he "would help where he could" - later supporting the passage of A17.

The critical thinker however, might wonder about the entire set of causes for this disaster in overcrowding and grinding poverty. Was a faulty Constitution, or the capitalism of free markets spawned by that document, the cause? To what extent should such things as inept immigration policies, money management issues, language barriers and human weaknesses be held responsible for these misfortunes?

What about the possibility of faulty judgement skewed by emotion and desperation for relief from the evil and squalor of NYC slums? Was it really necessary to speculate on an irreversible amendment to the Constitution when reasonable immigration regulation and official regard for its own rules, laws and zoning ordinances might have made more sense?

What about the unforeseen results of A17? Like the questionable outcomes of a later age which produced improperly funded programs and ballooning debt – the inflation of which, causes doubt about the efficacy and accuracy of poverty rate measurements? Today's poverty rates in New York City could soon rival those of 1890. A recent study found 45% of its citizens living at or near poverty despite massive debits on future citizens to cure the problem.

---

26 Riis, Jacob August, *How the Other Half Lives*, 1903

Have vengeful laws and attitudes evolved which compromised the ability of reviled entrepreneurs to produce the highest quality at the lowest price for consumers who, whether or not fettered by overcrowding, would nearly always vote with their hard-won dollar for the best entrepreneur?

The complete troubleshooter might also wonder about the wisdom of immigration allowances that fostered such a tidal wave of human misery. Now my mind switches to the almost forgotten, ghastly image of a lone surviving mouse discovered trapped in a large, open jug of the kind used to pickle cucumbers with a dozen half-chewed bones of relatives at his feet. What in God's name were those immigration regulators thinking about? According to Riis, the worst population densities recorded in London paled in comparison to those of 1880 New York, where the worst densities were found to be 350,000 souls per square mile.

The so-called Gilded Age in the United States (about 1870 to 1910) was not so gilded, but it was a period of unprecedented economic growth. Here, wages grew higher than in Europe, especially for skilled workers. The expansion of industrialization led to a 60% wage growth between 1860 and 1890. The annual wage gain between 1880 and 1890 was especially dramatic: $380 to $564 annually, or a gain of 48% in ten years with no inflation. Europeans, accordingly, immigrated to our shores by the millions on the promise of good jobs and a better life.

But such numbers, compounded by language barriers and communication difficulties, merely intensified an already existing shortage of city tenements which in turn produced obscene rent yields as workers were willing to pay whatever for scarce tenements, attics, sheds or even cellars in order to be closer to their jobs; or to their markets in those cases where tenements, hallways, cellars and attics were also used for producing items like cigars, clothing, button holes and other hand wrought goods.

The Riis revelations were so compelling that we should no longer wonder why such a large and distinguished army of Progressives like "Teddy" Roosevelt and Woodrow Wilson rose with such force, energy and eloquence to do something, anything, that might relieve such abominations — even if it meant taking a closer look at Marxist philosophy or a harmless (sic), low level patch on the Constitution that nine out of ten illustrious Constitutional Convention delegates had already rejected in 1787 after extensive detailed debate on the matter.

> *"In the tenements all the influences make for evil; because*
> *they are the hot-beds of the epidemics that carry death to*
> *rich and poor alike; the nurseries of pauperism and crime*
> *that fill our jails and police courts; that throw off a scum*
> *of forty thousand human wrecks to the island asylums and*
> *workhouses year by year; that turned out in the last eight*
> *years a round half million beggars to prey upon our charities;*
> *that maintain a standing army of ten thousand tramps with*
> *all that that implies; because, above all, they touch the family*
> *life with deadly moral contagion."*
> Jacob August Riis, 1903

Eloquent penmanship and superb intellect dedicated to such noble ideas as pursuit of happiness and a more perfect union made little sense to the illiterate immigrant family unable to pay the rent or properly communicate with their oppressors. Self-evident truths about blessings, liberty, domestic tranquility, equality and questionable Senate election problems seemed as cruel jokes to would-be Bolsheviks hunkered in filthy, unheated New York tenements while bourgeoise counterparts admired their jewelry by the fireplace in gilded Newport mansions.

Ben Franklin's republic was insufficient. Madison was wrong about the dangers of pure democracy. And Tocqueville worried needlessly about the tyranny of the majority. The entire Constitutional Convention, by their unanimous 10 to 0 vote, erred in mandating State legislative control of the Senate. The public at large should be trusted more than a bunch of ancient, overfed white guys who owned slaves; and so, it goes, ad infinitum.

Orations and essays from influential leaders like "Teddy" and Franklin Roosevelt, Woodrow Wilson, John Dewey, Et al, alleged that Robber Barons were colluding with fraud infested political institutions in need of convincing lessons about income inequality – maybe even time in the big house.

The result of such influence? Passage of A17 and the false hope of improvements in wealth redistribution. One historian discovered that, in 1890, one (1) percent of Americans owned fifty (50) percent of the nation's wealth.[27] (See also https://www.history.com/news/second-gilded-age-income-inequality)

But wait, another amendment might be needed – one with more teeth in it. A new wave of industrialists, financiers and government welfare data enters the scene in the latter part of the 20th century to cast doubt about the long-term effectiveness and wisdom of A17. For it is true that in 2018, one (1) percent of the nation's population owned forty (40) percent of the nation's wealth, and the gap is rapidly widening. A cosmic instant from now, *the ratio will be the same as it was in 1890, i.e., 1% owning 50% of the wealth.* Time to rethink the amendment yet? (see: https://en.wikipedia.org/wiki/Wealth_inequality_in_the_United_States)

Then there's this graphic from Alvaredo et al showing concentrations of *family wealth* ratios (as opposed to *individual wealth*) thought to be ameliorated and redistributed by defenders of A17. Except for the temporary success as indicated for the 50-year trend between 1930 and 1970, the household income gap of 2010 is slightly higher than that of 1913. The justification for A17 gets weaker with every turn of the page.

---

27 O'Donnell, Edward T., Ph.D. *"Are We Living in the Gilded Age 2.0?"* Updated Jan 31, 2019

Figure 6:
Income share held by the richest one percent of American households

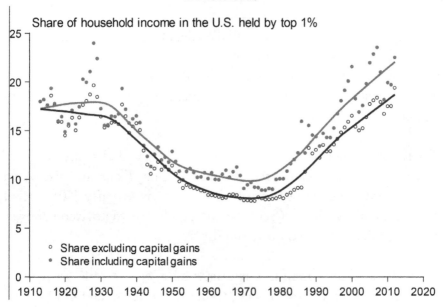

Share of household income in the U.S. held by top 1%

- ○ Share excluding capital gains
- • Share including capital gains

OPEN SOURCE: ALVAREDO ET AL. (2014); 20TH CENT ESTIMATES OF A NEAREST NEIGHBOR SMOOTHED SCATTER PLOT. HTTPS:// WWW.SCIRP.ORG/JOURNAL/OPENACCESS.ASPX)

What about Inflation, virtually non-existent prior to the enactment of A17 thanks to a wiser Senate? In 2018 the cost to service the national debt – considered by many economists to be a major contributor to infla-tion - was about $300 billion dollars; enough to rebuild our bridges and roads twice. Ten years hence, in 2028, that cost will be the better part of a trillion dollars.

The poverty problem gives the illusion of improvement because of constant fiddling with the funding required to stay ahead of the costs-post-benefits spiral. To illustrate the difficulty in getting a proper mea-surement of poverty rates while annual injections of new money are added to treat the tail-chasing problem of rising prices every year, ask yourself what the poverty rate, presently just under 15%, would be in 2028 if no new funds were added for each of the next ten years. Would it still be just under 15%? Or the same as the Progressive era when inflation, for the most part, was under control– roughly 50%? Or somewhere in between?

> *"Total welfare costs have risen from $671 per person*
> *in poverty in 1963 to $19,355 per person in 2018.*
> *That totals $77,418 for a family of four even though*
> *the Poverty Threshold for such a family is $25,701. Total*
> *federal welfare costs include the expenditures of 13 large*
> *government programs (See the Safety Net Page) plus the*
> *Medicaid Program which supplies health care to low-income*
> *Americans. The figures have been adjusted for the costs of*
> *inflation and stated in 2018 dollars."*
> http://federalsafetynet.com/poverty-and-spending-
> over-the-years.html

In an essay published at peoplespunditdaily.com economist Daniel Mitchell convincingly asserts that real progress against poverty won't be realized until the federal government, by way of block grants, gets "out of the business of redistributing income to let state and local governments decide how best to deal with the issue."[28]

Figure 7

---

28 Mitchell, Daniel, *"Poverty, the Welfare State, and the Failure of Centralized Government,"*

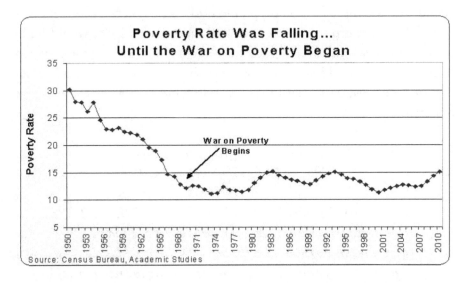

NOTE THE DECLINE IN THE POVERTY RATE UNTIL THE WAR ON POVERTY BEGINS

(Mitchell, D., 2015)
In other words, before the huge growth in government spending on poverty programs, poverty was declining rapidly in America. After the new programs were fully implemented, the poverty rate stopped declining.

It's important to note that poverty rates everywhere have been falling consistently ever since the advent of the industrial age and full-blown capitalism (from approximately 90%), mostly in capitalist countries – even in countries who claim to be governed under communist principles but allow a robust form of capitalism to exist. In Communist China, where some form of capitalism is allowed, poverty rates are reported to have fallen sharply from about 80% in 1980 to less than 10% today.

The following chart provides a graphic example of how capitalism, even when operating under a so-called communist government, serves to resolve poverty problems.

Figure 8:
Poverty rate in China since 1980

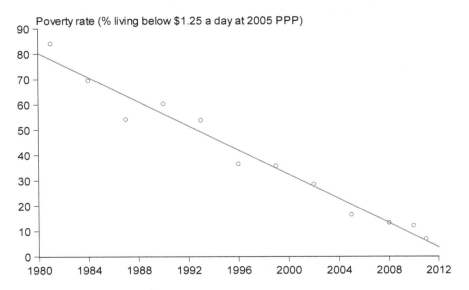

SOURCE: THE ECONOMICS OF POVERTY: HISTORY, MEASUREMENT, AND POLICY, MARTIN RAVALLION, 2016

"He who despises his neighbor is a sinner, but he who has mercy on the poor blesses him." (Proverbs 14:21)

THE NATURAL POVERTY RATE

Remember the old adage about fools and their money being soon parted? This section will explore the classic problem of personal poverty while simultaneously calling attention to the likelihood that no amendment – not a hundred such amendments – can be trusted to fix natural or unnatural tragedies like universal fiscal foolishness (governments especially), overpopulated hovels or hurricanes. This segment is presented to inspire otherwise good and faithful servants of God and family who have money enough, but manage unwisely, to improve asset management skills through education – much of which can be self-taught on the cheap.

This is not about the poverty stricken who have perpetual funding problems. These are special cases requiring special attention – and of course, the availability of jobs. This is about avoiding that condition where possible by ordinary means.

The following simple 3 question quiz, excerpted from an article by Moises Naim, illustrates the likelihood that most folks are, shall we say, insufficiently literate in financial matters (60% of Americans did not ace this quiz as they should have – easily); and to demonstrate the possibility that financial education should be pursued with a little more energy. The article, *"Most People in the World Have No Idea How to Manage Their Money,"* was originally published on the website, TheAtlantic.com by Moises Naim, and is republished here with The Atlantic's permission:

1. Suppose you had $100 in a savings account and the interest rate was 2 percent per year. After five years, how much do you think you would have in the account if you left the money to grow? A) more than $102; B) exactly $102; C) less than $102; D) do not know; refuse to answer.

2. Imagine that the interest rate on your savings account is 1 percent per year and inflation is 2 percent per year. After one year, would you be able to buy A) more than, B) exactly the same as, or C) less than today with the money in this account? D) do not know; refuse to answer.

3. Do you think that the following statement is true or false? "Buying a single company stock usually provides a safer return than a stock mutual fund." A) true; B) false; C) do not know; refuse to answer.

The correct answers are 1-A; 2-C; and 3-B.

Holding on to assets achieved by whatever means (inheritances, successful business, lottery winnings, even regular or irregular paychecks) can be challenging. Young adults who receive large inheritances should immediately consult with a parent, if available, or a financial advisor. The worst thing anyone (or any government) can do, according to financial managers, is to run out and spend money lavishly. Eliminating or avoiding debt should be priority one.

Most folks are wired for instant gratification. Nature made us that way uncounted eons ago and no constitutional amendment – not a hundred such amendments - will change that fact.

Financial advisors will tell you to understand the difference between wants and needs. Do we "want" a big house or SUV when all that's really "needed" is the smaller? Live within your means and make short term sacrifices.

People should invest and save automatically. By making saving a priority, spending will be less. The important thing is to spend less than you make. It has been proven historically that a 20-year-old who begins and holds to investing a lousy $25 weekly will be a millionaire at age 65.

People should better understand the cost of debt. As a financial virgin in desperate need of a reliable car for my DeVry Tech classes in Chicago, I discovered late in that game that the total of my payments to GMAC, who financed its purchase, amounted to double the original price tag for the car over 3 years. The experience was both a shock and a learning experience for me.

Run the numbers where necessary. Some believe that when a car begins to have problems, it's better to get a newer car to minimize maintenance and repair bills. This is not necessarily true. A few hundred dollars a year in repairs might prove to be wise when compared to the cost of a replacement.

Financially savvy people know that IRA's and 401k's are tax-free or tax-deferred and take full advantage of them. Lessons on money management are widely available. https://www.daveramsey.com/ or https://www.suzeorman.com might be good places to start.

To better comprehend the eternal nature of poverty, we will briefly explore the condition of lottery jackpot winners. The researchers are all over the place on this issue. Some report higher levels of happiness, others report pain and sorrow in the extreme. But one sad fact stands out as supremely avoidable: too many jackpot winners manage their winnings unwisely, ending up in bankruptcy court, or at least see all of their jackpot winnings disappear for one dumb reason or another within 5 years or so. One study claimed the financial failure rate of lottery jackpot winners to be as high as 70%.

These factors should be included in any effort to fully understand the justification for A17, and to devise a formula that would calculate, or estimate, the natural poverty rate. When I get properly schooled in mathematics and statistics, I will hazard an attempt at it. Is it not a curious coincidence that the poverty rate for much of the 19th century, while declining thanks to the influence of capitalism, was estimated to be about 50 to 70 percent?

Let's try a simple fantasy to demonstrate poverty as intractable by giving each citizen the equivalent of an imaginary lottery jackpot, say $1 million tomorrow. This jejune experiment of the mind will stimulate feelings of euphoria, at the outset at least. If the above research is any indication however, a large percent of the population would eventually fall economically and maybe even be in a worsened condition of want because of the fact that changes in money supplies are closely related to price changes. In 1880 for example, a quart of milk, in a reflection of the money supply for that era, could be had for 3 or 4 pennies; while today's printing press economy requires 2 dollars and rising for the same. What would the overall cost of living be 5 years after giving everyone a million dollars each? And what would the poverty rate be, given the inflation that's sure to track that injection of money into the economy compounded by the foolish spending habits revealed by the research for too large a part of the population?

When influential Henry George inquired with considerable energy into the causes of "Increase of Want with Increase in Wealth," he never had the advantage of Google search revelations that might have given him a better understanding about personal financial management skills and a more complete set of the causes of poverty. If he had, he might have had a better understanding about the reasons for the "Want/Wealth" dichotomy that influenced passage of A17, and, by his own admission, boggled his mind.[29]

And we might have had a better grip on the entire set of unjustifiable motivators that brought us a change in the way we elect our Senators.

---

29 George, Henry, *Progress and Poverty: An Inquiry into the Cause of Industrial Depressions and of Increase of Want with Increase of Wealth: The Remedy,* 1879.

Chapter 17

DEMONIZING SENATORS AND ROBBER BARONS

After reviewing the history of American attitudes and motivators over the past few centuries, it could be fairly estimated that the pendulum of political correctness and justice swings not only back and forth, but all around in a series of glancing blows from one sin or virtue to the next depending on the motivator or the season.

At times, these blows would be severe enough to rouse the image of that proverbial bull in a china shop. And it often proved necessary that that bull be programmed to steer clear of embarrassing facts in order to avoid the painful reality of ordinary common sense.

Abolishing slavery was one such motivator, the bull for which denied self-evident truths in mutual dignity and respect that, regrettably, demanded a shooting war to demonstrate the seriousness of the issue. So also, was the effort to rid ourselves of the English crown, the bull for that manifesting in bullets and bloodshed, too. The "need" for an amendment to repair real, induced or imagined bribery and corruption in Senate elections followed suit, with sharpened horns manifesting in the form of a clumsy federal election law compounded by vicious, exaggerated, libelous, yellow journalism to get it done.

After lo, so many years of failed efforts, mainly due to lack of respect for what our founders gave us and visions of how we could damage that legacy, it became apparent that a more powerful force would be required to get A17 enacted; and that this force would need to get down and dirty in keeping with the dictum that all's fair in love and war.

It appeared mainly in the form of a 1906 series of "muckraking" articles published by Cosmopolitan Magazine which would become known as *"The Treason of the Senate."* These caustic, "overstated" essays were powerful enough to subdue and cripple the reputation of stubborn Senators who were repeatedly rejecting amendment resolutions over many years.

But what about corruption in the House of Representatives; the judiciary and other federal and state administrations? Why should those unrefined assaults against the Senate, while partly true (to give the devil his due), not include the surprising level of crime and corruption in the House of Representatives and other appendages of government? Would the whole truth dilute the energy to get A17 enacted? If corruption repair was the true motivator, shouldn't the muckraking have included the House of Representatives and any or all other sources, as well?

Sarcastic efforts to mock amendment resolutions by using another resolution to improve the honesty of Representatives, as well as the Senate, was gaining traction. So, only the Senate would be targeted. Only the Senate was to be more closely controlled by the people. The House of Representatives already had that control. But it wasn't corruption in the Senate or the House or anywhere else that mattered for determined advocates. Their only concern was to get closer control of the Senate, corruption and bribery rates elsewhere notwithstanding. (see: https://en.wikipedia.org/wiki/Corruption_in_the_United_States)

Not that anyone determined to confirm popular Senate elections and a revamped constitution would have cared, but one recent survey of federal offences found that 60 U.S. Representatives were convicted

MICHAEL JAMES GEANOULIS, SR.

of a variety of federal crimes while only 8 U.S. Senators were so convicted over the same 200-year time span - a ratio of more than 7 to 1. If it could have been shown that a constitutional amendment could solve corruption problems, the House of Representatives would have been the first target, not the Senate. (https://en.wikipedia.org/wiki/List_of_American_federal_politicians_convicted_of_crimes)

Nor would the giants of American industry be spared the illogicality of the times, or the horns of that vicious bull. In the late 19th Century, the public mood turned against wealthy entrepreneurs as irately as it did against the Senate. They both got it with spades, and both barrels.

The term "Robber Barons" was a derogatory epithet applied to powerful, wealthy industrialists - the captains of industry who, it was alleged, "monopolized" the railroads, the steel industry, the tobacco industry, the oil industry and the financiers who controlled the banks using alleged unfair business practices, or rather untoward efforts DiLorenzo described as "political entrepreneur" tactics – i.e., colluding with politicians to compensate for an inability to compete fairly and openly with "market entrepreneurs" using the advantages of "crony capitalism" which then evolved into monopolies.[30]

"Robber Barons engaged in unethical practices having widespread political influences," it was said. John D. Rockefeller was the head of the Standard Oil Company, the first great U.S. business trust. It was alleged that he was ruthless and used questionable and crazy methods and would be included in the list of Robber Barons. But DiLorenzo demonstrated that it was Rockefeller's competitors who gained political influence (aka crony capitalism) - not Rockefeller, who competed using greater efficiency through vertical integration as a "market entrepreneur" thereby obviating the need for political help.

---

30 DiLorenzo, Thomas J., Ph.D., *"How Capitalism Saved America: The Untold Story of Our Country from the Pilgrims to the Present,"* 2004

Robber Barons used bribery and corruption to gain support from politicians and government officials – Senators, Representatives, judges and administrators alike. It was a free-for-all in repulsive immorality that could have inspired a dozen amendment efforts, or rather, higher levels of law enforcement – not just an amendment for the Senate that may well prove to be a self-inflicted curse in the final analysis.

The more famous of the so-called "Robber Barons" were J. P. Morgan, or "Rich Uncle Pennybags," as he is called in the Monopoly board game, Andrew Carnegie, Andrew M. Mellon, Cornelius Vanderbilt, and John D. Rockefeller – all very successful businessmen in the 19th Century.

These "criminals" cared little for the working conditions and safety of their employees, and some were manipulating the stock market. "And they were very wealthy," came another reproach reflecting one of the seven deadly sins: envy. They all had an unquenchable thirst for power and fame and needed a darn good dressing down. Criticism from newspapers intensified. Even the courts were biased. Henry Ford once won a libel suit for the Chicago Tribune's disparaging remarks against him but was awarded only 6 cents (which was never paid).

Museums, libraries and educational institutions – even Alaskan fjords, and glaciers and a small town in the Amazon were named to honor their memory. But a few were vilified as they should have been if the stories are true.

They kept wages at a minimum, even reduced them. Many families were on the edge of squalor and survival; their children forced to work in order to maintain a minimal existence. Workers were banned from joining unions or labor movements. Monopolists were exploiting workers, it was commonly asserted.

And yet they came – by the millions - as massive testimony to even harsher conditions from a prior existence overseas; and evidence, as demonstrated by their determination to immigrate, that there might well be another side to the aforementioned popular portrayal of Scrooge-like behavior here.

The Gilded Age was no picnic to be sure. Even well-to-do entrepreneurs were taking hits. In addition to the occasional bankruptcy, many of these hits took the form of exaggerated epithets and damaged reputations, however deserved, for so-called "Robber Barons" who were rewarded for their abilities in improving living standards (even those trapped in high density hovels) with epithets denoting a variety of evils and wrongdoings – both real and imagined.

Free markets forces can be very unkind. Business competitors and workers alike were sparring everywhere like chickens scrambling for potato chips. Inferior efficiencies and decisions would result in bankruptcies, job losses and debilitation. Unemployment and dread would accrue to all sides in like kind. Even one of our founders was threatened with debtor's prison because of a poor business decision. Where is it written that capitalism, free markets, football, hockey, wrestling or any other form of rigorous competition should be cake walks?

And why did they keep coming? Were things really that bad in America? Maybe the law could have paid closer attention to bribery, excessive immigration quotas, language barriers, fraud and corruption - but a speculative, unproven amendment for that hard-won, respectable Constitution of the United States of America?

It would take a hundred years, but authors and researchers are beginning to discover that the industry and capitalism of the "Gilded Age" of the late 19th century was a net good thing for the United States in spite of those inflammatory and derogatory reports. The men who were called Robber Barons were often portrayed as tough, self-seeking egotists, like many fullbacks worthy of their letters. But they created good jobs for

American workers and slowly raised living standards everywhere, as well.

They were very sharing and benevolent in many constructive ways, too. I could find only one financial wizard (I won't call them Robbers anymore) who was not generous with his wealth – harboring it instead for his many children and grandchildren who squandered it all over many years. He will remain unidentified on the grounds that he, too, was nonetheless a net positive, increasing living standards for Americans everywhere with cheaper goods and services of every kind.

Burton Folsom, who holds the Charles F. Kline chair in history and management at Hillsdale College won't call them robbers either.[31] He tells an important side of the Progressive story in 2018, that, had it been told in 1906 (the year of Cosmopolitan's smear of America's Senators and industrial wizards), A17 might never have passed muster. I was personally psyched to discover that his book is widely used in high schools and universities.

Tom DiLorenzo is an American economics professor at the Loyola University Maryland Sellinger School of Business who identifies with the Austrian School of economics. He is a research fellow at The Independent Institute, a senior fellow of the Ludwig von Mises Institute, and an associate of the Abbeville Institute. Tom's book is especially valuable for the way it parses the difference between "market entrepreneurs" and "political entrepreneurs" – the former more upright and successful than the political chicanery of the monopolistic latter for interesting and revealing reasons based on "crony capitalism."

DiLorenzo, like Folsom, might have doomed the chancy A17 with his revealing account about Laissez-Faire Capitalism had it been available in 1906. He showed how free markets actually improved the lives of

31 Burton W. Folsom, Jr., *The Myth of the Robber Barons: The Untold History of Our Country, From the Pilgrims to the Present,"* 2004)

millions of Americans by providing jobs, newer and better products at higher wages and lower prices resulting in higher living standards. And he provides compelling evidence describing how price fixing and the socialist philosophy of Roosevelt and the New Deal actually made the Great Depression worse.

Attacks on Capitalism have been relentless and hateful ever since the 19th century. DiLorenzo invents a new word to describe the phenomenon: Anticapitalism - inspired by the exaggerated narratives of Michael Moore, modern media and Hollywood movie producers who depict Capitalism as a negative on consumers and the working-class. *"How Capitalism Saved America in Spite of the Influence of Anticapitalists"* would have been a more fitting title for DiLorenzo's book. Those who care about a better understanding of America's former greatness should consider both DiLorenzo and Folsom.

ANDREW CARNEGIE: ROBBER? OR BENEVOLENT INDUSTRIAL GENIUS?

The example of Andrew Carnegie[32] gives us reason to suspect that those malicious muckraking reports were somewhat less than honest. The worst that could be said about Carnegie was that he worked very hard; had a sharp eye for investment opportunities; was skillful in innovation and vertical integration; was a serious competitor who kept costs at a minimum – including labor costs that should be governed by market forces, not unilateral union or political forces; and he read voraciously. As his wealth grew, Carnegie, who began his career working for about 3 cents an hour ($1.20 a week), developed the principles of giving that would define him. America was fortunate to have neighbors like Andrew Carnegie.

When he was 33, Andrew Carnegie wrote a ***Letter to Himself***, urging himself to live modestly and charitably:

---

32 McCreary, Matthew, *"How Andrew Carnegie Went From $1.20 a Week to $309 Billion ... Then Gave It All Away,"* 2018) (see also: https://www.entrepreneur.com/article/317827)

December, 1868
St. Nicholas Hotel, New York
Thirty-three and an income of $50,000 per annum.

By these two years I can so arrange all my business as to secure at least 50,000 per annum. Beyond this never earn -- make no effort to increase fortune, but spend the surplus each year for benevolent purposes. Cast aside business forever except for others. Settle in Oxford and get a thorough education, making the acquaintance of literary men this will take three years active work -- pay especial attention to speaking in public.

Settle then in London & purchase a controlling interest in some newspaper or live review & give the general management of it attention, taking a part in public matters especially those connected with education & improvement of the poorer classes. Man must have an idol -- the amassing of wealth is one of the worst species of idolatry. No idol more debasing than the worship of money. Whatever I engage in I must push inordinately therefore should I be careful to choose that life which will be the most elevating in its character.

To continue much longer overwhelmed by business cares and with most of my thoughts wholly upon the way to make more money in the shortest time, must degrade me beyond hope of permanent recovery. I will resign business at 35, but during the ensuing two years, I wish to spend the afternoons in securing instruction, and in reading systematically.

———

Carnegie did not retire by the age of 35, as he had planned. Instead, he continued to grow his influence within the steel industry over the course of three decades. He opened his first steel plant in 1875, bought a rival steel company, the Homestead Steel Works, in 1883, and formed the Carnegie Steel Company in 1892.

Using technological advances including the Bessemer process and vertical integration, Carnegie built the largest steel empire in American history. When he eventually sold his company to John Pierpont Morgan, it was the largest deal in American history -- $480 million, of which Carnegie's share was worth more than $225 million.

Carnegie was 66 when he sold his company in 1901, retiring 31 years later than he had predicted. However, he did spend the rest of his career in philanthropic pursuits. In his most famous piece of writing, *The Gospel of Wealth*, Carnegie said that "The man who dies thus rich dies disgraced," and he spent the rest of his life doing his best to live by that code. From 1901 until his death in 1919, Carnegie distributed $350 million to schools, libraries, colleges and other public works, primarily across the English-speaking world. He believed that the best way to spend what he called "excess wealth" was to put it to long-lasting causes for world peace, art and education. Despite his efforts, Carnegie still died rich. In his will, Carnegie gave $30 million, the bulk of his remaining fortune, to the Carnegie Corporation, which he hoped would help establish international laws and foster world peace.

THE GOSPEL OF WEALTH
By Andrew Carnegie
North American Review, June, 1889

[Note: This eloquent Carnegie essay is resurrected from the forgotten dust bin of history and posted here for the purpose of presenting another side of the story about those so-called "Robber Barons"; to assist in defending this gentleman's reputation; to cast doubt on the integrity and honesty of Progressive Era muckrakers who tried, using the bad examples of a few, to bury the entire lot of valuable industrialists, inventors and innovators as sinners who should be remembered only in terms of criminal activity, guilt, shame and dishonor. After reading Carnegie's philosophy, you might be given to wonder who the real sinners were in those days – and what the real basis for A17 was. Carnegie gave away virtually all of his billions before he died, (as did many of his fellow victims of vicious yellow journalism), but he did so judiciously, being very careful to avoid doing more harm than good – but I'll let this honorable baron have the floor.]

—

"The problem of our age is the proper administration of wealth, so that the ties of brotherhood may still bind together the rich and poor in harmonious relationship. The conditions of human life have not only been changed, but revolutionized, within the past few hundred years. In former days there was little difference between the dwelling, dress, food, and environment of the chief and those of his retainers. The Indians are to-day where civilized man then was. When visiting the Sioux, I was led to the wigwam of the chief. It was just like the others in external appearance, and even within the difference was trifling between it and those of the poorest of his braves. The contrast between the palace of the millionaire and the cottage of the laborer with us today measures the change which has come with civilization.

This change, however, is not to be deplored, but welcomed as highly beneficial. It is well, nay, essential for the progress of the race, that the houses of some should be homes for all that is highest and best in literature and the arts, and for all the refinements of civilization, rather than that none should be so. Much better this great irregularity than universal squalor. Without wealth there can be no Mæcenas. The "good old times " were not good old times. Neither master nor servant was as well situated then as today. A relapse to old conditions would be disastrous to both--not the least so to him who serves--and would Sweep away civilization with it. But whether the change be for good or ill, it is upon us, beyond our power to alter, and therefore to be accepted and made the best of. It is a waste of time to criticize the inevitable.

It is easy to see how the change has come. One illustration will serve for almost every phase of the cause. In the manufacture of products, we have the whole story. It applies to all combinations of human industry, as stimulated and enlarged by the inventions of this scientific age. Formerly, articles were manufactured at the domestic hearth or in small shops which formed part of the household. The master and his apprentices worked side by side, the latter living with the master, and therefore subject to the same conditions. When these apprentices rose to be masters, there was little or no change in their mode of life, and they, in turn, educated in the same routine succeeding apprentices. There was, substantially social equality, and even political equality, for those engaged in industrial pursuits had then little or no political voice in the State. But the inevitable result of such a mode of manufacture was crude articles at high prices.

Today the world obtains commodities of excellent quality at prices which even the generation preceding this would have deemed incredible. In the commercial world similar causes have produced similar results, and the race is benefited thereby. The poor enjoy what the rich could not before afford. What were the luxuries have become the necessaries of life. The laborer has now more comforts than the landlord had a few generations ago. The farmer has more luxuries than the landlord had, and is more richly clad and better housed. The landlord has books and pictures rarer, and appointments more artistic, than the King could then obtain. The price we pay for this salutary change is, no doubt, great. We assemble thousands of operatives in the factory, in the mine, and in the counting-house, of whom the employer can know little or nothing, and to whom the employer is little better than a myth.

All intercourse between them is at an end. Rigid Castes are formed, and, as usual, mutual ignorance breeds mutual distrust. Each Caste is without sympathy for the other, and ready to credit anything disparaging in regard to it. Under the law of competition, the employer of thousands is forced into the strictest economies, among which the rates paid to labor figure prominently, and often there is friction between the employer and the employed, between capital and labor, between rich and poor. Human society loses homogeneity.

The price which society pays for the *law of competition*, like the price it pays for cheap comforts and luxuries, is also great; but the advantage of this law is also greater still, for it is to this law that we owe our wonderful material development, which brings improved conditions in its train. But, whether the law be benign or not, we must say of it, as we say of the change in the conditions of men to which we have referred: It is here; we cannot evade it; no substitutes for it have been found; and while the law may be sometimes hard for the individual, it is best for the race, because it insures the survival of the fittest in every department.

We accept and welcome therefore, as conditions to which we must accommodate ourselves, great inequality of environment, the concentration of business, industrial and commercial, in the hands of a few, and the law of competition between these, as being not only beneficial, but essential for the future progress of the race. Having accepted these, it follows that there must be great scope for the exercise of special ability in the merchant and in the manufacturer, who has to conduct affairs upon a great scale. *That this talent for organization and management is rare among men is proved by the fact that it invariably secures for its possessor enormous rewards, no matter where or under what laws or conditions.*

The experienced in affairs always rate the MAN whose services can be obtained as a partner as not only the first consideration, but such as to render the question of his capital scarcely worth considering, for such men soon create capital; while, *without the special talent required, capital soon takes wings.* Such men become interested in firms or corporations using millions; and estimating only simple interest to be made upon the capital invested, it is inevitable that their income must exceed their expenditures, and that they must accumulate wealth. Nor is there any middle ground which such men can occupy, because the great manufacturing or commercial concern which does not earn at least interest upon its capital soon becomes bankrupt. It, must either go forward or fall behind: to stand still is impossible. It is a condition essential for its successful operation that it should be thus far profitable, and even that, in addition to interest on capital, it should make profit. It is a law, as certain as any of the others named, that men possessed of this peculiar talent for affair, under the free play of economic forces, must, of necessity, soon be in receipt of more revenue than can be judiciously expended upon themselves; and this law is as beneficial for the race as the others.

Objections to the foundations upon which society is based are not in order, because the condition of the race is better with these than it has been with any others which have been tried. Of the effect of any new substitutes proposed we cannot be sure. *The Socialist or Anarchist who seeks to overturn present conditions is to be regarded as attacking the foundation upon which civilization itself rests,* for civilization took its start from the day that the capable, industrious workman said to his incompetent and lazy fellow, *"If thou dost not sow, thou shalt not reap," and thus ended Communism by separating the drones from the bees.*

One who studies this subject will soon be brought face to face with the conclusion that *upon the sacredness of property civilization itself depends- -the right of the laborer to his hundred dollars in the savings bank, and equally the legal right of the millionaire to his millions.*

To these who propose to substitute Communism for this intense Individualism the answer, therefore, is: The race has tried that. All progress from that barbarous day to the present time has resulted from its displacement. *Not evil, but good, has come to the race from the accumulation of wealth by those who have the ability and energy that produce it.*

But even if we admit for a moment that it might be better for the race to discard its present foundation, Individualism,--that it is a nobler ideal that man should labor, not for himself alone, but in and for a brotherhood of his fellows, and share with them all in common, realizing Swedenborg's idea of Heaven, where, as he says, the angels derive their happiness, not from laboring for self, but for each other,--even admit all this, and a sufficient answer is, This is not evolution, but revolution. It necessitates the changing of human nature itself a work of eons, even if it were good to change it, which we cannot know. It is not practicable in our day or in our age. Even if desirable theoretically, it belongs to another and long-succeeding sociological stratum.

Our duty is with what is practicable now; with the next step possible in our day and generation. *It is criminal to waste our energies in endeavoring to uproot, when all we can profitably or possibly accomplish is to bend the universal tree of humanity a little in the direction most favorable to the production of good fruit under existing circumstances. We might as well urge the destruction of the highest existing type of man because he failed to reach our ideal as favor the destruction of Individualism, Private Property, the Law of Accumulation of Wealth, and the Law of Competition; for these are the highest results of human experience, the soil in which society so far has produced the best fruit. Unequally or unjustly, perhaps, as these laws sometimes operate, and imperfect as they appear to the Idealist, they are, nevertheless, like the highest type of man, the best and most valuable of all that humanity has yet accomplished.*

We start, then, with a condition of affairs under which the best interests of the race are promoted, but which inevitably gives wealth to the few. Thus far, accepting conditions as they exist, the situation can be surveyed and pronounced good. The question then arises, --and, if the foregoing be correct, it is the only question with which we have to deal, --What is the proper mode of administering wealth after the laws upon which civilization is founded have thrown it into the hands of the few? And it is of this great question that I believe I offer the true solution. It will be understood that fortunes are here spoken of, not moderate sums saved by many years of effort, the returns on which are required for the comfortable maintenance and education of families. *This is not wealth, but only competence which it should be the aim of all to acquire.*

There are but three modes in which surplus wealth can be disposed of. It will be left to the families of the decedents; or it can be bequeathed for public purposes; or, finally, it can be administered during their lives by its possessors. Under the first and second modes most of the wealth of the world that has reached the few has hitherto been applied. Let us in turn consider each of these modes.

The first is the most injudicious. In monarchical countries, the eStates and the greatest portion of the wealth are left to the first son, that the vanity of the parent may be gratified by the thought that his name and title are to descend to succeeding generations unimpaired. The condition of this class in Europe to-day teaches the futility of such hopes or ambitions. The successors have become impoverished through their follies or from the fall in the value of land. Even in Great Britain the strict law of entail has been found inadequate to maintain the status of a hereditary class. Its soil is rapidly passing into the hands of the stranger. Under republican institutions the division of property among the children is much fairer, but the question which forces itself upon thoughtful men in all lands is: Why should men leave great fortunes to their children? If this is done from affection, is it not misguided affection?

Observation teaches that, generally speaking, it is not well for the children that they should be so burdened. Neither is it well for the state. Beyond providing for the wife and daughters moderate sources of income, and very moderate allowances indeed, if any, for the sons, men may well hesitate, for it is no longer questionable that great suns bequeathed oftener work more for the injury than for the good of the recipients. Wise men will soon conclude that, for the best interests of the members of their families and of the state, such bequests are an improper use of their means. It is not suggested that men who have failed to educate their sons to earn a livelihood shall cast them adrift in poverty. If any man has seen fit to rear his sons with a view to their living idle lives, or, what is highly commendable, has instilled in them the sentiment that they are in a position to labor for public ends without reference to pecuniary considerations, then, of course, the duty of the parent is to see that such are provided for in *moderation*. There are instances of millionaires' sons unspoiled by wealth, who, being rich, still perform great services in the community. Such are the very salt of the earth, as valuable as, unfortunately, they are rare; still it is not the exception, but the rule, that men must regard, and, looking at the usual result of enormous sums conferred upon legatees, the thoughtful man must shortly say, "I would as soon leave to my son a curse as the almighty dollar," and admit to himself that it is not the welfare of the children, but family pride, which inspires these enormous legacies.

As to the second mode, that of leaving wealth at death for public uses, it may be said that this is only a means for the disposal of wealth, provided a man is content to wait until he is dead before it becomes of much good in the world. Knowledge of the results of legacies bequeathed is not calculated to inspire the brightest hopes of much posthumous good being accomplished. The cases are not few in which the real object sought by the testator is not attained, nor are they few in which his real wishes are thwarted. In many cases the bequests are so used as to become only monuments of his folly. It is well to remember that it requires the exercise of not less ability than that which acquired the wealth to use it so as to be really beneficial to the community. Besides this, it may fairly be said that no man is to be extolled for doing what he cannot help doing, nor is he to be thanked by the community to which he only leaves wealth at death. Men who leave vast sums in this way may fairly be thought men who would not have left it at all, had they been able to take it with them. The memories of such cannot be held in grateful remembrance, for there is no grace in their gifts. It is not to be wondered at that such bequests seem so generally to lack the blessing.

The growing disposition to tax more and more heavily large eStates left at death is a cheering indication of the growth of a salutary change in public opinion. The State of Pennsylvania now takes--subject to some exceptions--one-tenth of the property left by its citizens. The budget presented in the British Parliament the other day proposes to increase the death-duties; and, most significant of all, the new tax is to be a graduated one. Of all forms of taxation, this seems the wisest. Men who continue hoarding great sums all their lives, the proper use of which for public ends would work good to the community, should be made to feel that the community, in the form of the state, cannot thus be deprived of its proper share. By taxing eStates heavily at death, the state marks its condemnation of the selfish millionaire's unworthy life. It is desirable; that nations should go much further in this direction. Indeed, it is difficult to set bounds to the share of a rich man's estate which should go at his death to the public through the agency of the state, and by all means such taxes should be graduated, beginning at nothing upon moderate sums to dependents, and increasing rapidly as the amounts swell, until of the millionaire's hoard, as of Shylock's, at least "The other half Comes to the privy coffer of the state."

This policy would work powerfully to induce the rich man to attend to the administration of wealth during his life, which is the end that society should always have in view, as being that by far most fruitful for the people. Nor need it be feared that this policy would sap the root of enterprise and render men less anxious to accumulate, for to the class whose ambition it is to leave great fortunes and be talked about after their death, it will attract even more attention, and, indeed, be a somewhat nobler ambition to have enormous sums paid over to the state from their fortunes.

There remains, then, only one mode of using great fortunes; but in this we have the true antidote for the temporary unequal distribution of wealth, the reconciliation of the rich and the poor--a reign of harmony--another ideal, differing, indeed, from that of the Communist in requiring only the further evolution of existing conditions, not the total overthrow of our civilization. It is founded upon the present most intense individualism, and the race is projected to put it in practice by degree whenever it pleases. Under its sway we shall have an ideal state, in which the surplus wealth of the few will become, in the best sense the property of the many, because administered for the common good, and this wealth, passing through the hands of the few, can be made a much more potent force for the elevation of our race than if it had been distributed in small sums to the people themselves. Even the poorest can be made to see this, and to agree that great sums gathered by some of their fellow-citizens and spent for public purposes, from which the masses reap the principal benefit, are more valuable to them than if scattered among them through the course of many years in trifling amounts.

If we consider what results flow from the Cooper Institute, for instance, to the best portion of the race in New York not possessed of means, and compare these with those which would have arisen for the good of the masses from an equal sum distributed by Mr. Cooper in his lifetime in the form of wages, which is the highest form of distribution, being for work done and not for charity, we can form some estimate of the possibilities for the improvement of the race which lie embedded in the present law of the accumulation of wealth. Much of this sum if distributed in small quantities among the people, would have been wasted in the indulgence of appetite, some of it in excess, and it may be doubted whether even the part put to the best use, that of adding to the comforts of the home, would have yielded results for the race, as a race, at all comparable to those which are flowing and are to flow from the Cooper Institute from generation to generation. Let the advocate of violent or radical change ponder well this thought.

We might even go so far as to take another instance, that of Mr. Tilden's bequest of five millions of dollars for a free library in the city of New York, but in referring to this one cannot help saying involuntarily, how much better if Mr. Tilden had devoted the last years of his own life to the proper administration of this immense sum; in which case neither legal contest nor any other cause of delay could have interfered with his aims. But let us assume that Mr. Tilden's millions finally become the means of giving to this city a noble public library, where the treasures of the world contained in books will be open to all forever, without money and without price. Considering the good of that part of the race which congregates in and around Manhattan Island, would its permanent benefit have been better promoted had these millions been allowed to circulate in small sums through the hands of the masses? Even the most strenuous advocate of Communism must entertain a doubt upon this subject. Most of those who think will probably entertain no doubt whatever.

Poor and restricted are our opportunities in this life; narrow our horizon; our best work most imperfect; but rich men should be thankful for one inestimable boon. They have it in their power during their lives to busy themselves in organizing benefactions from which the masses of their fellows will derive lasting advantage, and thus dignify their own lives. The highest life is probably to be reached, not by such imitation of the life of Christ as Count Tolstoi gives us, but, while animated by Christ's spirit, by recognizing the changed conditions of this age, and adopting modes of expressing this spirit suitable to the changed conditions under which we live; still laboring for the good of our fellows, which was the essence of his life and teaching, but laboring in a different manner.

This, then, is held to be the duty of the man of Wealth: First, to set an example of modest, unostentatious living, shunning display or extravagance; to provide moderately for the legitimate wants of those dependent upon him; and after doing so to consider all surplus revenues which come to him simply as trust funds, which he is called upon to administer, and strictly bound as a matter of duty to administer in the manner which, in his judgment, is best calculated to produce the most beneficial results for the community--the man of wealth thus becoming the mere agent and trustee for his poorer brethren, bringing to their service his superior wisdom, experience and ability to administer, doing for them better than they would or could do for themselves.

We are met here with the difficulty of determining what are moderate sums to leave to members of the family; what is modest, unostentatious living; what is the test of extravagance. There must be different standards for different conditions. The answer is that it is as impossible to name exact amounts or actions as it is to define good manners, good taste, or the rules of propriety; but, nevertheless, these are verities, well known although undefinable. Public sentiment is quick to know and to feel what offends these. So, in the case of wealth. The rule in regard to good taste in the dress of men or women applies here. Whatever makes one conspicuous offends the canon. If any family be chiefly known for display, for extravagance in home, table, equipage, for enormous sums ostentatiously spent in any form upon itself, if these be its chief distinctions, we have no difficulty in estimating its nature or culture. So likewise, in regard to the use or abuse of its surplus wealth, or to generous, freehanded cooperation in good public uses, or to unabated efforts to accumulate and hoard to the last, whether they administer or bequeath. The verdict rests with the best and most enlightened public sentiment. The community will surely judge and its judgments will not often be wrong.

The best uses to which surplus wealth can be put have already been indicated. These who would administer wisely must, indeed, be wise, for one of the serious obstacles to the improvement of our race is indiscriminate charity. It were better for mankind that the millions of the rich were thrown in to the sea than so spent as to encourage the slothful, the drunken, the unworthy. Of every thousand dollars spent in so called charity today, it is probable that $950 is unwisely spent; so spent, indeed as to produce the very evils which it proposes to mitigate or cure. A well-known writer of philosophic books admitted the other day that he had given a quarter of a dollar to a man who approached him as he was coming to visit the house of his friend. He knew nothing of the habits of this beggar; knew not the use that would be made of this money, although he had every reason to suspect that it would be spent improperly. This man professed to be a disciple of Herbert Spencer; yet the quarter-dollar given that night will probably work more injury than all the money which its thoughtless donor will ever be able to give in true charity will do good. He only gratified his own feelings, saved himself from annoyance, -- and this was probably one of the most selfish and very worst actions of his life, for in all respects he is most worthy.

In bestowing charity, the main consideration should be to help those who will help themselves; to provide part of the means by which those who desire to improve may do so; to give those who desire to use the aids by which they may rise; to assist, but rarely or never to do all. Neither the individual nor the race is improved by alms-giving. Those worthy of assistance, except in rare cases, seldom require assistance. The really valuable men of the race never do, except in cases of accident or sudden change. Everyone has, of course, cases of individuals brought to his own knowledge where temporary assistance can do genuine good, and these he will not overlook. But the amount which can be wisely given by the individual for individuals is necessarily limited by his lack of knowledge of the circumstances connected with each. He is the only true reformer who is as careful and as anxious not to aid the unworthy as he is to aid the worthy, and, perhaps, even more so, *for in alms-giving more injury is probably done by rewarding vice than by relieving virtue.*

The rich man is thus almost restricted to following the examples of Peter Cooper, Enoch Pratt of Baltimore, Mr. Pratt of Brooklyn, Senator Stanford, and others, *who know that the best means of benefiting the community is to place within its reach the ladders upon which the aspiring can rise--parks, and means of recreation, by which men are helped in body and mind; works of art, certain to give pleasure and improve the public taste, and public institutions of various kinds, which will improve the general condition of the people;--in this manner returning their surplus wealth to the mass of their fellows in the forms best calculated to do them lasting good.*

Thus is the problem of Rich and Poor to be solved. The laws of accumulation will be left free; the laws of distribution free. *Individualism will continue, but the millionaire will be but a trustee for the poor; entrusted for a season with a great part of the increased wealth of the community, but administering it for the community far better than it could or would have done for itself.* The best minds will thus have reached a stage in the development of the race in which it is clearly seen that there is no mode of disposing of surplus wealth creditable to thoughtful and earnest men into whose hands it flows save by using it year by year for the general good. This day already dawns. But a little while, and although, without incurring the pity of their fellows, men may die sharers in great business enterprises from which their capital cannot be or has not been withdrawn, and is left chiefly at death for public uses, *yet the man who dies leaving behind many millions of available wealth, which was his to administer during life, will pass away " unwept, unhonored, and unsung," no matter to what uses he leaves the dross which he cannot take with him. Of such as these the public verdict will then be: "The man who dies thus rich dies disgraced."*

Such, in my opinion, is the true Gospel concerning Wealth, obedience to which is destined someday to solve the problem of the Rich and the Poor, and to bring 'Peace on earth, among men of Good-Will.'"

Andrew Carnegie

———

The mystery of the Soviet Union or any other communist country is not why it produced so little, but why it produced anything at all.
Theodore Dalrymple, English Cultural Critic and Psychiatrist

THEODORE "Teddy" ROOSEVELT

The below quote from Teddy Roosevelt illustrates the bias and selective attention often given to the dichotomy between the rich and the poor. Here, from a 1912 campaign speech, Roosevelt capitalizes on popular sentiment by castigating the small minority (industrialists who "grab" our coal deposits and water power) when in fact it is the majority, not the minority, who "grab," by way of proxy and popular demands for a better life. And in the process, Teddy, and the spiteful and envious public he hopes to win the support of, forgets that those demands can only be facilitated by consumption of the very coal deposits and water power needed to provide for those demands. Teddy and his followers, moreover, seemed to forget that the rich became that way because the majority rewarded the best producer of quality and economy with their dollar vote. Presto, chango: one efficient entrepreneur who wins a dollar of profit by the dollar vote of one million satisfied customers each, likely produces one competent millionaire. Teddy would not have agreed, but America was lucky to have had such efficient millionaires.

> "I have scant patience with this talk of the tyranny of the majority. Whenever there is tyranny of the majority, I shall protest against it with all my heart and soul.... It is a small minority that is grabbing our coal deposits, our water powers, our harbor fronts.... The only tyrannies from which men, women and children are suffering in real life are the tyrannies of minorities."
>
> (Theodore Roosevelt, Campaign Speech, 1912; as reported by Hillsdale College in *The US Constitution: A Reader*, p. 683)

HENRY GEORGE, EXODUS OF BUSINESS, AND THE 20/2 WAGE CONTRAST

So, how do we explain the concurrence of abject poverty with dramatic wealth formation and wage growth? Henry George, previously cited, comes up with a plausible explanation:

*"I asked a passing teamster, for want of something better to
say, what land was worth there. He pointed to some cows
grazing so far off that they looked like mice, and said, "I
don't know exactly, but there is a man over there who will
sell some land for a thousand dollars an acre." Like a flash
it came over me that there was the reason of advancing
poverty with advancing wealth. With the growth of
population, land (or real estate) grows in value, and the
men who work it must pay more for the privilege."*
George, Henry, 1879

Henry George wrote *Progress and Poverty* in order to identify and resolve
the great paradox of modern industrial life. How was it possible that
abject poverty, financial instability, and extreme economic inequality
could co-exist with rising productivity and technological progress? He
analyzed and rejected the widely held beliefs that poverty inevitably followed from the laws of economics or from a Darwinian struggle for survival of the fittest. George concluded that at the heart of this dilemma
was how society treated natural resources, especially urban land. He did
not succumb to the panacea of arbitrarily confiscating property or taking from the rich to give to the poor. George argued that taxes on productive labor and capital should be drastically reduced. His "sovereign
remedy" declared that public goods could be adequately funded from the
returns to land and other natural resources. The activities of society as a
whole give land its value. It is therefore both equitable and efficient for
the community to tax or recapture land values to support the activities
of government.

George's book was so popular that its sales volume was exceeded only
by the Bible during the Progressive Era. His complicated formulas for
taxes seemed to be biased more for labor and less for business; and may
have been, in addition to A17, indirectly responsible for the slow decay
and disappearance of formerly vigorous native commerce like the old
textile and shoe industries of New England, the ship builders of New

Jersey, the automobile, electronics and steel industries, and so on. The Wagner Act, minimum wage laws, ensuing wage/post/price spirals and the 20/2 wage dichotomy - $20 per hour here; $2 a day overseas – together and separately might have been partly responsible for the decay, as well. Such laws and conditions might have evolved differently under the more visionary wisdom of a clearer thinking, pre-1913 Senate.

Harry, my old legal beagle buddy (not his real name) once expressed it best to me during a hypothetical discussion over a cup of coffee.

"Lordy," he proclaimed with wide, bloodshot eyes, "I think I would rather be ruled by one millionaire like Andrew Carnegie or Bill Gates than a hundred of the lower east side residents that resided in Manhattan and voted during the Progressive Era."

"Gosh," I said, then asked, "can I echo that in my book?"

"No," he responded. "Not unless you want your house set on fire. If you do, keep me out of it. I don't need the hassle."

We then devolved into a discussion about qualifiers for voters which, in colonial days, required that voters be owners of property to demonstrate a modicum of ability. We both agreed that a minimum qualifier these days should be home ownership and a certificate in History 101. But then we were forced to reject the idea because most folks cared little about the basics that qualified our supremely educated founders to set the stage for us.

> *"If the people of the United States have enough intelligence to choose their representatives in the state legislature, . . . they have enough intelligence to choose the men (to) represent them in the U.S. Senate."*
> (Senator William Jennings Bryan; from Rossum, R. A.; p. 191)

Chapter 18

THE ROLE OF THE SUPREME COURT

"The enumeration in the Constitution of certain rights, shall not be construed To deny or disparage others retained by the people."
The Constitution of the United States of America, Amendment IX

"The powers not delegated to the United States by the Constitution, nor prohibited by it to the States, are reserved to the States respectively, or to the people."
The Constitution of the United States of America, Amendment X

"I, _____, do solemnly swear (or affirm) that I will support and defend the   Constitution of the United States against all enemies, foreign and domestic; that I will bear true faith and allegiance to the same; that I take this obligation freely, without any mental reservation or purpose of evasion; and that I will well and faithfully discharge the duties of the office on which I am about to enter. So help me God."
(Oath in support of the Constitution required of all federal officials, Article VI)

As it was in the Frank Sinatra song, *High Hopes*, and that little old ram who kept buttin' that dam, so also was it with Progressives who kept arguing forcefully and persistently, over many years, that a critical obstruction in our Constitution had to be removed. As that stubborn goat seemed unwilling to trouble himself with the vision of a busted dam, so also did Progressives not bother about making any estimates of possible long-term damage to a Constitution modified in a way the founders would have rejected as demonstrated by their detailed notes on the subject from the Convention of 1787. Any possible damage caused by that modification, or even an objective estimate of its impact on the future of America, would have no standing whatever.

As no one could make that ram scram; so too, were Progressives persistent, unrelenting and determined to get State legislators out of the way of "progress." And by golly, just as Sinatra philosophized musically about the need for gritty ambition to get things done as in "oops, there goes a billion-kilowatt dam," there went part of a brilliant plan.

Though it took a while, their arguments were so compelling and brought with such emotional force as to be undeniable in the end; that nothing should stand in the way: not federalism; not republicanism; not Senates; not free markets; not founders' intentions; not empty treasuries; not common sense; and certainly not property rights or Amendment IX or Amendment X or prescribed oaths intended to protect, defend, retain, honor, preserve and reserve powers not delegated to the United States *"to the States respectively, or to the people."*

As that goat overlooked the likely consequences of a broken dam, so also did Progressives forget to assess the possible costs of a Constitution damaged by A17, giving scant regard for the careful thought given to its construction. It weakened federalism, partially neutered the States as States, and paved the way for federal government overreach, unmanageable debt and inflation.

The founders anticipated such mischief. While they expected the potential for problems with checks, balances and federalism; they might have been inclined to say, if they had been present to observe the aforementioned Progressive determination: "Not to worry, good people. We anticipated such shenanigans and installed redundant safeguards. To Wit: The Ninth and Tenth Amendments and, for reinforcement, the Supreme Court which, together with all government officials, would be required to swear an oath to support and defend the United States Constitution which we equipped with clauses specifically designed to obviate any desire for the federal government, or any of its alliances, to interfere with property rights and freedoms we declared to be sacrosanct and inviolable."

Which brings us to an analysis of two primary remedies for the preservation of dual state/federal responsibilities, aka federalism: (1) Senators to serve, in part, as State ambassadors to, and checks on, the federal government, and (2) policing powers of the Supreme Court reinforced by Amendments IX, X and the specific enumeration of federal powers. But A17 changed Senate appointments from State legislatures to the People thereby creating a new kind of Senator who is now primarily responsible to the People; only secondarily to their respective States.

So, the first of those two leashes designed to check big government, in large part, is diminished. Before I comment on the possible decline of the second, and since it could rightfully be charged that I'm the least of all legal experts, I'd like to ask a truly simple question or two in order to set a simple theme: "How did it come to pass, given what we know about specified enumerated powers delegated to the United States, that the feds became so involved with the health of people, the education of people, and the welfare of people? Are these not powers reserved to the State, or to the People since they were not specifically enumerated for the United States?"

What is it about Amendments IX and X that makes it so difficult for U.S. Government officials, members of the U.S. Legislature and Supreme Court judges to understand? Or so easy to ignore? Was the Progressive movement so powerful and compelling that we should now ignore simple constitutional sentences written in a style nearly impossible to misconstrue?

I posed those questions to my old legal beagle buddy and favorite collaborator, Harold, for whom I have the highest regard.

"It partly boils down to the way the Supreme Court (SCOTUS) interprets the Commerce Clause," he said, "in combination with the powerful influence of the Progressive movement."

Harry further stated, "the health issue is a dizzying array of complex problems in education, funding, terrorism, overlapping responsibilities, and training, any of which could easily impact many States simultaneously." He stated emphatically that federal involvement and such things as federally sponsored research and the Center for Disease Control (CDC) are good things nonetheless. "It's important for people to have good health. It's a universal concern."

"Simply put," knowing me to be charged emotionally about these things, "pandemics, pollution and terrorism know no state boundaries." Harry continues, "that said, I do believe that the Supreme Court can be oppressive, even tyrannical. Exhibit A would be the SCOTUS decision in *Dred Scott v. Sanford* (1857) which affirmed the right for one human to own another. And I would nominate as Exhibit B, the recent SCOTUS decision affirming the right of government to penalize those who did not buy health insurance."

Harry went on, "There were education inequities in southern States during the Reconstruction Era which spawned the 14th Amendment and equal protection. Everywhere there were heinous persecutions of black people and miserable Jim Crow laws to contend with." After a short pause for a google search, he added, "In a 1954 decision, *Brown v. Board of Education,* the Supreme Court declared as unconstitutional the segregation of public schools and gave the executive branch legal precedent for enforcing equal access to education."

We both agreed with the SCOTUS decision, but I did a brief google search of my own to resurrect evidence about how that case led to questionable federal expansion.

The search verified the almost forgotten. President Johnson encouraged passage of *"The Elementary and Secondary Education Act"* (ESEA) in 1965. The justifiable bill was a key part of the War on Poverty, but it set the basic terms of the federal government's involvement in education and welfare. The incentives-with-caveats formula allowed the federal government to work around the 10th Amendment and have a greater hand in enforcing the 14th. It provided both the carrot of federal funds and the stick of their withdrawal. (see: https://www.gse.harvard.edu/news/ed/17/08/when-it-comes-education-federal-government-charge-um-what)

"What about the dozen, or more, federal welfare programs that belong more properly to the States?" I asked Harry. "You'd be correct to say that States were not required to adopt those programs; that they could have devised their own programs as they had the right to do. But they let the feds intervene because of so-called "carrot/stick" bribery facilitated with IOUs issued to those not yet born – an inflationary spectacle referred to as *"The Big Gorge"* by John J. DeIulio, Ph.D., of the Brookings Institute."

According to 18 U.S. Code § 201, bribery refers to the *offering, giving, soliciting, or receiving of any item of value as a means of influencing the actions of an individual holding a public or legal duty.*

"It's a fraud worth as much as 15 years in the big house," I alleged vehemently. (Too bad the code refers to the singular, which would undoubtedly exempt any collective practice of the art).

I continued, "If States denied the feds offer (a benevolent form of extortion), which they didn't, they wouldn't receive federal funding. If States were influenced to act by receiving any item(s) of value (federal programs), which they did, that's called bribery, Harry, pure and simple, by both parties – the giver and the receiver to quote Wes Law." I claimed that bribery is at work here – a synonym of corruption. Both bribery and corruption can be used synonymously in the same sentence. Both are classified as federal crimes. Harry seemed unimpressed.

In an expression of empathy, Harry responded, "Look, I agree that government can be somewhat invasive into powers not delegated to them, federal welfare programs would rank as primary examples with me."

"Hoover and Roosevelt started welfare because of the depression. They had good intentions. People were hurting. But I agree with you. The welfare of people is clearly a function of the State and its People. In my personal opinion, it should be reserved as such."

I fumed a little about some of the testimony I helped get on the record while serving on the world's first *New Hampshire Commission on the Status of Men* which was enacted, in part, "to bring fathers and their children closer together." [Chapter 19-I, NH Statutes, 2010] (Four biennial reports can be seen at: www.nhmenscommission.org)

"We should consider the distinct possibility, Harry, that while those programs did help many single mothers who were having serious problems with poverty, they also discouraged, to a considerable degree, the formation of the more economically viable traditional family while facilitating single lifestyles and fatherlessness which David Blankenhorn wrote about in his book, *Fatherless America: Confronting Our Most Urgent*

Social Problem. I believe Amendment Seventeen, which on its face was well-intentioned, unwittingly and indirectly influenced the unforeseeable." Harry seemed dumbstruck.

> *"That is not a just government, nor is property secure under*
> *it, where the Property which a man has in his personal*
> *safety and personal liberty, is violated by arbitrary seizures*
> *of one class of citizens for the service of the rest."*
> James Madison, 1792

THE COMMERCE CLAUSE

> *"To regulate Commerce with foreign Nations, and among*
> *the several States, and with Indian Tribes."*
> Constitution of the United States of America; Article I,
> Section 8

Rossum has shown how the Supreme Court, in efforts thought to be attempts at restoring the state/federal balance of old, struck down a dozen federal laws in recent years because of findings that the U.S. Government was interfering excessively with responsibilities belonging to the States, or its People. In one notable case, *United States v. Morrison*, Chief Justice Rehnquist stated that to uphold Congress's claim of authority under the commerce clause would "completely obliterate the Constitution's distinction between national and local authority." It could be reasonably alleged that a pre-A17 Senate might never have allowed the passage of such laws to begin with. (See Rossum, Ralph A., 2001, Chapter 1)

Those dozen SCOTUS cases were much-needed improvements in respect for the founder's design, but it may have been too little, too late. Where were SCOTUS judges in the 30s when inappropriate and downright illegal federal invasions into responsibilities belonging to the States and its People were building a head of steam into no-brainer state responsibilities like, umm, the education of people and the welfare of people?

> *The consequences of the ratification of the Seventeenth*
> *Amendment on Federalism went completely unexplored,*
> *and the people, in their desire to make the Constitution*
> *more democratic, inattentively abandoned what the framers*
> *regarded as the crucial constitutional means for protecting*
> *the state/federal balance and the interests of States as States.*
> Rossum, Ralph A., 2001

Some feel that our Constitution is outdated; that it was fabricated by a factious, selfish collection of "rich, educated white slave owners" who gave us a faulty document to begin with and who "cared little about the poor or disadvantaged." Others simply dismiss the controversy by saying, "The people have spoken. They want closer control over the Senate. It's democracy in action. Deal with it."

Rossum and others assert that the long struggle to transform the Framers' exquisite compound democratic/federal structure into a democratic form deadly to republics, culminated in the passage of A17.

Supporters of A17 allege that we should have a higher level of democracy. By right of reasonable inspection of age-old evidence exposing pure democracy as failures, however, we were given a republican tradition - until A17 came along.

The national debt (with its annual service costs) increased only slightly over the 100 years prior to 1913. In the 100-year period following 1913, the national debt grew from about $3 billion to more than $300 billion. Our debt now totals, by official estimates, more than $20 trillion. If standard accounting practices were used to include vested entitlement obligations, that indebtedness would be reported as a whopping $100 trillion according to estimates by conventionofStates.com.

Virtually no one from either side of the aisle in either the House or the Senate would dare give their blessings to such a debt even as they seem incapable or unwilling, under our partially damaged republic, to do anything about it. Such was not the case prior to 1913 and A17.

THE NECESSARY AND PROPER CLAUSE

The Necessary and Proper Clause allows Congress "To make all Laws which shall be *necessary and proper for carrying into Execution the <u>enumerated Powers</u>, (emphasis added) and all other Powers vested by this Constitution in the Government of the United States, or in any Department or Officer thereof.*" (Article I, Section 8, Clause 18). It is also sometimes called the "elastic clause." It grants Congress the powers that are *implied* in the Constitution, but that are not explicitly stated. That is why the powers derived from the Necessary and Proper Clause are referred to as implied powers.

The correct way to interpret the Necessary and Proper Clause was the subject of intense debate between Secretary of the Treasury Alexander Hamilton and Secretary of State Thomas Jefferson. Hamilton argued for an expansive interpretation of the clause. His view would have authorized Congress to exercise a broad range of implied powers. On the other hand, Jefferson was concerned about vesting too much power in any one branch of government. He argued that "necessary" was a restrictive adjective meaning *essential*. **Jefferson's interpretation would have strengthened States' Rights** (emphasis added). George Washington and James Madison favored Hamilton's more flexible interpretation, and subsequent events helped foster the growth of a strong central government.

THE GENERAL WELFARE CLAUSE

Article I, Section 8, reads, "The Congress shall have Power to lay and collect Taxes, Duties, Imposts and Excises, to pay the Debts and provide for the common Defense and General Welfare of the United States." This clause, called the General Welfare Clause or the Spending Power

Clause, does not grant Congress the power to legislate for the general welfare of the country; that is a power reserved to the States through the Tenth Amendment.

It only allowed Congress to spend federal money for the general welfare (as opposed to selected welfare). The principle underlying this distinction—the limitation of federal power—eventually inspired the only important disagreement over the meaning of the clause that persists to this day.

According to James Madison, the clause authorized Congress to spend money, but only to carry out the powers and duties specifically enumerated in the subsequent clauses of Article I, Section 8, and elsewhere in the Constitution, not to meet the seemingly infinite needs of the general public. Alexander Hamilton posited that the clause granted Congress the power to spend without limitation for the general welfare of the nation. The winner of this debate seems to have ended with the enactment of Amendment Seventeen on May 31, 1913.

Chapter 19

SUMMARY AND CONCLUSION

> *But the will so declared was to be mature, deliberate, well-considered—its sober second thought. They were building for centuries, not for hours. They were prescribing the laws of health and growth for a mighty national life, compared with whose duration years, terms of Presidential office, generations of men are but as the pulsation of an artery.*
> Senator George F. Hoar, 1890

We should not exit this dissertation without a further effort, however speculative or impossible to prove, in estimating what might have been if Amendment Seventeen had never been enacted. [Oh, what we wouldn't give to have a few founders presiding over this effort.]

It's true that the Senate of yore had to contend with difficult and contentious problems – especially those of the Civil War era. One eloquent northern abolitionist, Senator Sumner, was severely thrashed with the cane of a southern slavery zealot, Senator Brooks, who lost his cool. But they deliberated, in the main, with a higher level of wisdom, dignity and thought for the long term that seems to exist to a lesser extent in the Senate these days.

Today's Senators seem chained more to the factious passions of the public and less to the chains of the Constitution, even as it was revised by A17. Reelections now depend more on popular approval and less on State legislatures. A recently released book by Caldwell describes this phenomenon in considerable detail.[33]

Our mountain of debt gives mute testimony to that disorder. For the entire 19th century, under the supervision and influence of the Senate as structured by our founders, debt was virtually non-existent. Today, the national debt, along with its annual service costs would be totally out of control were it not for FED manipulation of interest rates that should be a function of the open market. The relatively sudden, exponential increase in federal deficit spending (and accompanying debt costs) should, by itself, suffice to justify a thorough review of A17's impact.

Poverty was a problem in the Gilded Age, even though GDP and wages were rising as never before. Poverty is a problem now, even as the debt balloons in efforts to fix it. Poverty has been a problem since before the Bible was written. Poverty is eternal – more or less depending on the inventive genius and efficiencies that seem to accompany free markets. Poverty and the benevolent desire to cure it gave us A17. But poverty was not cured by A17; nor will it be cured by a hundred such amendments. The attempt to fix poverty now seems to depend more on future incomes and less on the availability of jobs. As recently as 2014, New York City reported 45.1% of its residents living at or near poverty, a rate that would rival that of the Progressive Era but for the constant injections of new money borrowed from the future, at which time the cycle will repeat with inflated intensity.

Today's poverty measurements might well reflect the same as those of the Progressive Era were it not for those constant, enormous injections of fiat money casually and irreverently gorged from those not yet born.

33 Caldwell, Christopher, *The Age of Entitlement*, 2020

In the old days the poor relied on neighbors, family, marriage and/ or local charities. With the advent of A17, the poor rely on remotely controlled federal programs thereby obviating the need for family and neighbors – even discouraging father involvement and local charity in too many cases. While serving on the *New Hampshire Commission on the Status of Men* a few years ago, I heard a father painfully testify how his divorcing wife responded to his claim that he wasn't earning enough to support three kids and two households. "It's okay," she allegedly said, "I can get money from the government."

The well-circulated story of a charitable doctor is another important example. After becoming involved with Medicaid, he reported a notable income increase on his 1099 which flagged the IRS who then investigated this good doctor as a potential con man. Such charity is less likely thanks to poorly conceived, well intentioned programs and the invisible influence of A17.

The record for family formation in the old days is difficult to obtain. But it's a safe bet that marriage was seen as a better poverty program than what exists in too many American neighborhoods today, where too many unsupervised children from too many impoverished single-parent homes gravitate toward too many unsavory criminal activities – even murder in the streets.

In the so-called Gilded Age, people were left to their own devices and most responded responsibly and constructively as well as they could. The result? A level of prosperity and achievement that made us the envy of the world. Under today's invisible influence of A17 and the neo culture of dependency, too many are encouraged to look to others – even the unborn - for a higher measure of life satisfaction and too often end up addicted to a variety of drugs, alcohol opioids and doubts about self-worth.

THE DEPRESSIONS OF 1920 AND 1930

A sketch comparison of the 1920 and 1930 depressions might help illustrate the difference between an administration operating under the influence of the old versus that of the new. "Old," in this context, refers to the Harding era and Senators who were appointed by their respective State legislatures prior to A17 and reelected by their new constituents, the public, after 1913; while the "new," during the Hoover/Roosevelt administrations of the 30s, refers to Senators who were entirely elected by the demanding public as provided for by A17.

Much has been written and remembered about the disastrous Hoover/ Roosevelt depression of the 1930s which, according to scholarly estimates, might have persisted well into the 1940s but for the outbreak of WWII. It was a very difficult time.

But how much is written or remembered about the Harding depression of 1920, an economic decline every bit as serious in its beginnings as that which occurred in 1930 – even more so when comparing the wage and GDP downdraft and the record for federal intervention in the first year of each. Severe commodity inflation was the precursor for the former, while intense stock inflation staged the latter.

Even as prices and wages plunged, President Harding, with apparent backing from a Senate comprising a mixture of the "old" and the "new," did nothing except slash the budget 65% in one year and cut taxes. Hoover and Roosevelt, on other hand, supported in part, by the "new" Senate did the exact opposite, intervening massively with spending, wage/price controls and social programs.[34]

It's morbidly fascinating, yet instructive, to speculate about how things might have developed if Harding, together with remnants of the "old" Senate, were presiding over the economic decline of 1930. And

---

34 Grant, James, *The Forgotten Depression*, 2015

conversely, how things would have fared if the "new" A17 Senate, together with interventionist Hoover followed by Progressive Roosevelt, had been in charge during the economic downdraft of 1920. Would a Great Depression of the 20s and a Roaring 30s have been the results?

We should carefully study the history of this dichotomy. According to Robert Murphy, senior economist at the Independent Energy Institute and research assistant professor with the Free Market Institute at Texas Tech University, the price deflation of the 1920 depression was worse. The Consumer Price Index fell 15.8 percent during that year. In contrast, year-over-year price deflation never reached 11 percent at any point during the Great Depression.[35]

The Harding depression lasted only a year and a half and set the stage for the roaring twenties. The Hoover/Roosevelt depression, on the other hand, lingered for many years. For his "Hands Off" policy, Harding was vilified as a do-nothing president; while Roosevelt was seen as one of the best presidents we ever had primarily because he radiated good intentions (under the auspices of a "new" Senate).

Economist John Maynard Keynes, well respected for his theories on fiscal stimulus, was once asked during the worst of the Great Depression: "Has there ever been anything this bad in human history?" Keynes responded, apparently unaware of Harding's hands-off cure for an economic downdraft having the same potential: "Not since the Dark Ages." One of Keynes' disciples, New York Times economist Paul Krugman, won a Nobel Prize for recommending an equivalent fiscal stimulus to cure the Great Recession of 2008. The siren of debt as a source of economic relief knows no bounds it seems, not even in the magnificent halls of the Nobel Foundation.

---

35 Murphy, Robert P., *The Politically Incorrect Guide to the Great Depression*, 2009

The first federally dictated minimum wage came about as a result of the Fair Labor Standards Act of 1938, which guaranteed "employees who are engaged in interstate commerce or in the production of goods for commerce, or who are employed by an enterprise engaged in commerce or in the production of goods for commerce," 25 cents an hour. The next year, the minimum for these workers was raised a nickel to $0.30 an hour. This, despite the fact that prevailing market rates for entry level, low skilled jobs were 15 cents an hour.

Many workers in the United States were earning more than the minimum wage in 1938. But the marketplace, while showing signs of improvement around that time frame, could not sustain those wage minimums and suffered a further decline. Harding, apparently with the blessing of the "old" Senate, let wages and prices fall to levels that reignited the economy. Would it be unreasonable to speculate that Roosevelt should have echoed the same in order to reignite his economy; and that a wiser Senate might have helped pave the way?

THE MILITARY COMPLEX

It's hard to imagine a wiser, more deliberative Senate allowing such a buildup of the military complex we all know too well these days; or the sanction of policies and laws like the Gulf of Tonkin resolution, the War Powers Act or the Iraq War that arguably led to a permanent state of deadly entanglements most difficult to justify on hindsight. Could there be any doubt that the "old" Senate would have tolerated the shenanigans revealed in the Pentagon Papers or the more recent Afghanistan Papers?

The United States today has 72 nuclear powered submarines – 8 or 10 of which could kill the world 20 times. If that proved insufficient, we could unleash the whole lot of them. The development of such power is tremendously expensive, arguably unnecessary, and might have been more carefully reviewed under a wiser, clearer thinking Senate.

TO REPEAL OR NOT TO REPEAL?

"That should be the bottom-line question, shouldn't it?" I asked Harold, who seems to be tiring of the discussion. "Repeal, or at least redress and repair?"

"With what we know of the public's conviction that our founders erred in the way they constructed the Senate," he answered, "repeal is out of the question. You should just bring your account to the public and let it rest on the exposure you've given it. Just hope for more dialogue, good or bad. I think the former more likely than the latter might develop, if at all."

"That seems like a fair assessment, Harry," I said disappointedly. "But what if the public takes a closer look at the alleged differences between the old and the new, and the dubious way it was derived? Will they then be able to maintain that conviction in good conscience? Will they still believe, as Teddy Roosevelt believed, that the people 'will make fewer mistakes in governing themselves than any smaller class or body of men?' I don't think so, Harry. I think it's possible they would sanction at least a low-level repair that would restore some semblance of State legislative control over the Senate – like a short, bipartisan list approved by the legislature for the people to select from, or, inversely, the same brought instead, by the people to the legislature. Some States have already tried to move in that direction; New Hampshire being among the first, I'm proud to say."

"Whatever possessed you to tackle this mind-bender anyway?"

"The main prompt came when I read, '*Understanding the Dollar Crisis*,' where I discovered, much to my astonishment, that inflation rates were virtually zero throughout the entire 19th century. For sure, there were periodic and painful economic downdrafts with miserable poverty rates though declining over that time span in spite of the miserable conditions in crowded city slums. But the 20th century was even worse given the graphic descriptions of the 1920 depression, the 1930s depression; and we should include the Great Recession of 2008. Why should inflation be relatively stable throughout the 19th, then begin a trip to the moon in the 20th? Could A17 with its modified Senate be the root of these differences?"

"My interest with inflation began in 1944 and the busy bus and train stations of wartime Salem, Massachusetts where, as an 8-year-old, I hawked *The Salem Evening News* for 3 cents each. People would give me a nickel and wait patiently as I begged telepathically for them to let me keep the change. Pennies in those days meant something. Nine of them could buy a loaf of bread. Once in a while some nice little old lady would flip me a nickel and say, 'keep the change, sonny.'"

"Later on, I discovered how the Roman Empire allegedly fell into obscurity soon after debauching their own currency – somewhat like we're doing today. Copper and silver coins are no longer made of copper and silver; gold coins have disappeared; nobody can tell you what the basis for the dollar is; and the price for a cup of coffee at my favorite coffee shop just went up 50 percent to $1.50 just yesterday. In 1890, a cup of coffee could be bought for a penny. When my dad came home on leave from WWII, he threw a nickel on the counter for the same."

Today, people would scoff at questions to which I think I know the answer, but I raised them for Harry anyway for academic reasons (he often seems a little slow in the upstairs department):

"Why must we now - a cosmic instant later – pay a thirtyfold higher price for that same newspaper?" He had no answer – at least nothing that he cared to divulge.

Harry now displayed the demeanor of a psychiatrist. He wheedled as if to a peevish old man: "Why don't you forget about it. Go fishing or golfing. Life is good. Enjoy it. Let it go."

"Harry, for God's sake," I responded impatiently. "You might just as well try to stop a hound dog who thoroughly enjoys helping his master find an escaping criminal – even in alligator infested swamps."

I continued, "an anxious nose for clues soon brought me to the possibility that that obscure and forgotten Amendment Seventeen may rank as a primary cause for the negative symptoms I tried to described in detail. While the intense controversy that raged during most of the 19th century is virtually unknown today, the rationale used to downgrade our highly educated founders and our honorable Senators came as a profound shock to me. I couldn't stand the nauseating justification, the exaggeration and the damage we did to ourselves. I felt the need to do something, and so probed it."

"I often muse about what those 19th century operatives would have thought if they had been aware of the assessment described by Greaves in his 20th century book. Would they have fought so hard to change the method of electing the Senate?"

"And I often wonder as we all should wonder: How could we have generated such a great record for growth, innovation, constantly rising per capita GDP numbers, increasing wages, living standards and productivity while maintaining near-zero inflation rates? Why was the national debt, which hovered around only $1 or $2 billion throughout the entire 19th century, so much better managed than what appears to be the case after 1913? Why couldn't centuries 20 and 21 have echoed the same?" While he never mentioned A17, these questions bothered Percy Greaves, as well.

"You seem very confident about A17 being the root cause of many of our problems today, Mike. Maybe it was something else," said Harry, "like the growing world economy, world wars, ever increasing population numbers or the communist threat. It's a complicated world out there. Some claim we would have taken the exact same path, A17 or no A17 – old Senate or new Senate."

"I'll give you the complex," Harry, "But not the 'exact same path,' a position you yourself could validate by asking the next such supporter you meet to help you repeal A17 on the grounds that it made no difference. Only then will you understand, I guess."

"Didn't Alexander Hamilton recommend debt to stimulate business activity and facilitate government needs from the start?" Harry asked.

"Yes, he did," I answered. "But it came with the proviso that a sinking fund be established to properly manage and retire any debt deemed necessary by law. The Senate of old seems to have abided by those principles while the new seemingly abandoned it."

"Such questions, and more, need desperately to be properly examined, Harry," I alleged. "If I wasn't in such a rush to publish this book, I'd bring up more. Like what caused the 20/2 wage dichotomy; the steady decline - as evidenced by rusting factories and vacant mills seen everywhere - in our growing inability to compete in a world economy; our decline in education scores; our downgrade in the International *Index of Economic Freedoms*; could 9/11 have been avoided? We should also wonder how Senate positions on Johnson's War on Poverty may have been popularly influenced (Ref Hillsdale Letter, Chapter 10), etc. There, I set the stage for another possible edition. But I'll let you write it. I'm getting too old."

"Now you have the sum, substance and motivators for this book, Harry. I hope it has at least a small impact on the way we think about these things. We may otherwise go the way of the Romans."

"Prayers will be necessary," says Harry.

"Can do." says I.

> *"What bitter anguish would not the people of Athens have often escaped, if their government had contained so provident a safeguard (Senate) against the tyranny of their own passions?"*
> (James Madison, Federalist #63

EPILOGUE

America is still a standard of excellence and a beacon of hope for the world, but we need to be more careful about preserving that image. As we seem to have evolved ever so slowly from a manufacturing to a service economy, others now seem to have learned more than we forgot about how to maintain a healthy economy and prosperity for the multitude. As we have evolved away from a bias that favored business toward a deference for labor which includes wage rates difficult to justify in a world economy, countries like China, for example, do the opposite with a bias that prioritizes healthy businesses – something akin to our business philosophy prior to 1913 and the advent of Amendment Seventeen. With poverty rates less that 10 percent and declining, China emerges as a worthy economic opponent, penetrating with increasing business activity and influence around the world.

It seems somewhat ironic that Capitalist America drifts ever so slowly toward the communal philosophy of Karl Marx, or any of its more palliative spinoffs, while Communist countries like China evolve to include the maxims of Capitalism.

Social philosopher and communist Karl Marx knew more about manipulating the media than he knew about the generation of wealth and the true nature of slavery and poverty, but he nevertheless won the hearts and minds of many unhappy 19th century Americans. He accomplished this, in part, by winning the favor of *The New York Tribune*, America's leading newspaper of the era who published more than 400 articles written by him over a ten-year period (only 2 of these articles could be raised in a search of newspapers at the Library of Congress. It was necessary to enlist the help of a concerned librarian). While most of those articles focused on newsworthy developments in Europe, a word or two was occasionally injected in attempts to promote the philosophy of the collective for naïve, gullible American consumers of the news.

Marx, who had a history of instability in the workplace, influenced many disgruntled 19th century Americans who, in the main, were unable to digest the envious fact that in a free economy properly regulated by law, wealth accumulates more to some than to others. His denigration of the "despotism of Capital and the slavery of Labor" won enthusiastic popular support and no doubt encouraged the irrational and irreversible development of Amendment Seventeen as an unproven mechanism to get relief from said despotism and slavery. Indeed, as indicated by some modern scholars, Marx and his well-intentioned disciples may even have garnered more respect than the founders who facilitated the very prosperity many Americans tragically viewed as oppressive, even as their overall living standards, wages, innovation and personal GDP numbers inched constantly upward.

Let us examine the fundamental difference between the philosophies of Karl Marx and James Madison, each of whom personify and illuminate the irreconcilable. For the one camp, property is a private affair, for the other, not so much. The following selected essays by each might serve to better illustrate these differences; to provide a convenient reference for readers who may be interested in reviewing the basic tenets of each re labor, property distribution and excesses of power; and to encourage thought about which political system, or any of the infinite variations thereof, provides for the highest possible level of happiness and wellness for the highest number of people. They might also wonder conversely, which system, however constructed, modified or amended in the perpetually complex effort to make things better for everyone, is at greater risk for the despotism, excesses of power and slavery detested by both Marx and Madison.

The recent experience of Communist Russia would have given Karl Marx food for thought about his so-called "despotism of Capital" and the "slavery of Labor." There, despots ordered its citizens to work and comply with collective demands or suffer the Gulag. There, millions were ordered to give up their property and farms and to slave under state guidance or die from starvation.

Letter to the Labor Parliament
by Karl Marx
London, 1854

[**Submitted to, but rejected by,** *The New York Tribune and published in other places including The People's Paper* of March 18, 1854]

I regret deeply to be unable, for the moment at least, to leave London, and thus to be prevented from expressing verbally my feelings of pride and gratitude on receiving the invitation to sit as Honorary Delegate at the Labor Parliament. The mere assembling of such a Parliament marks a new epoch in the history of the world. The news of this great fact will arouse the hopes of the working-classes throughout Europe and America.

Great Britain, of all other countries, has been developed on the greatest scale, the *despotism of Capital and the slavery of Labor* (emphasis added). In no other country have the intermediate stations between the millionaire commanding whole industrial armies and the wages-slave living only from hand to mouth so gradually been swept away from the soil. There exist here no longer, as in continental countries, large classes of peasants and artisan, almost equally dependent on their own property and their own labor. A complete divorce of property from labor has been affected in Great Britain. In no other country, therefore, the war between the two classes that constitute modern society has assumed so colossal dimensions and features so distinct and palpable.

But it is precisely from these facts that the working-classes of Great Britain, before all others, are competent and called for to act as leaders in the great movement that must finally result in the absolute emancipation of Labor. Such they are from the conscious clearness of their position, the vast superiority of their numbers, the disastrous struggles of their past, and the moral strength of their present.

It is the working millions of Great Britain who first have laid down – the real basis of a new society – modern industry, which transformed the destructive agencies of nature into the productive power of man. The English working-classes, with invincible energies, by the sweat of their brows and brains, have called into life the material means of ennobling labor itself, and of multiplying its fruits to such a degree as to make general abundance possible.

By creating the inexhaustible productive powers of modern industry they have fulfilled the first condition of the emancipation of Labor. They have now to realize its other condition. They have to free those wealth-producing powers from the infamous shackles of monopoly, and subject them to the joint control of the producers, who, till now, allowed the very products of their hands to turn against them and be transformed into as many instruments of their own subjugation.

The laboring classes have conquered nature; they have now to conquer man. To succeed in this attempt they do not want strength, but the organization of their common strength, organization of the laboring classes on a national scale – such, I suppose, is the great and glorious end aimed at by the Labor Parliament.

If the Labor Parliament proves true to the idea that called it into life, some future historian will have to record that there existed in the year 1854 two Parliaments in England, a Parliament at London, and a Parliament at Manchester – a Parliament of the rich, and a Parliament of the poor – but that men sat only in the Parliament of the men and not in the Parliament of the masters.

Yours truly,
Karl Marx

PROPERTY
By James Madison, March, 1792

This term in its particular application means "that dominion which one man claims and exercises over the external things of the world, in exclusion of every other individual."

In its larger and juster meaning, it embraces everything to which a man may attach a value and have a right; and *which leaves to everyone else the like advantage.* In the former sense, a man's land, or merchandize, or money is called his property. In the latter sense, a man has property in his opinions and the free communication of them. He has a property of peculiar value in his religious opinions, and in the profession and practice dictated by them.

He has a property very dear to him in the safety and liberty of his person.

He has an equal property in the free use of his faculties and free choice of the objects on which to employ them.

In a word, as a man is said to have a right to his property, he may be equally said to have a property in his rights.

Where an excess of power prevails, property of no sort is duly respected. No man is safe in his opinions, his person, his faculties, or his possessions. Where there is an excess of liberty, the effect is the same, tho' from an opposite cause.

Government is instituted to protect property of every sort; as well that which lies in various rights of individuals, as that which the term particularly expresses. **This being the end of government, that alone is a *just* government, which *impartially* secures to every man, whatever is his.**

According to this standard of merit, the praise of affording a just security to property, should be sparingly bestowed on a government which, however scrupulously guarding the possessions of individuals, does not protect them in the enjoyment and communication of their opinions, in which they have an equal, and in the estimation of some, a more valuable property.

More sparingly should this praise be allowed to a government, where a man's religious rights are violated by penalties, or fettered by tests, or taxed by a hierarchy. Conscience is the most sacred of all property; other property depending in part on positive law, the exercise of that, being a natural and unalienable right.

To guard a man's house as his castle, to pay public and enforce private debts with the most exact faith, can give no title to invade a man's conscience which is more sacred than his castle, or to withhold from it that debt of protection, for which the public faith is pledged, by the very nature and original conditions of the social pact.

That is not a just government, nor is property secure under it, where the property which a man has in his personal safety and personal liberty, is violated by arbitrary seizures of one class of citizens for the service of the rest. A magistrate issuing his warrants to a press gang, would be in his proper functions in Turkey or Hindustan, under appellations proverbial of the most complete despotism.

That is not a just government, nor is property secure under it, where arbitrary restrictions, exemptions, and monopolies deny to part of its citizens that free use of their faculties, and free choice of their occupations, which not only constitute their property in the general sense of the word; but are the means of acquiring property strictly called.

What must be the spirit of legislation where a manufacturer of linen cloth is forbidden to bury his own child in a linen shroud, in order to favor his neighbor who manufactures woolen cloth; where the manufacturer and wearer of woolen cloth are again forbidden the economical use of buttons of that material, in favor of the manufacturer of buttons of other materials!

A just security to property is not afforded by that government, under which unequal taxes oppress one species of property and reward another species: where arbitrary taxes invade the domestic sanctuaries of the rich, and excessive taxes grind the faces of the poor; where the keenness and competitions of want are deemed an insufficient spur to labor, and taxes are again applied, by an unfeeling policy, as another spur; in violation of that sacred property, which Heaven, in decreeing man to earn his bread by the sweat of his brow, kindly reserved to him, in the small repose that could be spared from the supply of his necessities.

If there be a government then which prides itself in maintaining the inviolability of property; which provides that none shall be taken *directly* even for public use without indemnification to the owner, and yet *directly* violates the property which individuals have in their opinions, their religion, their persons, and their faculties; nay more, which *indirectly* violates their property, in their actual possessions, in the labor that acquires their daily subsistence, and in the hallowed remnant of time which ought to relieve their fatigues and soothe their cares, the influence will have been anticipated, that such a government is not a pattern for the United States.

If the United States mean to obtain or deserve the full praise due to wise and just governments, they will equally respect the rights of property, and the property in rights: they will rival the government that most sacredly guards the former; and by repelling its example in violating the latter, will make themselves a pattern to that and all other governments.

———

"...a well-constructed Senate...may be sometimes necessary as a defense to the people against their own temporary errors and delusions," (Hamilton or Madison, Federalist #63)

ACKNOWLEDGEMENTS

Kudos to the weekly "Men's Coffee" in New Castle, New Hampshire, who were very patient with me and enormously helpful in clarifying my thoughts on the controversial complexities I brought to the table. Special recognition and appreciation go out to Jim Cerny, neighbor and Men's Coffee member who stimulating my thinking like no other.

As I found myself being slowly mesmerized and somewhat emotionally crippled with what I thought to be incredibly important discoveries about the way A17 evolved, I adopted the philosophy of lawyers who believe they should never represent themselves in legal proceedings. So, I'd be less than honest if I didn't admit to soliciting the assistance of the Palmetto Publishing Group in efforts to increase the chances of exposure for the heady contents herein described. While I did not accept all of their advice and counsel, any measure of success in the distribution of this otherwise tyro effort to amend the history of A17, and to increase public vigilance, should be credited in large part to the detailed attention and quality of professional services I received from that important group.

Thanks also to employees at the Library of Congress who helped this amateur researcher find certain documents that were critical for a proper understanding of the tedious series of events that brought us Amendment Seventeen.

The Google search engine deserves Kudos, as well, for obvious reasons.

Special recognition to my wife Norma for her patient typing and proofing skills, for her ability in dealing with this personal heartburn of mine, and for being so adorable.

MJG

BIBLIOGRAPHY (ABRIDGED)

Amneus, Dan, *The Garbage Generation*, 1990

Bailey, Lonce H. and Mileur, Jerome M., *In Defense of the Founders Republic*

Barton, David. *America's Godly Heritage*, (Also a TV Series)

Beard, Charles A. and Mary R., *The Rise of American Civilization*, 2 vols.

Blankenhorn, David, *Fatherless America: Confronting Our Most Urgent Social Problem*

Bowen, Catherine Drinker, *Miracle at Philadelphia*

Bradford, William; *Of Plymouth Plantation*, (undated)

Bybee, Jay S., *Ulysses at the Mast: Democracy, Federalism, and the Sirens' Song of the Seventeenth Amendment (1997)*. Scholarly Works Paper 350.

Caldwell, Christopher, *The Age of Entitlement*

Charon, Mona, *Sex Matters*

De Tocqueville, Alexis, *Democracy in America*

Dilorenzo, Thomas J., *How Capitalism Saved America*

Dilorenzo, Thomas J., *The Problem with Socialism*

Marx, Karl and Engels, Frederick, *The Communist Manifesto*

Marx, Karl, *Dispatches for the New York Tribune:* (Incomplete and abridged)

Ellis, Joseph J., *Founding Brothers*

Epstein, Richard A., *How Progressives Rewrote the Constitution*

Folsom, Jr., Burton W., *The Myth of The Robber Barons: The untold Story of Our Country*

Franklin, Benjamin, *The Way to Wealth*

Friedman, Milton, *Why Government Is the Problem*

Garrison, W. P., *The Reform of the Senate*, 1891

Geanoulis, Michael J. Sr., *The Big Gorge* (An autobiography of sorts)

George, Henry, *Progress and Poverty: An Inquiry into the Cause of Industrial Depressions and of Increase of Want with Increase of Wealth: The Remedy.* (1879)

Goodnow, Frank J., *Politics and Administration: A Study in Government*

Grant, James, *The Forgotten Depression: 1921: The Crash that Cured Itself*

Greaves, Percy L., Jr., *Understanding the Dollar Crisis*, 1973

Hamilton, Alexander, Madison, James and Jay, John. *The Federalist*

Higgs, Robert, *Crisis and Leviathan*

Hillsdale College, *The U.S. Constitution: A Reader*

Hoebeke, C. H., *The Road to Mass Democracy*

Holcombe, Randall G., *The Growth of the Federal Government in the 1920s*

Kolko, G., *The Triumph of Conservatism*, (1963)

Larson, E. and Winship, M., Editors; *The Constitution Convention: Notes of James Madison*

Murphy, Robert P., *The Politically Incorrect Guide to the Great Depression*, 2009

Painter, Neil Irvin, *Standing at Armageddon: The United States: 1877-1919*

Pestritto, Ronald J. and Atto, William J, *American Progressivism*

Rand, Ayn, *We the Living*

Riis, Jacob A., *How the Other Half Lives*

Rossum, Ralph A., *Federalism, The Supreme Court and the Seventeenth Amendment*

Schiller, Wendy J. and Stewart, Charles III, *Electing the Senate: Indirect Democracy before the Seventeenth Amendment*

Tocqueville, Alexis, *Democracy in America*

Tocqueville, Alexis, *Memoir on Pauperism*, 1834

Skidmore, Thomas, *The Rights of Man to Property*, 1829

Zywicki, Todd J., *Beyond the Shell and Husk of History: The History of the Seventeenth Amendment and Its Implications for Current Reform Proposals.* 45 Clev. St. L. Rev. 165

ABOUT THE AUTHOR

Michael James Geanoulis, Sr.

For most of his life, Mr. Geanoulis worked as an electronics field engineer on nuclear submarines for the U. S. Navy, and automatic sorting machines for the U. S. Postal Service. After retiring in 1998, he pursued an interest in social issues, economics and low-level gardening. During a span of about thirty years he served on such New Hampshire agencies as the Governor's Commission on Child Support, the Strafford County Domestic Violence Coalition, a legislative Task Force on Family Law, and the world's first Commission on the Status of Men.

He authored a personal biography for his family, "The Big Gorge" in 2018, which detailed his personal learning experiences and philosophy.

He holds a degree in electronics technology from DeVry Technical Institute, a business degree from Southern New Hampshire University and is otherwise a self-appointed, self-taught Jack of all Liberal Arts, but master of none. He resides in historic New Castle, New Hampshire with his wife, Norma, and two amazingly talented black cats, who, after a year of patient tutoring, now roll over on command. Norma owns and cares for three equally talented and beautiful horses.

CPSIA information can be obtained
at www.ICGtesting.com
Printed in the USA
BVHW040054081021
618390BV00003B/14